1981

DEUTSCHLAND
Grenzen von 1937
und heute

NEW FUNCTIONAL GERMAN

TAPES

accompanying

New Functional German

NUMBER OF REELS: 30 (full-track)
SPEED: 3¾ IPS
RUNNING TIME: 24 hours (approximate)

MATERIALS RECORDED:

All Units of Speech and Vocabulary.
All Oral and Pattern Practice.
All Model Sentences.
All Comprehending and Speaking sections.

Oral and Pattern Practice and questions and answers are four-phased: cue — pause — correct response — pause. Units of Speech and Model Sentences have pauses for student repetition. Comprehending and Speaking sections are spoken at normal speed and repeated by phrases with pauses.

The American Book Company will provide, *free of charge*, a set of tapes for a college, school, instructor, or student requesting it for use in a course in which the text is adopted. Only an at-cost charge will be made to cover the raw tapes, handling, and mailing.

NEW FUNCTIONAL GERMAN

.

Max S. Kirch

University of Delaware

Rolf Kieser

Queens College of The City University of New York

AMERICAN BOOK COMPANY

New York

Preface

New Functional German represents a complete revision of the original text. The most obvious changes involve the use of German cues in the drills on Units of Speech and Vocabulary and Model Sentences (A II and B II sections). We have eliminated translation drills and replaced them with pattern practice, exclusively in German. The Comprehending and Speaking passages (E I and II) are completely new, too. The Units of Speech and Vocabulary have been modified by the addition of more common words and the deletion of others of lesser frequency. The Model Sentences have been revised and extended. The grammatical explanations (C) have been thoroughly rewritten, and new written Exercises (D) have been provided. In sum, the new edition represents a continuation of the principles of the first edition, with practical changes to provide greater effectiveness.

The materials have been carefully programmed. It is important that the student learn each section thoroughly before proceeding to the next section. Thus, the Units of Speech and Vocabulary (A I) should be committed to memory before going on to the Oral Practice (A II). Likewise, the Model Sentences (B I) must be learned by heart before going on to the Pattern Practice (B II). The grammatical analysis in Structure (C) is designed to help the student understand constructions he has already learned to use in the A and B sections. The A and B sections, once mastered, lead logically to the D sentences, which are variations of the grammatical structures exemplified in the Model Sentences, with different vocabulary. The new Comprehending and Speaking sections (E) provide contextual material and a wider range of idioms and vocabulary. Since this vocabulary is for recognition knowledge only, new words are identified in visible page vocabularies.

(*v*)

New Functional German is designed to develop the ability to understand, speak, read, and write German. A great deal of audio-lingual practice is provided, not only in order to develop the listening and speaking skills, but also because much more practice in structure can be achieved orally than is possible by other means in the same amount of time. All the materials have been tested and proved over several years. The book can be easily completed in one year in a class meeting three or four hours per week. A rapid pace should be maintained, so that students spend most of their class time *practicing* German, not just learning *about* German.

Information about the comprehensive tapes accompanying *New Functional German* appears opposite the title page of this book.

M. S. K.
R. K.

CONTENTS

(*vii*)

4. Dative of Personal Pronouns (Third Person). 5. Order of Direct and Indirect Objects. 6. Prepositions Requiring Dative (**aus, bei, mit**). 7. Possessive **sein** in the Dative.

Das Fernrohr

Beim Angeln

NEW FUNCTIONAL GERMAN

UNIT 1

A. UNITS OF SPEECH AND VOCABULARY

I. Study and Practice Aloud.

Guten Morgen!	Good morning.
Wie geht es Ihnen?	How are you?
Es geht mir gut. Und Ihnen?	I'm fine. (I'm well.) And you?
Auch gut.	(I'm) fine, too. (I'm well, too)
Danke.	Thanks. (Thank you.)
Auf Wiedersehen!	Good-by.

Herr Schmidt	Mr. Schmidt	**sagen**	say, are saying, do say
Frau Braun	Mrs. Braun		
Fräulein Meyer	Miss Meyer	**sagt**	says, is saying, does say
hat	has, is having, does have	**die Aufgabe**	the lesson
haben	have, are having, do have	**eine Aufgabe**	a lesson
		das Buch	the book
ist	is	**ein Buch**	a book
sind	are	**das Kind**	the child
machen	make, are making; do, are doing	**der Professor**	the professor
		ein Professor	a professor
		der Student	the student
macht	makes, is making; does, is doing	**ein Student**	a student
		die Studentin	the student (*f.*), coed

(*1*)

eine Studentin	a student (*f.*),	**wo?**	where?
	coed	**auch**	also, too
der Tisch	the table	**dort**	there
er	he, it	**hier**	here
sie	she, it, they	**ja**	yes
es	it, he, she	**nein**	no
was?	what?	**und**	and
wer?	who?		

II. Oral Practice. Repeat the pattern sentence. Then substitute the items listed below. Repeat the entire sentence with each substitute item, changing the verb where necessary.[1]

a. Guten Morgen, Herr Schmidt!
1. Frau Braun
2. Fräulein Meyer
3. Herr Meyer
4. Frau Schmidt

b. Der Professor sagt „Auf Wiedersehen!"
1. er
2. die Studentin
3. sie (*sing.*)
4. das Kind
5. ein Kind und eine Studentin
6. sie (*pl.*)

c. Der Student macht die Aufgabe.
1. die Studentin
2. das Kind
3. eine Studentin
4. ein Student
5. der Student und die Studentin
6. sie (*pl.*)

d. Das Kind hat ein Buch.
1. der Professor
2. er
3. die Studentin
4. sie (*sing.*)
5. der Student und die Studentin
6. sie (*pl.*)

e. Wer ist das Kind?
1. die Studentin
2. der Professor
3. der Student

[1] To illustrate the procedure in substitution drills, the student's responses in paragraphs "a" and "b" should be as follows:
a. Guten Morgen, Herr Schmidt!
1. Guten Morgen, Frau Braun!
2. Guten Morgen, Fräulein Meyer!
3. Guten Morgen, Herr Meyer!
4. Guten Morgen, Frau Schmidt!
b. Der Professor sagt „Auf Wiedersehen!"
1. Er sagt „Auf Wiedersehen!"
2. Die Studentin sagt „Auf Wiedersehen!"
3. Sie sagt „Auf Wiedersehen!"
4. Das Kind sagt „Auf Wiedersehen!"
5. Ein Kind und eine Studentin sagen „Auf Wiedersehen!"
6. Sie sagen „Auf Wiedersehen!"

f. Wo ist der Tisch?
1. das Kind
2. der Professor
3. er
4. die Studentin
5. sie (*sing.*)
6. der Student

g. Was hat die Studentin?
1. sie (*sing.*)
2. das Kind
3. der Student
4. er
5. der Professor und der Student
6. sie (*pl.*)

h. Ist der Professor hier?
1. er
2. das Kind
3. der Tisch
4. die Studentin
5. sie (*sing.*)
6. der Student

i. Nein, der Professor ist dort.
1. er
2. das Kind
3. der Tisch
4. die Studentin
5. sie (*sing.*)
6. der Student

B. MODEL SENTENCES

I. Study each sentence until you can reproduce it correctly.

1. **Guten Morgen, Herr Schmidt! Wie geht es Ihnen?**
2. **Danke, es geht mir gut. Und Ihnen, Fräulein Braun?**
3. **Macht der Student die Aufgabe? — Ja, er macht sie.**
4. **Wo ist der Tisch? — Er ist hier.**
5. **Hat die Studentin ein Buch? — Ja, sie hat ein Buch.**
6. **Was sagt das Kind? — Es sagt: „Wie geht es Ihnen?"**
7. **Wer hat das Buch? — Der Professor hat es.**

1. Good morning, Mr. Schmidt. How are you?
2. I'm fine, thanks. And you, Miss Braun?
3. Is the student doing the lesson? — Yes, he is doing it.
4. Where is the table? — It's here.
5. Does the student (*f.*) have a book? — Yes, she has a book.
6. What is the child saying? — He (she) is saying: "How are you?"
7. Who has the book? — The professor has it.

II. Pattern Practice. Repeat the model sentence. Then substitute the following items in the equivalent part of the model sentence. Repeat the entire sentence with each substitute item.

a. Guten Morgen, Herr Schmidt! Wie geht es Ihnen?
1. Frau Schmidt
2. Frau Meyer
3. Fräulein Braun
4. Herr und Frau Schwarz

b. **Danke, es geht mir gut. Und Ihnen, Fräulein Braun?**
    1. Herr Schmidt   3. Fräulein Meyer
    2. Frau Schwarz   4. Herr und Frau Bauer

c. **Macht der Student die Aufgabe? — Ja, er macht sie.**
    1. der Professor   3. Karl Meyer
    2. Herr Schmidt   4. Hans Bauer

d. **Wo ist der Tisch? — Er ist hier.**
    1. der Professor   3. Herr Schmidt
    2. der Student   4. Hans Meyer

e. **Hat die Studentin ein Buch? — Ja, sie hat ein Buch.**
    1. Fräulein Braun   3. Frau Schwarz
    2. Fräulein Meyer   4. Frau Bauer

f. **Was sagt das Kind? — Es sagt: „Wie geht es Ihnen?"**
    1. „Es geht mir gut."   3. „Guten Morgen!"
    2. „Auf Wiedersehen!"   4. „Danke."

g. **Wer hat das Buch? — Der Professor hat es.**
    1. der Student   3. die Studentin
    2. das Kind   4. Fräulein Bauer

C. STRUCTURE

1. German nouns are masculine, feminine, or neuter.

    a. Masculine nouns use **der** as the subject form of the definite article. Nouns denoting male beings are usually in this category:

        der Professor   *the professor*
        der Student   *the student*

    But many names of inanimate things are also masculine:

        der Tisch   *the table*

    b. Feminine nouns use **die** as the subject (and direct-object) form of the definite article. Nouns denoting female beings are usually in this category:

        die Studentin   *the student* (f.), *coed*

    The names of many inanimate things are also feminine:

        die Aufgabe   *the lesson*

    c. Neuter nouns use **das** as the subject (and direct-object) form of the definite article. Neuter nouns include mostly inanimate objects:

        das Buch   *the book*

The names of some animate beings are also neuter:

das Kind *the child*

Note: All nouns in German are capitalized.

2. Masculine nouns use **ein** (*a, an*) for the subject form of the indefinite article:

ein Professor *a professor*
ein Student *a student*
ein Tisch *a table*

Feminine nouns use **eine** (*a, an*) for the subject (and direct-object) form of the indefinite article:

eine Aufgabe *a lesson*
eine Studentin *a student* (f.), *coed*

Neuter nouns use **ein** (*a, an*) for the subject (and direct-object) form of the indefinite article:

ein Buch *a book*
ein Kind *a child*

3. The pronoun replacing the subject form of any masculine noun, regardless of whether it is animate or inanimate, is **er**. For example, **der Student** or **der Tisch** is replaced by **er**:

a. Macht **der Student** die Aufgabe? — Ja, **er** macht die Aufgabe.
Is the student doing the lesson? — Yes, he is doing the lesson.
b. Wo ist **der Tisch?** — **Er** ist hier.
Where is the table? — It is here.

Any feminine noun (subject and object forms) is replaced by **sie:**

a. Hat **die Studentin** ein Buch? — Ja, **sie** hat ein Buch.
Does the student (f.) *have a book? — Yes, she has a book.*
b. Macht **der Student die Aufgabe?** — Ja, **er** macht **sie.**
Is the student doing the lesson? — Yes, he is doing it.

Any neuter noun (subject and object forms) is replaced by **es:**

a. Was macht **das Kind?** — **Es** macht eine Aufgabe.
What is the child doing? — He (*she*) *is doing a lesson.*
b. Wer hat **das Buch?** — Der Professor hat **es.**
Who has the book? — The professor has it.

4. The German verb has only a single form; English has three equivalent forms. For example, German **sagt** may mean *says, is saying, does say.*

> Der Professor **sagt** ,,Auf Wiedersehen!"
> *The professor says "Good-by."*
> *The professor is saying "Good-by."*
> *The professor does say "Good-by."*

5. Questions often begin, as in English, with an interrogative element:

    a. **Wo** ist der Tisch?
      Where is the table?
    b. **Was** macht das Kind?
      What is the child doing?
    c. **Wer** hat das Buch?
      Who has the book?

Or, if there is no interrogative element, with the verb:

    d. **Macht** der Student die Aufgabe?
      Is the student doing the lesson?
    e. **Hat** die Studentin ein Buch?
      Does the student (f.) *have a book?*

D. EXERCISES

Write the following sentences in German and be able to express them orally.

1. Is the child there? — No, she is here.
2. Who has the book? — A student (*f.*) has the book.
3. Where is Mrs. Schmidt? — She is here.
4. Miss Braun says "Good-by."
5. A student and a coed are there.
6. Are they here?
7. What is the student doing?
8. He is doing the lesson.
9. We say "Good morning."   *we = WIR*
10. Where is Mr. Schmidt? — He is there.
11. A child is doing the lesson.
12. Does the student (*f.*) have the book? — Yes, she has it.
13. Where are Mr. and Mrs. Meyer?
14. Where are they?
15. Does the student have the lesson? — Yes, he has it.
16. What is the child saying? — He's saying "Good-by."

E. COMPREHENDING AND SPEAKING

I. Repeat the following after your instructor (or the speaker) and study thoroughly.

IM BÜCHERLADEN[1]

Der Student Peter lernt Deutsch. Auch die Studentin Erika lernt Deutsch. Sie sind im Bücherladen.

Frau Braun sagt: ,,Guten Morgen!"

,,Guten Morgen, Frau Braun", sagt Peter, ,,wie geht es Ihnen?"

5 ,,Danke, es geht mir gut. Und Ihnen, Erika?"

,,Danke, auch gut. Haben Sie das Buch für[2] die Deutschklasse?[3] Hier ist der Titel."

,,Ja", sagt Frau Braun, ,,ich habe es. Dort ist auch ein Buch für Peter."

10 ,,Danke, Frau Braun", sagt Peter. ,,Ich gehe jetzt.[4] Ich habe eine Aufgabe für morgen.[5] Auf Wiedersehen, Erika!"

II. Beantworten Sie die folgenden Fragen auf deutsch (*Answer the following questions in German.*)

1. Wer lernt Deutsch?
2. Was lernt Erika?
3. Wo sind Peter und Erika?
4. Wer sagt ,,Guten Morgen?"
5. Was sagt Peter?
6. Was hat Frau Braun?

[1]**im Bücherladen**	in the bookstore	[4]**jetzt**	now
[2]**für**	for	[5]**morgen**	tomorrow
[3]**die Deutschklasse**	the German class		

UNIT 2

A. UNITS OF SPEECH AND VOCABULARY

I. Study and Practice Aloud.

Wie heißen Sie?	What is your name?
Ich heiße Hans.	My name is Hans.
Wie heißt er?	What is his name?
Er heißt Karl.	His name is Karl.
Wie heißt sie?	What is her name?
Sie heißt Grete.	Her name is Grete.
in das Zimmer	into the room
an das Fenster	to the window

begrüßen	to greet, are greeting	**lernen**	to learn, to study, are learning, are studying
fragen	to ask, are asking		
fragt	asks, is asking, does ask	**schreiben**	to write, are writing
gehen	to go, are going		
heißen	to be called, are called	**der Brief**	the letter
		ein Brief	a letter
kommen	to come, are coming	**der Bruder**	the brother
		sein Bruder	his brother
		sein Buch	his book
		die Eltern	the parents

(8)

seine Eltern	his parents	**die Schülerin**	the pupil (*f.*), student
das Fenster	the window		
die Fenster	the windows	**die Schwester**	the sister
das Gebäude	the building	**seine Schwester**	his sister
die Gebäude	the buildings	**die Tür**	the door
der Lehrer	the teacher	**der Vater**	the father
die Lehrer	the teachers	**sein Vater**	his father
das Mädchen	the girl	**das Zimmer**	the room
die Mädchen	the girls	**die Zimmer**	the rooms
die Mutter	the mother	**ich**	I
seine Mutter	his mother	**mich**	me
der Onkel	the uncle	**wir**	we
sein Onkel	his uncle	**uns**	us
der Schüler	the pupil, student	**Sie**	you
		ihn	him, it
die Schüler	the pupils, students	**sie**	her, it, them
		wie?	how?

II. Oral Practice. Repeat the pattern sentence. Then substitute the items listed below. Repeat the entire sentence with each substitute item.

a. Wie heißen Sie? — Ich heiße Karl Schmidt.
1. Robert Meyer
2. Hans Braun
3. Erika Weiß
4. Grete Schwarz

b. Wie heißt er? — Er heißt Hans Meyer.
1. der Lehrer
2. der Schüler
3. der Professor
4. sein Bruder
5. sein Onkel
6. sein Vater

c. Wie heißt sie? — Sie heißt Grete Braun.
1. die Studentin
2. die Schülerin
3. seine Schwester
4. seine Mutter

d. Was fragt der Lehrer?
1. der Schüler
2. das Mädchen
3. die Schülerin
4. sein Onkel
5. sein Vater
6. sein Bruder
7. seine Schwester
8. seine Mutter

e. Was lernt das Mädchen?
1. das Kind
2. der Schüler
3. er
4. Fräulein Meyer
5. sie
6. die Studentin

f. Was schreiben die Schüler?
1. die Mädchen
2. die Lehrer
3. seine Eltern
4. sie

III. Oral Practice. Repeat the pattern sentence. Then substitute the items listed below in the appropriate places. Repeat the entire sentence with each substitute item.[1]

a. Sie kommen in das Zimmer.
    1. Die Schüler _____
    2. Die Mädchen _____
    3. Die Lehrer _____
    4. _____ das Gebäude.
    5. _____ die Gebäude.
    6. Die Mädchen _____
    7. _____ die Zimmer.

b. Wir gehen an das Fenster.
    1. Die Schüler _____
    2. Die Eltern _____
    3. _____ die Fenster.
    4. Die Mädchen _____
    5. _____ die Tür.
    6. Die Eltern _____
    7. Die Schüler _____

c. Sie begrüßen mich.
    1. Der Vater und die Mutter _____
    2. Seine Eltern _____
    3. _____ ihn.
    4. Der Bruder und die Schwester _____
    5. _____ uns.
    6. Das Mädchen und der Onkel _____
    7. _____ sie.
    8. Die Lehrer _____
    9. _____ Sie.

[1] To illustrate the procedure in these exercises, the student's responses to paragraphs "a" and "b" should be as follows:

a. Sie kommen in das Zimmer.
    1. Die Schüler kommen in das Zimmer.
    2. Die Mädchen kommen in das Zimmer.
    3. Die Lehrer kommen in das Zimmer.
    4. Die Lehrer kommen in das Gebäude.
    5. Die Lehrer kommen in die Gebäude.
    6. Die Mädchen kommen in die Gebäude.
    7. Die Mädchen kommen in die Zimmer.

b. Wir gehen an das Fenster.
    1. Die Schüler gehen an das Fenster.
    2. Die Eltern gehen an das Fenster.
    3. Die Eltern gehen an die Fenster.
    4. Die Mädchen gehen an die Fenster.
    5. Die Mädchen gehen an die Tür.
    6. Die Eltern gehen an die Tür.
    7. Die Schüler gehen an die Tür.

d. Hier ist der Brief.
1. _____ ein Brief.
2. Dort _____
3. _____ der Brief.
4. Wo _____ ?

B. MODEL SENTENCES

I. Study each sentence until you can reproduce it correctly.

8. **Der Lehrer schreibt einen Brief. Er schreibt ihn.**
9. **Die Eltern begrüßen den Lehrer.**
10. **Hans begrüßt seinen Onkel.**
11. **Der Schüler lernt seine Aufgabe.**
12. **Der Student hat sein Buch.**
13. **Herr Schmidt begrüßt seine Eltern.**
14. **Die Schüler gehen an die Tür.**

8. The teacher is writing a letter. He is writing it.
9. The parents are greeting the teacher.
10. Hans is greeting his uncle.
11. The pupil is studying his lesson.
12. The student has his book.
13. Mr. Schmidt is greeting his parents.
14. The pupils are going to the door.

II. Pattern Practice. Repeat the model sentence. Then substitute the following items in the equivalent part of the model sentence. Repeat the entire sentence with each substitute item.

a. Der Lehrer schreibt einen Brief. Er schreibt ihn.

1. der Schüler	4. sein Bruder
2. der Professor	5. sein Onkel
3. Herr Schmidt	6. sein Vater

b. Die Eltern begrüßen den Lehrer.

1. die Schüler	4. sein Vater und seine Mutter
2. sie (*pl.*)	5. sein Onkel und seine Eltern
3. wir	6. sein Bruder und seine Schwester

c. Hans begrüßt seinen Onkel.

1. der Professor	3. der Schüler
2. der Student	4. der Lehrer

d. Der Schüler lernt seine Aufgabe.

1. Hans	3. er
2. Karl	4. sein Bruder

e. Der Student hat sein Buch.
    1. der Schüler   3. der Lehrer
    2. der Professor   4. er

f. Herr Schmidt begrüßt seine Eltern.
    1. der Lehrer   4. der Student
    2. der Schüler   5. Herr Meyer
    3. der Professor   6. Karl

g. Die Schüler gehen an die Tür.
    1. die Eltern   5. das Mädchen und die Mutter
    2. die Lehrer   6. der Bruder und die Schwester
    3. sie (*pl.*)   7. die Mädchen
    4. der Vater und die Mutter   8. die Mutter und der Bruder

C. STRUCTURE

1. Present indicative of regular verb: **sagen** (*to say*):

ich sag**e**	*I say, am saying, do say*
du sag**st**	*you say, are saying, do say*
er, sie, es sa**gt**	*he, she, it says, is saying, does say*
wir sag**en**	*we say, are saying, do say*
ihr sag**t**	*you say, are saying, do say*
sie sag**en**	*they say, are saying, do say*
Sie sag**en**	*you say, are saying, do say*

Note 1: The present indicative of regular verbs is formed by dropping the **-en** of the infinitive and adding the endings shown above to the verb stem (**sag-**).

Note 2: The familiar forms **du** and **ihr** are used when addressing relatives, children, and close friends. For practice the familiar forms will be used in E passages, where appropriate, beginning with Unit 3. The direct-object form corresponding to **du** is **dich**, to **ihr** it is **euch**.

2. Present indicative of **sein** (*to be*):

ich **bin**	*I am*
du **bist**	*you are*
er, sie, es **ist**	*he, she, it is*
wir **sind**	*we are*
ihr **seid**	*you are*
sie **sind**	*they are*
Sie **sind**	*you are*

3. Present indicative of **haben** (*to have*):

ich **habe**	*I have, am having, do have*
du **hast**	*you have, are having, do have*
er, sie, es **hat**	*he, she, it has, is having, does have*
wir **haben**	*we have, are having, do have*
ihr **habt**	*you have, are having, do have*
sie **haben**	*they have, are having, do have*
Sie **haben**	*you have, are having, do have*

4. Many masculine and neuter nouns have the same form in the plural as in the singular. The plural form of the definite article for all genders is **die**:

der **Lehrer**	*the teacher*	die **Lehrer**	*the teachers*
der **Onkel**	*the uncle*	die **Onkel**	*the uncles*
der **Schüler**	*the pupil, student*	die **Schüler**	*the pupils, students*
das **Fenster**	*the window*	die **Fenster**	*the windows*
das **Gebäude**	*the building*	die **Gebäude**	*the buildings*
das **Mädchen**	*the girl*	die **Mädchen**	*the girls*

5. The subject of the verb is in the nominative case and the direct object is in the accusative case. The form of the noun is usually the same in both cases. The definite article has one form for both cases, except in the masculine singular, where the nominative form is **der,** the accusative **den:**

a. **Der Lehrer** schreibt einen Brief.
   The teacher is writing a letter.
   Die Eltern begrüßen **den Lehrer.**
   The parents are greeting the teacher.
b. Hier ist **die Aufgabe.**
   Here is the lesson.
   Macht der Schüler **die Aufgabe?**
   Is the student doing the lesson?
c. **Das Buch** ist dort.
   The book is there.
   Wer hat **das Buch?**
   Who has the book?

6. The indefinite article also has only one form for both the nominative and accusative cases, except in the masculine singular, where the nominative form is **ein,** the accusative **einen:**

a. Hier ist **ein Brief.**
   Here is a letter.

Der Lehrer schreibt **einen Brief.**
The teacher is writing a letter.
b. Hier ist **eine Aufgabe.**
Here is a lesson.
Das Kind macht **eine Aufgabe.**
The child is doing a lesson.
c. Hier ist **ein Buch.**
Here is a book.
Hat die Schülerin **ein Buch?**
Does the student (f.) *have a book?*

7. The possessive **sein,** like the indefinite article, has only one singular form for both the nominative and accusative cases, except in the masculine, where the nominative form is **sein,** the accusative **seinen:**

a. Wie heißt **sein Onkel?**
What is his uncle's name?
Hans begrüßt **seinen Onkel.**
Hans is greeting his uncle.
b. Hier ist **seine Aufgabe.**
Here is his lesson.
Der Schüler lernt **seine Aufgabe.**
The pupil is studying his lesson.
c. Hier ist **sein Buch.**
Here is his book.
Der Student hat **sein Buch.**
The student has his book.

The plural form, both nominative and accusative is **seine:**

d. **Seine Eltern** begrüßen mich.
His parents are greeting me.
Herr Schmidt begrüßt **seine Eltern.**
Mr. Schmidt is greeting his parents.

8. Certain prepositions — for example, **in** (*into*) and **an** (*to*) — frequently require the accusative form of the noun after the preposition:

a. Sie kommen **in das Zimmer.**
They are coming into the room.
b. Die Schüler gehen **an die Tür.**
The students are going to the door.
c. Die Schülerin geht **an den Tisch.**
The student (f.) *is going to the table.*

9. The nominative and accusative forms of the personal pronouns **sie** and **es,** respectively, are the same:

    a. Die Schülerin hat **das Buch. Sie** hat **es.**
       The student (f.) has the book. She has it.
    b. Das Kind macht **die Aufgabe. Es** macht **sie.**
       The child is doing the lesson. He (she) is doing it.

For the masculine, however, the nominative form is **er,** the accusative **ihn:**

    a. Wo ist **der Tisch? Er** ist hier.
       Where is the table? It is here.
    b. Der Lehrer schreibt **einen Brief. Er** schreibt **ihn.**
       The teacher is writing a letter. He is writing it.
    c. Die Schüler begrüßen **den Lehrer. Sie** begrüßen **ihn.**
       The students are greeting the teacher. They are greeting him.

D. EXERCISES

Write the following sentences in German and be able to express them orally.

1. Is Miss Meyer writing a letter?
2. His parents are coming to the window.
3. I am here.
4. What is the girl saying?
5. I'm saying "Good-by."
6. Are you greeting him?
7. Do the girls have a table?
8. The girls' names are Erika and Grete.
9. Do you have the book? — Yes, we have it here.
10. Where are you, Miss Schmidt?
11. Are the pupils going into the room?
12. She is coming and he is going.
13. We are greeting his father and his brother.
14. Are you writing the letter? — Yes, I am writing it.
15. We are here and he is there.
16. Are they saying "Good morning?"
17. His brother is going to the door.
18. I am asking his father and his uncle.
19. Are his mother and his sister going into the building?
20. My name is Hans and his name is Robert.
21. What do you have there, Mrs. Braun?
22. Who is greeting his father? — The teacher is greeting him.
23. Are you studying the lesson? — Yes, I'm studying it.
24. Are his parents there?

E. COMPREHENDING AND SPEAKING

I. Repeat the following after your instructor (or the speaker) and study thoroughly.

AM TELEPHON

Das Telephon läutet.[1] Peter geht an den Tisch und hebt den Hörer.[2]

„Hallo, hier ist Peter Schmidt", sagt er, „wer ist dort?"

„Guten Morgen", sagt eine Stimme,[3] „ich heiße Walter Meyer.

5   Ich lerne Deutsch wie Sie.[4] Ich mache jetzt gerade[5] die Aufgabe für die Deutschklasse. Haben Sie schon[6] die Aufgabe?"

„Nein", sagt Peter, „ich gehe jetzt in das Klassenzimmer, um die Aufgabe zu machen. Kommen Sie auch? Wir machen die Aufgabe zusammen."[7]

10   „Gut, ich komme!" sagt Walter. „Danke, und auf Wiedersehen!"

„Wer ist am Telephon?" fragt die Mutter.

„Ein Student." sagt Peter.

„Wie heißt er?"

„Er heißt Walter Meyer und lernt Deutsch wie ich."

II. Beantworten Sie die folgenden Fragen auf deutsch!

1. Was läutet?
2. Wer geht an den Tisch?
3. Wer ist am Telephon?
4. Was macht Walter Meyer jetzt gerade?
5. Ist Walter auch ein Student?
6. Hat Peter schon die Aufgabe?

[1]**läutet**	rings	[5]**jetzt gerade**	right now
[2]**hebt den Hörer**	lifts the receiver	[6]**schon**	already
[3]**die Stimme**	the voice	[7]**zusammen**	together
[4]**wie Sie**	like you		

UNIT 3

A. UNITS OF SPEECH AND VOCABULARY

I. Study and Practice Aloud.

Er lernt gerne.	He likes to learn (study).
Sie spielen gerne.	They like to play.
Schreibt sie gerne?	Does she like to write?
Sie schreiben der Frau; sie schreiben ihr.	They are writing to the woman; they are writing to her.
Sie schreibt dem Mann; sie schreibt ihm.	She is writing to the man; she is writing to him.
Er schreibt dem Mädchen; er schreibt ihm.	He is writing to the girl; he is writing to her.
aus der Schule	from school
bei Frau Meyer; bei ihr	at Mrs. Meyer's (house); at her house
bei seinem Onkel; bei ihm	at his uncle's house; at his house
bei mir	at my house
bei ihm	at his house
bei uns	at our house
bei ihnen	at their house
bei Ihnen	at your house
mit der Frau; mit ihr	with the woman; with her
nach Hause	home(ward)
zu Hause	at home

(*17*)

die **Brüder**	the brothers	**wohnen**	to dwell, live
die **Frau**	the woman	**mir**	(to) me
das **Haus**	the house	**ihm**	(to) him, (to) her,
der **Junge**	the boy		(to) it
der **Mann**	the man	**ihr**	(to) her, (to) it
die **Mütter**	the mothers	**uns**	(to) us
die **Schule**	the school	**ihnen**	(to) them
der **Sohn**	the son	**Ihnen**	(to) you
die **Tochter**	the daughter	**gerne**	gladly
die **Töchter**	the daughters	**aus**	from, out of
die **Väter**	the fathers	**bei**	at the house of
geben	to give	**mit**	with
spielen	to play		

II. Oral Practice. Repeat the pattern sentence. Then substitute the items listed below. Repeat the entire sentence with each substitute item.

a. Er lernt gerne.
1. der Junge
2. das Mädchen
3. das Kind
4. es
5. der Student
6. sein Sohn
7. seine Tochter
8. sie (*sing.*)

b. Sie spielen gerne.
1. die Mädchen
2. der Junge und das Mädchen
3. die Schüler
4. seine Töchter
5. seine Brüder
6. sein Sohn und seine Tochter

c. Schreibt sie gerne?
1. die Frau
2. der Mann
3. der Junge
4. er
5. sein Sohn
6. seine Tochter

d. Sie schreiben der Frau; sie schreiben ihr.
1. der Sohn und die Tochter
2. der Student und die Studentin
3. die Brüder
4. die Töchter

e. Sie schreibt dem Mann; sie schreibt ihm.
1. die Tochter
2. die Studentin
3. die Schülerin
4. die Frau

f. Er schreibt dem Mädchen; er schreibt ihm.
1. der Vater
2. der Bruder
3. der Junge
4. der Student

g. Sie kommen aus der Schule.
1. die Schüler
2. die Mädchen
3. die Lehrer
4. der Junge und das Mädchen
5. der Bruder und die Schwester
6. der Schüler und die Schülerin

h. Sie wohnt bei Frau Meyer.

1. bei ihr
2. bei mir
3. bei ihm
4. bei Ihnen
5. bei uns
6. bei ihnen

i. Er wohnt bei seinem Onkel.

1. bei seinem Bruder
2. bei seinem Sohn
3. bei ihm
4. bei mir

j. Sie kommt mit der Frau.

1. mit ihr
2. mit der Studentin
3. mit der Schülerin
4. mit Erika Meyer

k. Sie gehen nach Hause.

1. der Vater und sein Sohn
2. der Student und sein Vater
3. die Mutter und die Tochter
4. die Mütter
5. die Väter
6. die Brüder

l. Sie sind zu Hause.

1. die Brüder
2. die Mütter
3. die Töchter
4. die Väter

m. Der Student und die Studentin geben mir das Buch.

1. Ihnen
2. uns
3. ihm
4. ihnen

B. MODEL SENTENCES

I. Study each sentence until you can reproduce it correctly.

15. **Das Kind spielt gerne.**
16. **Der Student schreibt seiner Mutter einen Brief.**
17. **Der Lehrer schreibt einer Schülerin.**
18. **Der Student schreibt einem Professor.**
19. **Die Brüder geben es dem Kind.**
20. **Sie geben es ihm.**
21. **Der Lehrer kommt mit den Schülern.**
22. **Der Junge spielt mit seinen Brüdern.**

15. The child likes to play.
16. The student is writing his mother a letter.
17. The teacher is writing to a pupil (*f.*).
18. The student is writing to a professor.
19. The brothers are giving it to the child.
20. They are giving it to him.
21. The teacher is coming with the pupils.
22. The boy is playing with his brothers.

II. Pattern Practice. Repeat the model sentence. Then substitute the following items in the equivalent part of the model sentence. Repeat the entire sentence with the substitute item.

a. Das Kind spielt gerne.
1. das Mädchen
2. der Junge
3. der Schüler
4. die Schülerin

b. Der Student schreibt seiner Mutter einen Brief.
1. der Junge
2. das Kind
3. das Mädchen
4. der Professor
5. der Lehrer
6. der Schüler

c. Der Lehrer schreibt einer Schülerin.
1. er
2. Frau Meyer
3. sie (*sing.*)
4. Fräulein Schwarz

d. Der Student schreibt einem Professor.
1. er
2. Karl Schmidt
3. Hans Meyer
4. Herr Braun

e. Die Brüder geben es dem Kind.
1. der Bruder und die Schwester
2. der Junge und das Mädchen
3. der Schüler und die Schülerin
4. der Vater und die Mutter
5. die Eltern
6. sie (*pl.*)

f. Sie geben es ihm.
1. seine Brüder
2. seine Eltern
3. die Mädchen
4. die Mütter

g. Der Lehrer kommt mit den Schülern.
1. Herr Schmidt
2. Herr Meyer
3. Hans Braun
4. Karl Schmidt

h. Der Junge spielt mit seinen Brüdern.
1. er
2. Karl
3. Hans
4. der Schüler

C. STRUCTURE

1. The plural of some nouns is formed by changing the stem vowel to an umlaut vowel. This change occurs primarily in masculine nouns of more than one syllable and in the two feminine nouns **Mutter** and **Tochter:**

der Vater	*the father*	**die Väter**	*the fathers*
der Bruder	*the brother*	**die Brüder**	*the brothers*
die Mutter	*the mother*	**die Mütter**	*the mothers*
die Tochter	*the daughter*	**die Töchter**	*the daughters*

Note: Umlaut affects only **a, o, u,** or **au** and is indicated by two dots above the letter. For the pronunciation of **ä, ö, ü,** and **äu,** follow your instructor or imitate the speaker on the tape.

2. The indirect object of a verb is in the dative case. (In English the indirect object of a verb may be preceded by a preposition; in German, almost never.) The dative singular form of the definite article is **dem** for the masculine and neuter, **der** for the feminine. The dative plural form is **den** for all genders.

    a. Sie schreibt **dem Mann.**
   She is writing to the man.
    b. Sie schreiben **der Frau.**
   They are writing to the woman.
    c. Er schreibt **dem Mädchen.**
   He is writing to the girl.
    d. Der Lehrer schreibt **den Schülern.**
   The teacher is writing to the pupils.

Note: Nouns which do not end in **-n** in the nominative plural add **-n** in the dative plural.

3. The dative forms of the indefinite article are **einem** for masculine and neuter, **einer** for feminine:

    a. Der Student schreibt **einem Professor.**
   The student is writing to a professor.
    b. Der Lehrer schreibt **einer Schülerin.**
   The teacher is writing to a pupil (f.).
    c. Der Lehrer schreibt **einem Kind.**
   The teacher is writing to a child.

4. The dative forms of the personal pronoun:

mir	(*to*) *me*	**uns**	(*to*) *us*
dir	(*to*) *you*	**euch**	(*to*) *you*
ihm	(*to*) *him*, (*to*) *it*	**ihnen**	(*to*) *them*
ihr	(*to*) *her*, (*to*) *it*	**Ihnen**	(*to*) *you*

Note 1: **Dir** and **euch** are the dative forms of **du** and **ihr,** respectively. The observations which apply to **du** and **ihr** apply also to **dir** and **euch** (see Unit 2, p. 12).

Note 2: **Ihm** is the dative form of both **er** and **es.**

5. If there is a direct object noun and an indirect object noun or pronoun in the same clause, the indirect object precedes the direct object:

a. Der Student schreibt **seiner Mutter einen Brief.**
The student is writing a letter to his mother.

b. Der Student schreibt **ihr einen Brief.**
The student is writing her a letter.

If the direct object is a pronoun, it always precedes the indirect object:

c. Die Brüder geben **es dem Kind.**
The brothers are giving it to the child.

d. Sie geben **es ihm.**
They are giving it to him (*her*).

6. The dative is required after certain prepositions. Common among these are:

aus *from, out of* **bei** *at the house of* **mit** *with*

a. Die Schüler kommen **aus der Schule.**
The pupils are coming from school.

b. Er wohnt **bei seinem Onkel.**
He lives at his uncle's house.

c. Der Junge spielt **mit seinen Brüdern.**
The boy is playing with his brothers.

Note: One-syllable masculine and neuter nouns may add **-e** in the dative singular. The ending is regularly used in the phrases **zu Hause** and **nach Hause.**

7. The possessive **sein** has the same endings in the singular as the indefinite article. For masculine and neuter nouns the dative form is **seinem,** for feminine nouns **seiner:**

a. Er wohnt bei **seinem Onkel.**
He is living at his uncle's house.

b. Der Mann kommt mit **seinem Kind(e).**
The man is coming with his child.

c. Der Student schreibt **seiner Mutter.**
The student is writing to his mother.

In the plural the dative form is **seinen:**

d. Der Junge spielt mit **seinen Brüdern.**
The boy is playing with his brothers.

D. EXERCISES

Write the following sentences in German and be able to express them orally.

1. His brothers are coming with him.

2. Does she like to write?
3. His brother and his sister are playing at our house.
4. Are you living at home?
5. The child is playing with his sister.
6. The pupils are coming out of the room.
7. We are giving the pupil (*f.*) the letter.
8. What are the daughters' names?
9. Does the girl like to study?
10. They are writing us a letter. They are writing it to us.
11. Who lives at your house?
12. Are the mothers at home?
13. A student (*f.*) is coming out of the building.
14. His sisters are coming with us.
15. I am giving the child his book.
16. Who is going with you?
17. Does the father write to his daughters?
18. The girl and the boy are saying it to the teachers.
19. Their names are Klara Schmidt and Anna Braun.
20. Are you giving the woman a book?
21. The son lives at his parents' house.
22. Are we going home?
23. He is playing with his child.
24. The man and his son are at my house.

E. COMPREHENDING AND SPEAKING

I. Repeat the following after your instructor (or the speaker) and study thoroughly.

DAS FERNROHR[1]

Walter ist bei Peter. Die beiden[2] lernen die Aufgabe. Sie schreiben die Sätze[3] aus dem Buch in ein Heft.[4]

Peter sagt nach einer Weile:[5] „Ich habe genug.[6] Ich gehe an das Fenster, um den Mond zu beobachten.[7] Kommen Sie mit mir?"

5 „Gerne", sagt Walter, „aber warum[8] sagen Sie ‚Sie' zu mir? Sie sind Student wie ich. Ich sage jetzt du zu dir."

„Gut", sagt Peter, „kommst du nun[9] an das Fenster, Walter?"

[1]**das Fernrohr**	the telescope	[6]**ich habe genug**	I'm fed up
[2]**die beiden**	the two (*both of them*)	[7]**um den Mond zu**	in order to observe
[3]**die Sätze**	the sentences	**beobachten**	the moon
[4]**das Heft**	the notebook	[8]**warum?**	why?
[5]**nach einer Weile**	after a while	[9]**nun**	now

„Gerne. Wo hast du das Teleskop?"

„Hier ist es. Wie heißt ein Teleskop auf deutsch?"

10   Peter liest in einem Buch: „Ein Teleskop heißt auf deutsch Fernrohr."

Peter und Walter spielen eine Weile mit dem Fernrohr.

Der Vater kommt in das Zimmer. „Guten Abend!" sagt er.

„Guten Abend, Vater. Hier ist Walter Meyer. Wir machen unsere

15   Aufgaben zusammen."

Der Vater begrüßt Walter. „Macht ihr nun auch die Aufgabe?" fragt er.

„Nein, Vater. Wir beobachten jetzt den Mond. Wir machen die Aufgabe nachher."

II. Beantworten Sie die folgenden Fragen auf deutsch!

1. Was lernen Walter und Peter?
2. Wie machen sie ihre Aufgabe?
3. Was will (*wants*) Peter am Fenster beobachten?
4. Wer spielt mit dem Fernrohr?
5. Was fragt der Vater?
6. Haben Peter und Walter die Aufgabe schon gemacht?

UNIT 4

A. UNITS OF SPEECH AND VOCABULARY

I. Study and Practice Aloud.

Wieviel Uhr ist es?	What time is it?
Es ist ein Uhr.	It's one o'clock.
Um wieviel Uhr . . .?	At what time . . .?
um zwei Uhr	at two o'clock
in die Schule	to school
anstatt des Mannes	instead of the man
während des Tages	during the day
während des Morgens	during the morning
er arbeitet	he works, is working, does work

die Arbeit	the work	**ein**	one
die Familie	the family	**zwei**	two
der Freund	the friend	**drei**	three
die Freundin	the (girl) friend	**vier**	four
der Morgen	the morning	**fünf**	five
der Tag	the day	**dieser**	this, that
Deutsch	German	**jeder**	each, every
arbeiten	to work	**mancher**	many a
beginnen	to begin, to start	**manche**	some
besuchen	to visit	**welcher?**	which?
essen	to eat	**anstatt**	instead of
lehren	to teach	**während**	during
jetzt	now		

(25)

II. Oral Practice. Repeat the pattern sentence. Then substitute the items listed below. Repeat the entire sentence with each substitute item, making any other necessary changes.

a. Wieviel Uhr ist es? — Es ist ein Uhr.
  1. 5   3. 4
  2. 3   4. 2

b. Um wieviel Uhr kommt er?
  1. sein Freund   4. seine Freundin
  2. sein Student   5. Fräulein Meyer
  3. seine Familie   6. sie (*sing.*)

c. Wir essen um zwei Uhr.
  1. 4   4. 3
  2. 1   5. jetzt
  3. 5

d. Sie geht in die Schule.
  1. seine Freundin   4. das Mädchen
  2. sein Sohn   5. das Kind
  3. er   6. ich

e. Kommt ein Mädchen anstatt des Mannes?
  1. ein Junge   3. ein Kind
  2. eine Frau   4. ein Freund

f. Die Familie besucht ihn während des Tages.
  1. mich   3. uns
  2. sie (*sing.*)   4. Sie

g. Er arbeitet während des Morgens.
  1. der Mann   4. die Familie
  2. die Frau   5. die Studentin
  3. seine Freundin   6. sein Freund

h. Die Familie beginnt die Arbeit.
  1. der Junge   4. der Professor
  2. der Student   5. sein Freund
  3. der Lehrer   6. seine Freundin

i. Mancher Junge arbeitet.
  1. mancher Mann   7. dieser Student
  2. mancher Freund   8. dieser Bruder
  3. mancher Student   9. dieser Freund
  4. jeder Schüler   10. manche Schüler
  5. jeder Lehrer   11. manche Lehrer
  6. jeder Professor   12. manche Mütter

j. Er lehrt Deutsch.
  1. dieser Mann   4. sein Freund
  2. dieser Herr   5. seine Freundin
  3. dieser Professor   6. sie (*sing.*)

k. Was macht er?

1. der Professor
2. der Junge

3. sein Freund
4. dieser Schüler

B. MODEL SENTENCES

I. Study each sentence until you can reproduce it correctly.

23. **Die Frau des Bruders heißt Lotte.**
24. **Der Sohn der Frau besucht uns.**
25. **Die Familie des Kindes ist hier.**
26. **Der Bruder der Mädchen kommt mit ihnen.**
27. **Diese Studentin ist Maries Freundin.**
28. **Anstatt des Mannes kommt sein Sohn.**
29. **Während des Tages arbeiten wir.**
30. **Jetzt lehrt sie Deutsch.**
31. **Geht er um ein Uhr in die Schule?**

23. The brother's wife is called Lotte.
24. The woman's son is visiting us.
25. The child's family is here.
26. The brother of the girls is coming with them.
27. This coed is Marie's friend.
28. Instead of the man his son is coming.
29. We work during the day.
30. She is teaching German now.
31. Does he go to school at one o'clock?

II. Pattern Practice. Repeat the model sentence. Then substitute the following items in the equivalent part of the model sentence. Repeat the entire sentence with each substitute item.

a. Die Frau des Bruders heißt Lotte.

1. die Tochter, Gretchen
2. die Freundin, Marie
3. der Sohn, Hans

4. der Freund, Walter
5. der Onkel, Robert
6. das Kind, Karl

b. Der Sohn der Frau besucht uns.

1. das Kind
2. der Onkel
3. der Vater

4. die Schwester
5. die Tochter
6. die Mutter

c. Die Familie des Kindes ist hier.

1. die Mutter
2. die Schwester
3. der Vater

4. der Bruder
5. der Onkel
6. der Freund

d. Der Bruder der Mädchen kommt mit ihnen.

1. der Vater
2. der Freund
3. der Lehrer
4. die Mutter
5. die Freundin
6. der Onkel

e. Diese Studentin ist Maries Freundin.

1. Maries Schwester
2. Gretchens Schwester
3. Gretchens Freundin
4. Erikas Freundin
5. Erikas Schwester
6. Frau Meyers Schwester

f. Anstatt des Mannes kommt sein Sohn.

1. sein Freund
2. sein Kind
3. seine Tochter
4. seine Frau

g. Während des Tages arbeiten wir.

1. sie
2. die Eltern
3. die Väter
4. die Mütter
5. der Schüler und die Schülerin
6. der Student und die Studentin

h. Jetzt lehrt sie Deutsch.

1. die Frau
2. der Lehrer
3. er
4. der Mann
5. die Studentin
6. das Mädchen

i. Geht er um ein Uhr in die Schule?

1. er, fünf
2. sie, fünf
3. sie, zwei
4. das Kind, zwei
5. das Kind, vier
6. das Mädchen, vier
7. das Mädchen, drei
8. der Schüler, drei

C. STRUCTURE

1. Possession is indicated by the genitive case:

   a. Die Frau des Bruders heißt Lotte.
   The brother's wife is called Lotte.

   b. Der Sohn der Frau besucht uns.
   The woman's son is visiting us.

   c. Die Familie des Kindes ist hier.
   The child's family is here.

   d. Der Bruder der Mädchen kommt mit ihnen.
   The brother of the girls is coming with them.

Note: **Die Frau des Bruders** may mean *the brother's wife* or *the wife of the brother.*

The genitive forms of the definite article are **des** for the masculine and neuter singulars, **der** for the feminine singular and all plurals. The genitive forms of the indefinite article are **eines** for the masculine and neuter, **einer** for the feminine.

Most masculine and neuter nouns of one syllable add **-es** as the genitive singular ending: **des Mannes, des Kindes.** Those of two or more syllables usually add **-s** (sometimes **-es**): **des Vaters, des Mädchens.**

The genitive singular of feminine nouns and the genitive plural of any gender have no endings: **der Frau, der Mädchen.**

2. Full table of the definite and indefinite articles:

	MASCULINE		FEMININE		NEUTER		PLURAL
NOM.	**der**	**ein**	**die**	**eine**	**das**	**ein**	**die**
GEN.	**des**	**eines**	**der**	**einer**	**des**	**eines**	**der**
DAT.	**dem**	**einem**	**der**	**einer**	**dem**	**einem**	**den**
ACC.	**den**	**einen**	**die**	**eine**	**das**	**ein**	**die**

3. The possessive **sein** follows the pattern of the indefinite article:

	MASCULINE	FEMININE	NEUTER	PLURAL
NOM.	**sein**	**seine**	**sein**	**seine**
GEN.	**seines**	**seiner**	**seines**	**seiner**
DAT.	**seinem**	**seiner**	**seinem**	**seinen**
ACC.	**seinen**	**seine**	**sein**	**seine**

4. **Dieser** (*this, that*) follows the pattern of the definite article:

	MASCULINE	FEMININE	NEUTER	PLURAL
NOM.	**dieser**	**diese**	**dieses**	**diese**
GEN.	**dieses**	**dieser**	**dieses**	**dieser**
DAT.	**diesem**	**dieser**	**diesem**	**diesen**
ACC.	**diesen**	**diese**	**dieses**	**diese**

The same endings are used for:

jeder *each, every*   **mancher** *many a*   **welcher?** *which?*

Note: Because they have endings similar to those of the definite article, these words are called **der**-words.

5. The genitive of proper names, regardless of gender, is formed by adding **-s:**

> Diese Studentin ist **Maries Freundin.**
> *This coed is Marie's friend.*

Note: Proper names ending in **-s, -z,** or **-sch** do not add **-s** and indicate this omission by an apostrophe:

> **Hans' Freundin** heißt Marie Meyer.
> *The name of Hans' girl friend is Marie Meyer.*

6. The genitive is required after certain prepositions:

anstatt	*instead of*
anstatt des Mannes	*instead of the man*
während	*during*
während des Tages	*during the day*

7. Ordinarily, the subject precedes the verb in a statement. If, however, the clause begins with an emphatic element (such as an adverb or a prepositional phrase) the subject must follow the verb:

a. Während des Tages arbeiten wir.
  We work during the day.
b. Jetzt lehrt sie Deutsch.
  She is teaching German now.

8. In statements, adverbs and phrases of time often stand first (see examples in the preceding paragraph). If not in initial position, expressions of time normally precede other adverbial expressions and noun objects:

a. Er geht **um ein Uhr in die Schule.**
  He goes to school at one o'clock.
  Geht er **um ein Uhr in die Schule?**
  Does he go to school at one o'clock?

b. Sie lehrt **jetzt hier.**
  She is teaching here now.
  Lehrt sie **jetzt hier?**
  Is she teaching here now?

c. Sie lehrt **jetzt Deutsch.**
  She is teaching German now.
  Lehrt sie **jetzt Deutsch?**
  Is she teaching German now?

Note: Expressions of time must follow pronoun objects:

a. Ich besuche **ihn während des Tages.**
  I visit him during the day.
b. Besucht sie **ihn jetzt?**
  Is she visiting him now?

D. EXERCISES

Write the following sentences in German and be able to express them orally.

1. Which pupils are here now?
2. These girls like to study.
3. Many a boy goes home at three o'clock.
4. Every family has one child.
5. Is the son coming instead of his parents?
6. Now we are beginning the lesson.
7. Do you go home during the day?
8. The parents of the girls are visiting us.
9. Is she learning German now?
10. That girl is Hans' daughter.
11. Which child is writing this letter?
12. Instead of the girl a woman is coming.
13. At what time do we begin?
14. The daughter of a friend is teaching German here.
15. Which son is working?
16. They begin at two o'clock.
17. Every pupil (*f.*) comes into the room during the morning.
18. The name of Klara's father is Richard.
19. He's greeting his sister's three daughters.
20. The two brothers are giving the parents a house.
21. The daughter is visiting a girl friend instead of the mother.
22. Into which building are his parents going?
23. The girl's brothers go to school at nine o'clock.
24. The student has his girl friend's book.
25. Some mothers come during the day.

E. COMPREHENDING AND SPEAKING

I. Repeat the following after your instructor (or the speaker) and study thoroughly.

DIE DEUTSCHSTUNDE[1]

Um zwei Uhr beginnt die Deutschstunde. Anstatt des Professors kommt ein Fremder[2] in das Klassenzimmer. „Ich bin Professor Gerber", sagt er. „Professor Müller ist krank.[3] Ich lehre Sie heute[4] Deutsch. Wir beginnen auf Seite fünf.[5] Hat jeder ein Buch? Gut!"

[1]**die Deutschstunde**	the German class	[4]**heute**	today
[2]**ein Fremder**	a stranger	[5]**auf Seite fünf**	on page five
[3]**krank**	sick		

5   Peters Bank ist hinten im Zimmer.[6] Walter ist neben[7] ihm. Während der Stunde schaut Peter immer auf die Uhr.[8] Das Wetter[9] ist so schön. Draußen[10] spielen zwei Studenten Tennis. Aber es ist erst[11] zwei Uhr.

Peter sagt leise:[12] ,,Ich spiele nach der Deutschstunde Tennis.
10   Kommst du mit mir, Walter?''

,,Um wieviel Uhr gehst du?'' fragt Walter.

,,Um fünf.''

,,Gut, ich komme mit dir.''

,,Der Lehrer kommt mit dem Buch zu Walter. ,,Haben Sie die
15   Aufgabe?'' fragt er.

,,Wo sind wir?'' fragt Walter leise.

,,Auf Seite fünf'', sagt Peter.

,,Danke'', sagt Walter. Er liest[13] die Aufgabe.

,,Gut'', sagt Professor Gerber, ,,für morgen gebe ich Ihnen keine[14]
20   Aufgabe.''

II. Beantworten Sie die folgenden Fragen auf deutsch!

1. Um wieviel Uhr beginnt die Deutschstunde?
2. Wer kommt anstatt des Professors ins Klassenzimmer?
3. Welcher Student hat ein Buch?
4. Wo ist Peters Bank?
5. Was spielen die zwei Studenten draußen?
6. Gibt Professor Gerber Walter eine Aufgabe?

[6]**Peters Bank ist hinten im Zimmer.**	Peter's seat is in the back of the room.	[9]**das Wetter**	the weather
		[10]**draußen**	outside
		[11]**erst**	only
[7]**neben ihm**	next to him	[12]**leise**	softly
[8]**schaut . . . immer auf die Uhr**	keeps looking at his watch	[13]**er liest**	he reads
		[14]**keine Aufgabe**	no assignment

UNIT 5

A. UNITS OF SPEECH AND VOCABULARY

I. Study and Practice Aloud.

Er kommt nicht.	He isn't coming.
Die Söhne gehen nicht.	The sons aren't going.
Schreibt das Mädchen nicht?	Isn't the girl writing? Doesn't the girl write?
Lernen sie nicht?	Aren't they studying? Don't they study?
Wir essen zu Mittag.[1]	We are eating lunch (or dinner).
Essen sie zu Abend?[2]	Are they eating supper (or dinner)?
Er ist (schon) seit einem Jahr hier.	He has been here for one year.
Sie sind (schon) seit zwei Tagen hier.	They have been here for two days.
zu Bett	to bed

der Bleistift	the pencil	**die Hand**	the hand
die Bleistifte	the pencils	**die Hände**	the hands
die Briefe	the letters	**die Häuser**	the houses
das Brot	the bread	**das Jahr**	the year
die Bücher	the books	**die Jahre**	the years
die Freunde	the friends	**die Kinder**	the children

---

[1] This expression is used in German for the midday meal, which may be called "lunch" or "dinner" in the United States.

[2] This expression is used in German for the evening meal, which may be called "dinner" or "supper" in the United States.

die **Männer**	the men	**euer**	your
die **Söhne**	the sons	**Ihr**	your
die **Tage**	the days	**sechs**	six
die **Tische**	the tables	**sieben**	seven
alt	old	**acht**	eight
schön	beautiful, nice	**neun**	nine
nicht	not	**zehn**	ten
schon	already	**elf**	eleven
kein	no, not any	**zwölf**	twelve
mein	my	**wann?**	when? at what time?
dein	your		
ihr	her, its (*f.*), their	**seit** (+ *dat.*)	since
unser	our		

II. Oral Practice. Repeat the pattern sentence. Then substitute the items listed below. Repeat the entire sentence with each substitute item, changing the verb where necessary.

a. Er kommt nicht.

1. mein Sohn
2. ihr Sohn
3. ihr Junge
4. unser Junge
5. Ihr Junge
6. die Söhne
7. die Kinder
8. die Männer
9. die Freunde
10. mein Sohn und Ihr Sohn

b. Die Söhne gehen nicht.

1. die Freunde
2. die Männer
3. die Lehrer
4. die Kinder
5. sie (*pl.*)
6. wir

c. Schreibt das Mädchen nicht?

1. Ihr Bruder
2. unser Bruder
3. ihr Kind
4. ihr Vater
5. ihr Freund
6. mein Freund

d. Lernen Sie nicht?

1. die Schüler
2. die Kinder
3. seine Kinder
4. seine Söhne
5. seine Freunde
6. seine Schüler

e. Wir essen zu Mittag.

1. die Männer
2. die Kinder
3. die Mädchen
4. seine Onkel
5. seine Freunde
6. seine Kinder

f. Essen sie zu Abend?

1. seine Söhne
2. seine Freunde
3. seine Eltern
4. seine Kinder
5. die Kinder
6. die Männer

g. **Er ist (schon) seit einem Jahr hier.**
  1. der Student   4. das Mädchen
  2. der Junge   5. die Studentin
  3. die Schülerin   6. der Professor

h. **Sie sind (schon) seit zwei Tagen hier.**
  1. seine Freunde   4. die Häuser
  2. die Kinder   5. die Bücher
  3. die Männer   6. die Briefe

i. **Geht er zu Bett?**
  1. Ihr Sohn   4. sein Kind
  2. unser Junge   5. mein Kind
  3. ihr Kind   6. unser Kind

j. **Er schreibt sechs Briefe.**
  1. 7   3. 9
  2. 8   4. 11

k. **Wir haben neun Bücher.**
  1. 10 Tische   4. 12 Bleistifte
  2. 2 Häuser   5. einen Bleistift
  3. 2 Hände

l. **Die Häuser sind schön.**
  1. die Gebäude   4. sie
  2. die Tische   5. die Mädchen
  3. die Bücher   6. die Kinder

m. **Die Bücher sind alt.**
  1. die Briefe   4. das Brot
  2. die Tische   5. das Haus
  3. die Häuser   6. das Gebäude

n. **Kein Brot ist hier.**
  1. kein Tisch   4. kein Bleistift
  2. kein Mann   5. kein Kind
  3. kein Haus   6. kein Mädchen

B. MODEL SENTENCES

I. Study each sentence until you can reproduce it correctly.

32. **Meine Freunde sind seit neun Tagen hier.**
33. **Ihr Bruder lernt schon seit drei Jahren Deutsch.**
34. **Haben Sie kein Brot?**
35. **Seine Schwester schreibt ihm nicht.**
36. **Sie spielt jetzt nicht, sie lernt.**

37. Unsere Kinder lernen nicht gerne.
38. Die Männer gehen nicht in das Haus.
39. Dieser Mann ist nicht mein Onkel.

32. My friends have been here for nine days.
33. Her brother has been studying German for three years.
34. Have you no bread?
35. His sister is not writing to him.
36. She isn't playing now; she is studying.
37. Our children don't like to study.
38. The men are not going into the house.
39. This man is not my uncle.

II. Pattern Practice. Repeat the model sentence. Then substitute the following items in the equivalent part of the model sentence. Repeat the entire sentence with each substitute item, changing the verb where necessary.

a. Meine Freunde sind seit neun Tagen hier.

1. zehn	4. sechs
2. zwölf	5. elf
3. acht	6. sieben

b. Ihr Bruder lernt schon seit drei Jahren Deutsch.

1. sechs	4. zwei
2. neun	5. fünf
3. vier	6. sieben

c. Haben Sie kein Brot?

1. Buch	3. Zimmer
2. Haus	4. Fenster

d. Seine Schwester schreibt ihm nicht.

1. Mutter	3. Familie
2. Tochter	4. Freundin

e. Sie spielt jetzt nicht; sie lernt.

1. er	4. die Mädchen
2. wir	5. der Schüler und die Schülerin
3. die Kinder	6. die Freunde

f. Unsere Kinder lernen nicht gerne.

1. Töchter	3. Brüder
2. Söhne	4. Freunde

g. Die Männer gehen nicht in das Haus.

1. die Väter	4. die Mädchen
2. die Mütter	5. die Eltern
3. die Kinder	6. die Brüder

h. Dieser Mann ist nicht mein Onkel.

1. mein Bruder
2. mein Vater
3. mein Freund
4. mein Lehrer
5. mein Sohn
6. mein Student

C. STRUCTURE

1. An action which began in the past and continues into the present is expressed in the present tense. Duration of time is indicated by **seit** plus dative case:

   Meine Freunde **sind seit neun Tagen hier.**
   My friends have been here for nine days.

   To emphasize duration, **schon** (*already*) may be added before **seit.**

   Ihr Bruder **lernt schon seit drei Jahren** Deutsch.
   Her brother has been studying German for three years.

2. Most German nouns form their plurals by adding a letter or a syllable. Many nouns add **-e.** The masculine nouns in this group frequently take umlaut, the feminine nouns wherever possible, the neuter nouns never:

der Bleistift	*the pencil*	**die Bleistifte**	*the pencils*
der Sohn	*the son*	**die Söhne**	*the sons*
der Tag	*the day*	**die Tage**	*the days*
die Hand	*the hand*	**die Hände**	*the hands*

3. Some nouns add **-er** to form the plural:

der Mann	*the man*	**die Männer**	*the men*
das Kind	*the child*	**die Kinder**	*the children*
das Buch	*the book*	**die Bücher**	*the books*

   There are no feminine nouns in this group. The masculine and neuter nouns take umlaut wherever possible.

4. One cannot tell by simply looking at a noun what plural ending, if any, it will take. It is therefore best to memorize the plural along with the singular when you learn a new noun:

NOM. SING.	NOM. PLURAL
der Lehrer	**die Lehrer**
die Hand	**die Hände**
das Haus	**die Häuser**

In vocabularies and word lists the plural endings are usually abbreviated as follows:

> **der Lehrer, -**
> **die Hand, ⁼e**
> **das Haus, ⁼er**

5. The negative indefinite article **kein** (*no, not any*) is declined in the singular like the indefinite article **ein** (*a, an*), in the plural like the **der**-words:

	Singular			Plural
	MASCULINE	FEMININE	NEUTER	ALL GENDERS
NOM.	kein	keine	kein	keine
GEN.	keines	keiner	keines	keiner
DAT.	keinem	keiner	keinem	keinen
ACC.	keinen	keine	kein	keine

Note 1: The case endings of **der**-words and **ein**-words are identical in all forms except the three boxed above: nominative masculine singular, nominative and accusative neuter singular. For these forms, **ein**-words have no case endings at all.

Note 2: The sentence **Ich habe keine Bücher** means either *I don't have* (or *haven't*) *any books* or *I have no books.*

6. The possessive adjectives are as follows:

mein	*my*	**unser**	*our*
dein	*your*	**euer**	*your*
sein	*his, its*	**ihr**	*their*
ihr	*her, its*	**Ihr**	*your*

mein is the possessive adjective for **ich**
dein is the possessive adjective for **du**
sein is the possessive adjective for **er** and **es**
unser is the possessive adjective for **wir**
euer is the possessive adjective for **ihr**
ihr is the possessive adjective for **sie** (sing. and pl.)
Ihr (always capitalized) is the possessive adjective for **Sie**

Note 1: Possessive adjectives have the same endings as **ein** and **kein**.

Note 2: The possessive adjective must be repeated before each noun in a series:

> **mein Vater und meine Mutter**
> *my father and mother*

7. The negative word **nicht** (*not*) usually *follows* the verb, its objects, and adverbs of time:

   a. Seine Schwester schreibt ihm **nicht.**
      His sister is not writing to him.
   b. Sie spielt jetzt **nicht,** sie lernt.
      She isn't playing now; she is studying.

Nicht usually *precedes* adverbs of manner or place:

   c. Unsere Kinder lernen **nicht gerne.**
      Our children don't like to study.
   d. Unsere Kinder sind **nicht hier.**
      Our children are not here.

Nicht usually *precedes* prepositional phrases:

   e. Die Männer gehen **nicht in das Haus.**
      The men are not going into the house.

Nicht usually *precedes* predicate nouns and adjectives.

   f. Dieser Mann ist **nicht mein Onkel.**
      This man is not my uncle.
   g. Dieser Mann ist **nicht alt.**
      That man is not old.

D. EXERCISES

Write the following sentences in German and be able to express them orally.

1. His child is ten days old.
2. We have no tables in these rooms.
3. When do your children go to bed?
4. Her son and her daughter do not eat any bread.
5. That child is not their brother.
6. She is writing her daughter seven letters.
7. Do your parents eat at twelve o'clock?
8. The man is working with one hand.
9. Is your brother going to bed now?
10. At what time do you eat lunch?
11. Aren't her mother's hands beautiful?
12. My father and mother eat at eight o'clock.
13. These books are not old.
14. Our friends have been at our house for three days.
15. They are giving the books to their pupils.

16. She has been writing this letter for four days.
17. Their children don't have any bread.
18. This pupil (*f.*) has been going to school for five years.
19. My daughter's children are not here.
20. These houses have six rooms.
21. These men have been living here for two years.
22. No student is there now.
23. Doesn't your girl friend have a book?
24. Are their houses beautiful?

E. COMPREHENDING AND SPEAKING

I. Repeat the following after your instructor (or the speaker) and study thoroughly.

EIN BESUCH AUS DEUTSCHLAND[1]

Um acht Uhr essen Peter und seine Familie zu Abend.[2] Heute ist ein Gast da. Er heißt Georg Hauser und wohnt seit zehn Jahren in Deutschland. Peters Vater und Georg Hauser sind schon lange[3] Freunde. Peter begrüßt die Familie und den Gast.

5 „Guten Abend, Peter", sagt Herr Hauser, „Sie lernen Deutsch, sagt Ihr Vater. Haben Sie Deutsch gern?"

„Oh ja", sagt Peter, „ich verstehe und spreche schon manches."[4]

„Das ist schön!" sagt Herr Hauser. „Wann besuchen Sie mich in Deutschland? Dort lernen Sie leicht[5] Deutsch. Warum kommen Sie 10 nicht schon dieses Jahr?"

„Gern", sagt Peter, „aber ich habe leider kein Geld.[6] Ich frage meinen Vater."

Der Vater ist nicht begeistert.[7] Er macht ein ernstes Gesicht:[8] „Ich habe kein Geld für eine Deutschlandreise."[9]

15 „Ich verdiene das Geld selbst",[10] sagt Peter, „ich arbeite gerne."

[1]**Ein Besuch aus Deutschland**	a visitor from Germany	[7]**begeistert**	enthusiastic
[2]**essen . . . zu Abend**	eat dinner	[8]**ein ernstes Gesicht machen**	to look serious
[3]**schon lange**	for a long time	[9]**die Deutschlandreise**	the trip to Germany
[4]**ich verstehe und spreche schon manches**	I already understand and speak a lot	[10]**ich verdiene das Geld selbst**	I'll earn the money myself
[5]**leicht**	easily		
[6]**Gern . . . aber ich habe leider kein Geld**	I would like to, but unfortunately I have no money		

II. Beantworten Sie die folgenden Fragen auf deutsch!

1. Wann essen Peter und seine Familie zu Abend?
2. Wer ist heute bei Peters Familie?
3. Wie heißt der Gast?
4. Seit wann wohnt Herr Hauser in Deutschland?
5. Was sagt Herr Hauser zu Peter?
6. Warum ist der Vater nicht begeistert?

REVIEW UNIT 1

A. *Supply the proper endings.*

1. Er wohnt seit ein— Jahr hier.
2. Das Kind besucht d— Mann.
3. Sein Onkel hat kein— Freunde.
4. Wann beginnt er d— Aufgabe?
5. Sie besuchen uns während d— Jahr—.
6. Welch— Junge hat d— Buch?
7. Der Vater schreibt sein— Söhn— zwei Briefe.
8. Haben Sie d— Bücher?
9. Hans ist jetzt bei sein— Freundin.
10. Mit welch— Mädchen spielt Klara?
11. Was sag— du, Marie?
12. Der Schüler lern— seine Aufgabe.
13. Meine Freunde schreib— jetzt Briefe.
14. Ich ess— jetzt.
15. Die Schule beginn— um neun Uhr.
16. Manch— Mädchen heißt Marie.
17. Welch— Freund besucht er jetzt?
18. Jed— Schülerin macht ihre Arbeit.
19. Wir geben dies— Kind das Brot.
20. Wie heißt die Schwester sein— Freund—?

B. *Supply the proper form of the word in parentheses in the place indicated.*

1. (sein) Vater, wo ———— du?
2. (Bruder) Sie haben vier ————.

(*42*)

3. (Haus) Sie gehen jetzt nach _____.
4. (Kind) Der Bruder des _____ heißt Hans.
5. (essen) Wann _____ ihr zu Abend, Karl und Robert?
6. (Buch) Diese _____ sind schön.
7. (Sohn) Die Frau begrüßt ihre _____.
8. (Vater) Wir geben den _____ die Briefe.
9. (haben) Mein Onkel _____ zwei Freunde.
10. (Mann) Anstatt des _____ kommen ihre Kinder.

C. *Supply in each case one word to complete the meaning of the sentence.*
   1. Wann kommt er _____ dieses Zimmer?
   2. Hat Frau Schmidt _____ Kind oder (*or*) zwei Kinder?
   3. Zwei und drei ist _____.
   4. Besucht er jetzt seine Eltern? — Nein, er besucht _____ nicht.
   5. Wir essen jetzt _____ Mittag.
   6. Wo ist der Brief? — _____ ist dort.
   7. Ihr Onkel wohnt _____ einem Jahr in Berlin.
   8. Frau Meyer ist _____ meine Schwester, sie ist Karls Schwester.
   9. Wann geht Robert _____ Bett?
   10. _____ Morgen, Fräulein Karsten.
   11. Sie ist _____ seit drei Stunden bei uns.
   12. _____ geht es Ihnen, Herr Müller?
   13. Jetzt geht er _____ Hause.
   14. _____ hat mein Buch? — Karl hat es.
   15. Die Schüler kommen _____ das Fenster.
   16. Wohnt er _____ Hause?
   17. Nein, er wohnt _____ Frau Schmidt.
   18. Die Lehrer gehen _____ die Schule.
   19. _____ Wiedersehen.
   20. Drei und vier ist _____.

D. *Beantworten Sie die folgenden Fragen auf deutsch!*
   1. Um wieviel Uhr essen Sie zu Abend?
   2. Was lernen Sie hier?
   3. Schreiben Sie gerne Briefe?
   4. Wohnen Sie zu Hause?
   5. Um wieviel Uhr gehen Sie zu Bett?
   6. Wie geht es Ihnen?
   7. Wie heißen Sie?
   8. Wieviel Uhr ist es?
   9. Wann kommen Sie in die Schule?
   10. Wann gehen Sie nach Hause?

E. *Make the following statements questions.*
1. Das Mädchen ist ihre Schwester.
2. Ihr Bruder lernt schon seit drei Jahren Deutsch.
3. Anstatt des Mannes kommt das Mädchen.
4. Jetzt machen sie die Arbeit.
5. Um zwei Uhr essen die Kinder.

F. *Make the following statements questions, using the interrogative element indicated. Make all other necessary changes.*
1. (Wann) Frau Schmidt spielt mit den Kindern.
2. (Wo) Jetzt lehrt Fräulein Meyer Deutsch.
3. (Um wieviel Uhr) Die Schüler gehen nach Hause.
4. (Was) Der Lehrer schreibt seinen Freunden einen Brief.
5. (Wer) Die Eltern begrüßen die Kinder.

G. *Change the following sentences by putting the indicated words in their proper places.*
1. Seine Eltern kommen in das Wohnzimmer. (jetzt)
2. Sie lehrt seit neun Jahren Deutsch. (schon)
3. Die Mädchen schreiben einen Brief. (uns)
4. Die Kinder gehen zu Bett. (wann)
5. Der Junge schreibt zwei Briefe. (seinen Freunden)
6. Er beginnt jetzt. (es)

H. *Make the following sentences negative.*
1. Es geht mir gut.
2. Er macht die Aufgabe.
3. Ja, er kommt heute.
4. Der Tisch ist hier.
5. Die Brüder geben es dem Kind.
6. Die Studentin hat ein Buch.
7. Der Lehrer hat das Buch.
8. Er hat es.
9. Die Mütter kommen aus dem Hause.
10. Diese Schülerin ist Maries Freundin.
11. Der Lehrer schreibt den Brief.
12. Er schreibt ihn.
13. Die Lehrer gehen an die Tür.
14. Der Student schreibt der Mutter einen Brief.
15. Der Junge wohnt bei seinem Onkel.
16. Sie arbeitet jetzt.
17. Er spielt gerne mit den Kindern.

I. *Change the following sentences to plural.*
1. Das Kind besucht seinen Freund.

2. Dieses Zimmer hat kein Fenster.
3. Wo ist das Haus?
4. Der Tisch ist alt.
5. Wer begrüßt den Mann?
6. Der Vater spielt mit seinem Sohn.
7. Die Mutter besucht ihre Tochter.
8. Der Schüler kommt aus dem Gebäude.
9. Ich habe das Buch des Mädchens.
10. Sie schreibt mir.

UNIT 6

A. UNITS OF SPEECH AND VOCABULARY

I. Study and Practice Aloud.

Er legt es auf den Tisch.	He is putting it on the table.
im Zimmer	in the room
ins Zimmer	into the room
am Fenster	at the window
ans Fenster	to the window

die Aufgaben	the lessons	**sitzen**	to sit
die Familien	the families	**stehen**	to stand
die Frauen	the women	**verstehen**	to understand
der Herr	the gentleman	**groß**	big, large, tall
die Herren	the gentlemen	**gut**	good
die Jungen	the boys	**jung**	young
die Schulen	the schools	**klein**	small, little
die Schülerinnen	the pupils (*f.*)	**an**	at, to
die Schwestern	the sisters	**auf**	on
die Studenten	the students	**hinter**	behind
die Studentinnen	the students (*f.*), coeds	**in**	in, into
		neben	next to, near
finden	to find	**über**	above, over
legen	to lay, put	**unter**	under
liegen	to lie, to be (situated)	**vor**	in front of
		zwischen	between, among

II. Oral Practice. Repeat the pattern sentence. Then substitute the items listed below. Repeat the entire sentence with each substitute item, changing the verb where necessary.

a. Er legt es auf den Tisch.

1. der Junge	4. der Herr
2. das Mädchen	5. wir
3. die Frau	6. Sie

b. Die Studenten sitzen im Zimmer.

1. die Studentinnen	4. die Frauen
2. die Schwestern	5. die Schülerinnen
3. die Herren	6. sie (*pl.*)

c. Die Jungen kommen ins Zimmer.

1. die Schülerinnen	4. die Herren
2. die Studentinnen	5. die Mädchen
3. die Frauen	6. meine Schwestern

d. Er steht am Fenster.

1. der Herr	4. sie (*sing.*)
2. der Lehrer	5. wir
3. die Studentin	6. ich

e. Sie geht ans Fenster.

1. er	3. die Frau
2. der Herr	4. wir

III. Oral Practice. Repeat the pattern sentence. Then substitute the following items in the appropriate places. Repeat the entire sentence with each substitute item, changing the verb where necessary.

a. Die Jungen sind groß.

1. Die Häuser _____	6. _____ jung.
2. Die Familien _____	7. Die Studentinnen _____
3. Ihre Schwestern _____	8. Die Herren _____
4. Die Fenster _____	9. Die Schülerinnen _____
5. Die Frauen _____	

b. Meine Schwestern sind klein.

1. Ihre Familien _____	5. _____ gut.
2. Ihre Häuser _____	6. Die Aufgaben _____
3. Die Schülerinnen _____	7. Sie _____
4. Die Schulen _____	

c. Die Jungen finden ihre Schwestern.

1. _____ ihre Bücher.	4. _____ ihre Aufgaben.
2. Die Frauen _____	5. Die Schüler _____
3. Die Schülerinnen _____	6. Die Mädchen _____

d. Die Aufgaben liegen hier.

1. Die Bücher _____   4. Die Bücher _____
2. Sie _____   5. Das Buch _____
3. _____ dort.   6. Es _____

e. Die Herren verstehen uns.

1. _____ Sie.   3. _____ die Herren.
2. Wir _____   4. Die Frauen _____

B. MODEL SENTENCES

I. Study each sentence until you can reproduce it correctly.

40. Die Studentinnen verstehen den Herrn.
41. Herrn Brauns Jungen sind groß.
42. Die Frauen gehen ans Fenster.
43. Die Frau steht am Fenster.
44. Die Schüler legen die Aufgaben auf den Tisch.
45. Ihre Aufgaben liegen auf dem Tisch.
46. Gehen Sie ins Zimmer!

40. The coeds understand the gentleman.
41. Mr. Braun's boys are big.
42. The women are going to the window.
43. The woman is standing at the window.
44. The students are putting the lessons on the table.
45. Their lessons are lying on the table.
46. Go into the room.

II. Pattern Practice. Repeat the model sentence. Then substitute the following items in the equivalent part of the model sentence. Repeat the entire sentence with each substitute item, changing the verb where necessary.

a. Die Studentinnen verstehen den Herrn.

1. die Studenten   4. die Lehrer
2. die Schüler   5. sie (*pl.*)
3. die Schülerinnen   6. wir

b. Herrn Brauns Jungen sind groß.

1. Eltern   4. Freunde
2. Brüder   5. Söhne
3. Schwestern   6. Kinder

c. Die Frauen gehen ans Fenster.

1. die Männer   4. die Schülerinnen
2. die Studenten   5. die Schüler
3. die Studentinnen   6. die Herren

d. Die Frau steht am Fenster.

1. sie (*sing.*)	4. das Mädchen
2. der Herr	5. das Kind
3. er	6. es

e. Die Schüler legen die Aufgaben auf den Tisch.

1. die Schülerinnen	4. die Mädchen
2. die Kinder	5. sie (*pl.*)
3. die Jungen	6. wir

f. Ihre Aufgaben liegen auf dem Tisch.

1. die Bücher	4. es
2. sie	5. der Brief
3. das Buch	6. er

g. Gehen Sie ins Zimmer!

1. ans Fenster	4. in die Stadt
2. ins Gebäude	5. anstatt des Mannes
3. in sein Zimmer	6. während des Tages

C. STRUCTURE

1. Most feminine nouns form their plurals by adding **-n** or **-en**. Those of more than one syllable ending in **-e**, **-l**, or **-r** take the plural ending **-n;** others take **-en:**

die Aufgabe	*the lesson*	**die Aufgaben**	*the lessons*
die Schwester	*the sister*	**die Schwestern**	*the sisters*
die Frau	*the woman*	**die Frauen**	*the women*

2. Feminine nouns ending in **-in** add **-nen:**

die Schülerin	*the pupil* (f.)	**die Schülerinnen**	*the pupils* (f.)
die Studentin	*the student* (f.)	**die Studentinnen**	*the students* (f.)

3. Masculine nouns ending in **-e** form their plural by adding **-n:**

der Junge	*the boy*	**die Jungen**	*the boys*

Some other masculine nouns, especially those of more than one syllable with the accent on the last syllable, form their plural by adding **-en:**

der Student	*the student*	**die Studenten**	*the students*

These nouns usually add the same endings for the genitive, dative, and accusative singulars, so that there are two forms: the nominative singular and a form ending in **-n** or **-en** for all other cases:

	SINGULAR		PLURAL	
NOM.	**der Junge**	**der Student**	**die Jungen**	**die Studenten**
GEN.	**des Jungen**	**des Studenten**	**der Jungen**	**der Studenten**
DAT.	**dem Jungen**	**dem Studenten**	**den Jungen**	**den Studenten**
ACC.	**den Jungen**	**den Studenten**	**die Jungen**	**die Studenten**

Note: **Der Herr** (*the gentleman*) adds **-n** for singular genitive, dative and accusative, but **-en** for *all* plural forms. The vocabulary entry is **der Herr, -n, -en.** The title **Herr** (*Mr.*) also adds **-n** in the singular forms, except the nominative.

4. Certain prepositions may combine with the definite article. Though these contractions are optional, they are preferred in colloquial German:

$$\text{an} + \text{dem} = \text{am} \qquad \text{an} + \text{das} = \text{ans}$$
$$\text{in} + \text{dem} = \text{im} \qquad \text{in} + \text{das} = \text{ins}$$
$$\text{auf} + \text{das} = \text{aufs}$$

5. Certain prepositions require the accusative case when expressing motion toward the object and the dative case when expressing position:

   a. Die Frauen gehen **ans** Fenster. (motion)
   The women are going to the window.

   b. Die Frau steht **am** Fenster. (position)
   The woman is standing at the window.

   c. Die Jungen kommen **ins** Zimmer. (motion)
   The boys are coming into the room.

   d. Die Studenten sitzen **im** Zimmer. (position)
   The students are sitting in the room.

   e. Die Schüler legen die Aufgaben **auf den** Tisch. (motion)
   The pupils are putting the lessons on the table.

   f. Ihre Aufgaben liegen **auf dem** Tisch. (position)
   Their lessons are lying on the table.

   Included in this category are the following prepositions:

an	*at, to*	**über**	*above, over*
auf	*on*	**unter**	*under*
hinter	*behind*	**vor**	*in front of, before*
in	*in, into*	**zwischen**	*between, among*
neben	*near, next to*		

6. Direct commands are conventionally expressed by putting the pronoun **Sie** after the verb:

   Gehen Sie ins Zimmer!
   Go into the room.

Such sentences usually end with an exclamation mark.

D. EXERCISES

Write the following sentences in German and be able to express them orally.
1. Don't put the book on the letters.
2. Do your friends understand Mr. Schmidt?
3. My sister likes to sit at the window.
4. Is your family sitting at the table now?
5. Some schools begin at nine o'clock.
6. These pupils are going with Mr. Meyer.
7. His sisters are standing behind my uncle.
8. Above the table are two windows.
9. Every boy's father is here.
10. Begin the letter now.
11. The women are standing next to the building.
12. Find the bread, Miss Braun.
13. We are at the teacher's house now.
14. The women are not young. They are old.
15. Her brothers write letters to the student (*f.*).
16. Are the women coming to the door?
17. The children are putting the lessons between the books.
18. My sisters' families are small.
19. They are giving the student the book.
20. We are putting the boy's books under the tables.
21. The mothers of the pupils (*f.*) are going into the teacher's house.
22. Are the gentlemen sitting at the windows?
23. The school is between these two buildings.
24. Is the boy standing in front of the girls?

E. COMPREHENDING AND SPEAKING

I. Repeat the following after your instructor (or the speaker) and study thoroughly.

BEIM ANGELN[1]

Seit zwölf Jahren geht Herr Schmidt fast jedes Wochenende[2] an einen See,[3] um Fische zu fangen.[4] Peter und Walter kommen oft[5] auch mit ihm. Am See steht ein Haus. Dort verwahrt[6] Herr Schmidt seine Angelruten.[7]

[1]**beim Angeln**	catching fish	[4]**fangen**	to catch
[2]**fast jedes Wochenende**	almost every weekend	[5]**oft**	often
		[6]**verwahren**	to keep
[3]**der See**	the lake	[7]**die Angelruten**	fishing rods

5 „Ich finde meine Angelrute nicht", sagt Peter, „Vater, wo ist sie?"

Herr Schmidt antwortet: „Liegt sie nicht dort unter dem Tisch, Peter?"

„Ich sehe sie nicht."

10 Die drei suchen Peters Angelrute, und Walter findet sie schließlich[8] hinter dem Haus.

Jetzt gehen die Jungen mit dem Vater an den See. Drei Stunden lang[9] sitzen sie am See. Während dieser Zeit sehen sie manchen Fisch, aber sie fangen keinen.

15 „Wir haben heute leider kein Glück!"[10] sagt schließlich der Vater. „Wir essen jetzt zu Mittag. Vielleicht[11] fangen wir unsere Fische am Nachmittag."

Peter und Walter haben auch am Nachmittag kein Glück. Aber neben Herrn Schmidt liegen am Abend zehn Fische auf dem Tisch.

20 „Wie machst du es, Vater?" fragt Peter.

„Es ist nicht so schwer. Meine Angel ist gut und meine Geduld[12] groß", lacht[13] Herr Schmidt.

II. Beantworten Sie die folgenden Fragen auf deutsch!

1. Seit wann geht Herr Schmidt fast jedes Wochenende an einen See?
2. Was steht am See?
3. Wo verwahrt Herr Schmidt seine Angelruten?
4. Was findet Walter schließlich hinter dem Haus?
5. Wer hat Glück beim Angeln?
6. Wie macht es der Vater?

[8]**schließlich**	eventually	[11]**vielleicht**	perhaps
[9]**drei Stunden lang**	for three hours	[12]**die Geduld**	patience
[10]**wir haben heute leider kein Glück**	we are not lucky today, unfortunately	[13]**lachen**	to laugh

---

UNIT 7

A. UNITS OF SPEECH AND VOCABULARY

I. Study and Practice Aloud.

wir müssen essen	we must eat, we have to eat
so groß wie	as big as
in die Stadt	to town, downtown
in der Stadt	in town
noch ein Glas	another glass
noch eine Tante	another aunt
wenig Geld	little money

das Geld, -er	the money	**kalt**	cold
das Glas, ⸗er	the glass	**neu**	new
die Kusine, -n	the cousin (*f.*)	**reich**	rich, wealthy
der Vetter, -n	the cousin	**viel**	much
die Tante, -n	the aunt	**viele**	many
die Stadt, ⸗e	the town, city	**warm**	warm
das Wasser, -	the water	**wenig**	little (in number)
bringen	to bring	**wenige**	few
müssen	must, to have to	**dreizehn**	thirteen
trinken	to drink	**vierzehn**	fourteen
wessen?	whose	**noch**	still, yet
wem?	(to) whom?	**aber**	but
wen?	whom?	**denn**	for, because, since
arm	poor	**warum?**	why?

II. Oral Practice. Repeat the pattern sentence. Then substitute the items listed below. Repeat the entire sentence with each substitute item, changing the verb where necessary.

a. Wir müssen essen.

1. trinken
2. lernen
3. schreiben
4. spielen
5. kommen
6. gehen

b. Er ist so groß wie sie.

1. klein
2. jung
3. alt
4. arm
5. reich
6. gut

c. Warum geht sie in die Stadt?

1. Ihre Tante
2. Ihre Kusine
3. seine Kusine
4. sein Vetter
5. unser Vetter
6. unser Onkel

d. Er bringt noch ein Glas.

1. noch ein Kind
2. noch ein Buch
3. noch einen Tisch
4. noch einen Brief
5. noch eine Tante
6. noch eine Kusine

e. Sie hat wenig Geld.

1. Ihre Tante
2. seine Familie
3. mein Vetter
4. meine Freunde
5. wir
6. ich

f. Wessen Tante wohnt in der Stadt?

1. Kusine
2. Schwester
3. Onkel
4. Vetter
5. Bruder
6. Sohn

g. Wem bringen Sie das Wasser?

1. das Geld
2. das Glas
3. das Buch
4. die Bücher
5. die Gläser
6. die Briefe

h. Wen lehrt er?

1. besucht
2. begrüßt
3. fragt
4. bringt

III. Oral Practice. Repeat the pattern sentence. Then substitute the items below in the appropriate places. Repeat the entire sentence with each substitute item, changing the verb where necessary.

a. Ich trinke viel Wasser.

1. Er _____
2. Meine Schwester _____
3. Sie _____
4. _____ wenig _____
5. Wir _____
6. Ich _____

b. **Das Wasser ist kalt.**

1. _____ warm.
2. _____ noch warm.
3. _____ noch kalt.
4. _____ im Glas.
5. _____ noch im Glas.
6. _____ noch auf dem Tisch.

c. **Die Schule ist neu.**

1. Das Glas _____
2. Das Buch _____
3. Die Bücher _____
4. Die Gläser _____
5. Die Schulen _____
6. Die Städte _____

d. **Ich habe dreizehn Vettern.**

1. _____ 14 _____
2. _____ Tanten.
3. _____ 15 _____
4. _____ 13 Tanten und 14 Vettern.

e. **Er hat kein Geld.**

1. _____ wenig Geld.
2. Sie (*sing.*) _____
3. _____ kein Geld.
4. _____ viel _____
5. Sie (*pl.*) haben _____
6. Seine Eltern _____

B. MODEL SENTENCES

I. Study each sentence until you can reproduce it correctly.

47. **Hier ist mein Brief. Wo ist Ihrer?**
48. **Er hat zwei Bücher und ich habe eins.**
49. **Sein Onkel hat wenig Geld, aber viele Freunde.**
50. **Alte Häuser sind nicht so gut wie neue Häuser.**
51. **Ihr alter Vater wohnt bei ihnen.**
52. **Sein altes Haus ist so groß wie mein neues Haus.**
53. **Mein Vetter Franz und meine Kusine Anna müssen nach Hause gehen.**
54. **Er schreibt gerne Briefe.**

47. Here is my letter. Where is yours?
48. He has two books and I have one.
49. His uncle has little money, but many friends.
50. Old houses are not as good as new houses.
51. Their old father lives at their house.
52. His old house is as big as my new house.
53. My cousin Franz and my cousin Anna must go home.
54. He likes to write letters.

II. Pattern Practice. Repeat the model sentence. Then substitute the following items in the equivalent part of the model sentence. Repeat the entire sentence with each substitute item.

a. Hier ist mein Brief. Wo ist Ihrer?

1.	mein Tisch	4.	mein Vetter
2.	mein Sohn	5.	mein Bruder
3.	mein Freund	6.	mein Vater

b. Er hat zwei Bücher und ich habe eins.

1.	zwei Gläser	4.	zwei Häuser
2.	zwei Kinder	5.	zwei Zimmer
3.	zwei Mädchen		

c. Sein Onkel hat wenig Geld, aber viele Freunde.

1.	sein Vetter	4.	seine Tante
2.	sein Freund	5.	seine Kusine
3.	sein Vater	6.	seine Familie

d. Alte Häuser sind nicht so gut wie neue Häuser.

1.	Gebäude	3.	Tische
2.	Schulen	4.	Gläser

e. Ihr alter Vater wohnt bei ihnen.

1.	sein alter Vater	3.	ihr alter Onkel
2.	sein alter Onkel	4.	ihr alter Vetter

f. Sein altes Haus ist so groß wie mein neues Haus.

1. mein altes Haus, ihr neues Haus
2. ihr altes Haus, sein neues Haus
3. ihr altes Haus, unser neues Haus
4. unser altes Haus, ihr neues Haus

g. Mein Vetter Franz und meine Kusine Anna müssen nach Hause gehen.

1. sein Vetter Franz und seine Kusine Anna
2. sein Vetter Franz und seine Kusine Marie
3. unser Vetter Hans und unsere Kusine Marie
4. ihr Vetter Robert und ihre Kusine Grete

h. Er schreibt gerne Briefe.

1.	ihr Vetter	4.	seine Kusine
2.	mein Freund	5.	ihre Tante
3.	meine Freundin	6.	das Mädchen

C. STRUCTURE

1. The interrogative pronoun **wer?** (*who?*) is inflected as follows:

NOMINATIVE   **wer?**   *who?*

GENITIVE	**wessen?**	*whose?*
DATIVE	**wem?**	*(to) whom?*
ACCUSATIVE	**wen?**	*whom?*

2. An **ein**-word used as a pronoun has the same endings as a **der**-word. In the nominative singular masculine, the **ein**-word pronoun ends in **-er,** (the **ein**-word adjective has no ending in the nominative masculine singular):

   a. Hier ist mein Brief. Wo ist **Ihrer?**
     Here is my letter. Where is yours?

In the nominative and accusative singulars of the neuter, the **ein**-word pronoun ends in **-(e)s** (the **ein**-word adjective has no ending):

   b. Ein Kind ist dort und **ein(e)s** ist hier.
     One child is there and one is here.
   c. Er hat zwei Bücher und ich habe **kein(e)s.**
     He has two books and I have none.

In all other cases, the **ein**-word pronoun has the same form as the adjective:

   d. Sie hat ihre Aufgabe und ich habe **meine.**
     She has her lesson and I have mine.

Note: Articles, **ein**-words, **der**-words, and cardinal numbers are called limiting adjectives because they limit the number, position, or ownership of things. Adjectives which describe some quality of a noun are called descriptive adjectives.

3. **Viel** and **wenig** are limiting adjectives which usually have no endings in the singular but are inflected like **der**-words in the plural:

   Sein Onkel hat **wenig Geld,** aber **viele Freunde.**
   His uncle has little money, but many friends.

4. Descriptive adjectives that modify and precede a noun have certain endings. Descriptive adjectives not preceded by a definite article, a **der**-word, or an inflected **ein**-word have "strong" endings, which are usually identical with **der**-word endings:

   a. **Alte Häuser** sind nicht so gut wie **neue Häuser.**
     Old houses are not as good as new houses.
   b. **Ihr alter Vater** wohnt bei ihnen.
     Their old father lives at their house.
   c. **Sein altes Haus** ist so groß wie **mein neues Haus.**
     His old house is as big as my new house.

5. In comparisons, **so ... wie** is equivalent to English *as ... as* (see examples 4a and 4c).

6. Present indicative of the irregular verb **müssen** (*must, to have to*):

ich **muß**	*I must, have to*
du **mußt**	*you must, have to*
er, sie, es **muß**	*he, she, it must, has to*
wir **müssen**	*we must, have to*
ihr **müßt**	*you must, have to*
sie **müssen**	*they must, have to*
Sie **müssen**	*you must, have to*

7. In a main clause, the infinitive stands last:

Mein Vetter Franz und meine Kusine Anna müssen nach Hause **gehen.**
My cousin Franz and my cousin Anna must go home.

8. **Gern(e)** usually precedes noun objects:

Er schreibt **gern(e)** Briefe.
He likes to write letters.

D. EXERCISES

Write the following sentences in German and be able to express them orally.

1. Their uncle has fourteen houses, but they have none.
2. My cousin (*f.*) likes to live in town.
3. Is he learning much German?
4. The pupil (*f.*) must study her lessons.
5. Are good books good friends?
6. His brother is not as tall as mine.
7. I must bring another glass.
8. The parents of many pupils are here.
9. One young student is still standing there.
10. My aunt is as old as your aunt.
11. To whom do you have to bring water?
12. Your friends have to eat now.
13. Do little boys like to play with little girls?
14. My cousin is coming home, for he has to study.
15. Does your uncle have a new house?
16. Is our old teacher still teaching German?
17. Our cousins live in old houses.
18. Does his school have many rooms? — No, it has few.

19. Whose child is here now? — His.
20. His old uncle has rich daughters.
21. Three books are lying on the table, and I have one here.
22. Whom is his new friend visiting?
23. Does your girl friend like to study her lessons?
24. Our old friend has little money.
25. Is our house as warm as theirs?

E. COMPREHENDING AND SPEAKING

I. Repeat the following after your instructor (or the speaker) and study thoroughly.

BEIM FRISEUR[1]

Walter geht gerne zum Friseur. Er findet dort immer andere Jungen, und er kann mit seinen Freunden viel diskutieren. Inzwischen schneidet Herr Bauer, der Friseur, den Jungen die Haare.[2]

Vor dem Friseurladen[3] steht heute ein neues Auto. Im Laden
5 trifft[4] Walter seinen Vetter Hans. „Hallo, Hans!" sagt er, „wessen Auto steht dort vor dem Laden?"

„Es gehört[5] meinem Onkel Fred", antwortet Hans, „er hat sehr viel Geld, denn er ist ein guter Geschäftsmann.[6] Aber er ist gutmütig.[7] Er gibt mir oft sein Auto.

10 „Bitte bewegen Sie den Kopf nicht!"[8] sagt der Friseur zu Walter, denn er dreht[9] seinen Kopf immer zum Fenster, um das Auto zu sehen.

„Entschuldigen Sie!"[10] sagt Walter.

Jetzt ist Herr Bauer fertig.[11] Walter legt das Geld für das Haarschneiden[12] auf den Tisch und gibt dem Friseur auch ein Trinkgeld.[13]

15 „Ich muß jetzt noch schnell in die Bibliothek gehen,[14] aber ich bringe dich mit dem Auto nach Hause."

„Danke, Hans", sagt Walter, „ich fahre gerne mit dir."

[1]**beim Friseur**	at the barber's	[8]**bitte bewegen Sie den Kopf nicht**	please do not move your head
[2]**inzwischen schneidet Herr Bauer den Jungen die Haare**	meanwhile Mr. Bauer cuts the boys' hair		
[3]**der Friseurladen, ⸗**	barbershop	[9]**drehen**	to turn
[4]**trifft**	meets	[10]**entschuldigen Sie!**	excuse me!
[5]**es gehört** (+ *dat.*)	it belongs (to)	[11]**jetzt ist Herr Bauer fertig**	Mr. Bauer is finished now
[6]**der Geschäftsmann, Geschäftsleute**	the businessman	[12]**das Haarschneiden, -**	the haircut
[7]**gutmütig**	good-natured	[13]**das Trinkgeld, -er**	the tip
		[14]**die Bibliothek, -en**	the library

II. Beantworten Sie die folgenden Fragen auf deutsch!

1. Warum geht Walter gerne zum Friseur?
2. Was steht heute vor dem Friseurladen?
3. Wen trifft Walter beim Friseur?
4. Gehört das Auto Hans?
5. Warum dreht Walter seinen Kopf immer zum Fenster?
6. Wem gibt Walter ein Trinkgeld?

UNIT 8

A. UNITS OF SPEECH AND VOCABULARY

I. Study and Practice Aloud.

Ich habe Hunger.	I am hungry.
Er hat Durst.	He is thirsty.
Sie hat recht.	She is right.
Sie haben unrecht.	They are wrong.
Heute kommt er.	He is coming today.
Morgen geht sie.	She is going tomorrow.
ein anderer Hut	a different hat
eine andere Studentin	a different student (*f.*)
ein anderes Kino	a different movie theater

das Auto, -s	the car	**kaufen**	to buy
der Hut, ⸚e	the hat	**reden**	to talk
das Kino, -s	the movie, movie theater	**werden**	to become, to get
der Laden, ⸚	the store	**anderer, andere, anderes**	other, different
die Leute (*pl.*)	(the) people		
das Restaurant, -s	the restaurant	**fünfzehn**	fifteen
		sechzehn	sixteen
die Straße, -n	the street	**siebzehn**	seventeen
der Verkäufer, -	the salesman	**achtzehn**	eighteen
die Verkäuferin, -nen	the salesgirl	**neunzehn**	nineteen
		heute	today
antworten	to answer	**morgen**	tomorrow

(*61*)

II. Oral Practice. Repeat the pattern sentence. Then substitute the items listed below. Repeat the entire sentence with each substitute item, changing the verb where necessary.

a. Ich habe Hunger.

1. er	5. der Junge
2. das Kind	6. die Schüler
3. es	7. sie (*pl.*)
4. das Mädchen	8. wir

b. Er hat Durst.

1. der Verkäufer	4. wir
2. die Verkäuferin	5. die Leute
3. sie (*sing.*)	6. sie (*pl.*)

c. Sie hat recht.

1. die Studentin	4. der Lehrer
2. der Verkäufer	5. die Leute
3. er	6. sie (*pl.*)

d. Sie haben unrecht.

1. die Leute	4. Sie
2. die Verkäuferinnen	5. das Kind
3. die Verkäuferin	6. der Junge

e. Heute kommt er.

1. mein Onkel	4. ihre Tochter
2. sein Bruder	5. fünfzehn Leute
3. ihr Vater	6. sechzehn Leute

f. Morgen geht sie ins Kino.

1. er	3. seine Kusine
2. wir	4. meine Tante

g. Hier ist ein anderer Hut.

1. ein anderer Laden	3. ein anderer Lehrer
2. ein anderer Verkäufer	4. ein anderer Tisch

h. Sie begrüßt eine andere Studentin.

1. eine andere Verkäuferin	3. eine andere Frau
2. eine andere Schülerin	4. eine andere Lehrerin

i. Wir finden ein anderes Kino.

1. ein anderes Restaurant	3. ein anderes Gebäude
2. ein anderes Haus	4. ein anderes Kind

j. Wir werden alt.

1. die Verkäuferinnen	3. sie (*pl.*)
2. die Verkäufer	4. seine Eltern

III. Oral Practice. Repeat the pattern sentence. Then substitute the items listed below in the appropriate places. Repeat the entire sentence with each substitute item, changing the verb where necessary.

a. Die Straße ist groß.

1. _____ klein.
2. _____ alt.
3. _____ neu.
4. Das Auto _____
5. _____ alt.
6. _____ klein.

b. Sie antworten.

1. Die Studenten _____

2. Die Leute _____
3. Der Verkäufer und die Verkäuferin _____
4. Wir _____

c. Die Leute kaufen Hüte.

1. Er _____
2. Sie (*sing.*) _____
3. _____ 19 Hüte.
4. Wir _____ 6 Gläser.
5. _____ 17 Bücher.
6. _____ zwei Autos.

d. Er redet viel.

1. Der Verkäufer _____
2. Die Verkäuferin _____
3. Ich _____
4. _____ wenig
5. Wir _____
6. Die Jungen _____

B. MODEL SENTENCES

I. Study each sentence until you can reproduce it correctly.

55. Die andere Tochter besucht die neue Schule.
56. Das junge Mädchen lehrt das kleine Kind.
57. Der arme Vater hat einen reichen Sohn.
58. Der Onkel des jungen Mannes ist reich.
59. Die jungen Leute essen in den guten Restaurants.
60. Das Kind schreibt gut.
61. Gehen wir ins Kino!
62. Morgen kauft er ein neues Auto.

55. The other daughter attends the new school.
56. The young girl is teaching the little child.
57. The poor father has a rich son.
58. The young man's uncle is rich.
59. The young people are eating in the good restaurants.
60. The child writes well.
61. Let's go to the movies.
62. He will buy a new car tomorrow.

II. Pattern Practice. Repeat the model sentence. Then substitute the following items in the equivalent part of the model sentence. Repeat the entire sentence with each substitute item.

a. Die andere Tochter besucht die neue Schule.

1. die andere Schwester	3. die andere Freundin
2. die andere Kusine	4. die andere Schülerin

b. Das junge Mädchen lehrt das kleine Kind.

1. besucht	4. fragt
2. begrüßt	5. findet
3. versteht	6. bringt

c. Der arme Vater hat einen reichen Sohn.

1. der arme Mann	4. der arme Verkäufer
2. der arme Herr	5. der arme Freund
3. der arme Lehrer	6. der arme Bruder

d. Der Onkel des jungen Mannes ist reich.

1. der Vater	4. die Kusine
2. der Bruder	5. die Tante
3. der Vetter	6. die Schwester

e. Die jungen Leute essen in den guten Restaurants.

1. die jungen Männer	4. die jungen Frauen
2. die jungen Studenten	5. die jungen Verkäuferinnen
3. die jungen Mädchen	6. die jungen Studentinnen

t. Das Kind schreibt gut.

1. das Mädchen	4. die Schülerin
2. der Junge	5. sein Bruder
3. der Schüler	6. meine Schwester

g. Gehen wir ins Kino!

1. ins Restaurant	4. ins Zimmer
2. ins Haus	5. in den Laden
3. ins Gebäude	6. in die Stadt

h. Morgen kauft er ein neues Auto.

1. der Student	5. sie (*sing.*)
2. der Lehrer	6. meine Tante
3. der Verkäufer	7. ihr Vater
4. die Verkäuferin	8. sein Sohn

C. STRUCTURE

1. Descriptive adjectives preceded by an article, a **der**-word, or an inflected **ein**-word have "weak" endings.

The "weak" adjective ending is **-e** in the nominative singular of all genders and in the accusative singular of the feminine and neuter:

a. Die **andere** Tochter besucht die **neue** Schule.
    The other daughter attends the new school.
b. Das **junge** Mädchen lehrt das **kleine** Kind.
    The young girl is teaching the little child.
c. Der **arme** Vater hat einen **reichen** Sohn.
    The poor father has a rich son.

In all other cases, the "weak" adjective ending is **-en**: the masculine singular accusative (c, above); the genitive and dative singulars of all genders; all cases in the plural:

d. Der Onkel des **jungen** Mannes ist reich.
    The young man's uncle is rich.
e. Die **jungen** Leute essen in den **guten** Restaurants.
    The young people are eating in the good restaurants.

2. Descriptive adjectives are generally used without endings as adverbs:

    Das Kind schreibt **gut.**
    The child writes well.

3. A few masculine and neuter nouns form their plural by adding **-s:**

das Auto, -s	*the car*
das Kino, -s	*the movies*
das Restaurant, -s	*the restaurant*

    Note: These nouns do not add **-n** to the dative plural:

    Die jungen Leute essen in den guten **Restaurants.**
    The young people eat in the good restaurants.

4. The command form of the first person plural is the same as the indicative form, with the verb preceding the subject:

    Gehen wir ins Kino!
    Let's go to the movies.

5. The present tense is frequently used with future meaning, especially when the future is made clear by an adverb:

    Morgen kauft er ein neues Auto.
    He will buy a new car tomorrow.

6. Verbs whose stems end in **-d** or **-t** add **-e** before the endings **-st** and **-t** to facilitate pronunciation:

ich rede	*I talk, am talking, do talk*
du red**est**	*you talk, are talking, do talk*
er, sie, es red**et**	*he, she, it talks, is talking, does talk*
wir reden	*we talk, are talking, do talk*
ihr red**et**	*you talk, are talking, do talk*
sie reden	*they talk, are talking, do talk*
Sie reden	*you talk, are talking, do talk*

ich antworte	*I answer, am answering, do answer*
du antwort**est**	*you answer, are answering, do answer*
er, sie, es antwort**et**	*he, she, it answers, is answering, does answer*
wir antworten	*we answer, are answering, do answer*
ihr antwort**et**	*you answer, are answering, do answer*
sie antworten	*they answer, are answering, do answer*
Sie antworten	*you answer, are answering, do answer*

7. The present indicative of **werden** (*to become, get*):

ich **werde**	*I become, am becoming, do become; get, am getting, do get*
du **wirst**	*you become, are becoming, do become; get, are getting, do get*
er, sie, es **wird**	*he, she, it becomes, is becoming, does become; gets, is getting, does get*
wir **werden**	*we become, do become, are becoming; get, are getting, do get*
ihr **werdet**	*you become, are becoming, do become; get, are getting, do get*
sie **werden**	*they become, are becoming, do become; get, are getting, do get*
Sie **werden**	*you become, are becoming, do become; get, are getting, do get*

D. EXERCISES

Write the following sentences in German and be able to express them orally.

1. The new teacher's pupils talk well.
2. Eighteen boys are answering.
3. The salesgirl is talking with an old woman.
4. I am bringing you the cold water.

5. The salesman is getting old.
6. These new restaurants are good.
7. Let's talk now.
8. The little girl understands German well.
9. Do you see the two movie houses?
10. Seventeen people will come tomorrow.
11. Is he buying a new hat?
12. Let's drink no water.
13. Do you understand the little child?
14. The new stores are small.
15. We'll talk with her tomorrow.
16. My cousin (*f.*) teaches in the other school.
17. Let's eat in the new restaurant.
18. His other sister will become nineteen tomorrow.
19. The little girl's hat is new.
20. Her sons are getting big.
21. He is talking with the other saleswoman.
22. The young woman's daughter doesn't answer.
23. Let's buy a new car.
24. She is buying a beautiful hat in the little store.

E. COMPREHENDING AND SPEAKING

I. Repeat the following after your instructor (or the speaker) and study thoroughly.

DER GEBURTSTAG[1]

Peter trifft seine Freundin Käthe in der Stadt. Sie gehen zusammen in einen Hutladen, denn Käthe muß einen neuen Hut kaufen.
Die Verkäuferin zeigt[2] ihr fünfzehn Hüte, aber Käthe ist nicht zufrieden.[3] Sie sagt zu Peter: ,,Ich suche einen besonders schönen
5   Frühlingshut,[4] denn heute ist ein besonderer Tag.''[5]

,,Was für ein Tag[6] ist heute?'' fragt Peter.

[1]**der Geburtstag**	the birthday	[5]**ein besonderer**	
[2]**zeigen**	to show	**Tag**	a special day
[3]**zufrieden**	content	[6]**was für ein Tag**	what kind of day
[4]**ich suche einen**	I am looking for an		
besonders	especially nice		
schönen	spring hat		
Frühlingshut			

„Mein Geburtstag! Ich werde heute neunzehn." Käthe ist beleidigt.[7]

„Wie dumm von mir![8] Du mußt entschuldigen, Käthe, ich
10   vergesse Geburtstage immer."[9]

Peter geht aus dem Laden und über die Straße. Dort kauft er
einen großen Strauß Rosen.[10] Er gibt seiner Freundin die Rosen.

„Wie schön sie sind!" sagt Käthe. „Danke vielmals,[11] Peter."

„Hast du Hunger?" fragt Peter. „Gehen wir in ein gutes Restau-
15   rant und essen wir zu Abend! Nachher suchen wir uns einen guten Film
und gehen ins Kino. Wir müssen deinen Geburtstag feiern!"[12]

II. Beantworten Sie die folgenden Fragen auf deutsch!

1. Wen trifft Peter in der Stadt?
2. Was zeigt ihnen die Verkäuferin?
3. Warum sucht Käthe einen besonders schönen Frühlingshut?
4. Wessen Geburtstag ist heute?
5. Wie alt wird Käthe?
6. Was kauft Peter für Käthe?

[7]**beleidigt**	offended	[10]**ein Strauß Rosen**	a bouquet of roses
[8]**wie dumm von mir!**	how stupid of me!	[11]**danke vielmals**	thank you very much
[9]**ich vergesse Geburtstage immer**	I always forget birthdays	[12]**feiern**	to celebrate

UNIT 9

A. UNITS OF SPEECH AND VOCABULARY

I. Study and Practice Aloud.

er dankt mir	he thanks me
ich helfe ihm	I help him
Sie macht eine Reise.	She is taking a trip.
nach Deutschland	to Germany
nach Frankreich	to France
nach Italien	to Italy
nach Spanien	to Spain
nach den Vereinigten Staaten	to the United States
in die Schweiz	to Switzerland
älter als	older than
ein älterer Mann	an elderly man

Berlin	Berlin	**die Reise, -n**	the trip
Deutschland	Germany	**die Tasche, -n**	the pocket
England	England	**danken**+*dat.*	to thank
Europa	Europe	**helfen**+*dat.*	to help
Frankreich	France	**reisen**	to travel
Italien	Italy	**stecken**	to put, to stick
Österreich	Austria	**hoch**	high
die Schweiz	Switzerland	**als**	than
Spanien	Spain	**zu**	too, excessively
die Vereinigten	the United		
Staaten (*pl.*)	States		

II. Oral Practice. Repeat the pattern sentence. Then substitute the items listed below.
Repeat the entire model with each substitute item, changing the verb where necessary.

a. Er dankt mir.

1. Der Junge		4. Die Studentin
2. Meine Freundin		5. Sein Vater
3. Sie		6. Der Verkäufer

b. Ich helfe ihm.

1. Wir
2. Der Vater und die Mutter
3. Sie
4. Meine Brüder
5. Seine Eltern
6. Sein Bruder und seine Schwester

c. Sie macht eine Reise.

1. Die Studentin
2. Der Lehrer
3. Er
4. Ihre Lehrer
5. Sie
6. Wir

d. Reisen Sie in die Schweiz?

1. er
2. Ihr Onkel
3. sein Bruder
4. Ihr Vetter
5. seine Mutter
6. ihr Vater

e. Er ist älter als sie.

1. Mein Vetter
2. Ihr Bruder
3. Ihre Freundin
4. Ihre Schwester
5. Meine Tante
6. Meine Kusine

f. Er ist ein älterer Mann.

1. Herr Braun
2. Ihr Onkel
3. Sein Vetter
4. Der Verkäufer
5. Ihr Freund
6. Sein Vater

g. Sie besucht die Vereinigten Staaten.

1. Die Studentin
2. Die Studentinnen
3. Sie (*pl.*)
4. Wir
5. Ich
6. Er

h. Er steckt den Brief in die Tasche.

1. Der Junge
2. Das Kind
3. Es
4. Das Mädchen
5. Die Frau
6. Sie (*sing.*)

i. Das Haus ist zu hoch.

1. Das Gebäude
2. Dieses Gebäude
3. Die Häuser
4. Die Gebäude

III. Oral Practice. Repeat the pattern sentence. Then substitute the items listed below
in the appropriate places. Repeat the entire sentence with each substitute item.

a. Wir reisen nach Deutschland.

1. Meine Freunde _____
2. Meine Eltern _____
3. _____ nach Frankreich.
4. Seine Brüder _____

5. Ihre Freunde _____
6. Meine Vettern _____
7. _____ nach Italien.
8. Seine Kusinen _____
9. Ihre Tanten _____
10. _____ nach Spanien.

b. Sie ist jetzt in Berlin.

1. Die Verkäuferin _____
2. Der Verkäufer _____
3. Er _____
4. _____ in Europa.
5. Mein Freund _____
6. Seine Tante _____
7. _____ in Italien.
8. Sie _____

11. Wir _____
12. Unsere Freunde _____
13. _____ nach den Vereinigten Staaten.
14. Diese Leute _____
15. Meine Schwestern _____

9. _____ in Spanien.
10. Ihre Freundin _____
11. Unser Vetter _____
12. _____ in Österreich.
13. Meine Mutter _____
14. _____ in England.
15. Meine Freundin _____
16. Die Studentin _____

B. MODEL SENTENCES

I. Study each sentence until you can reproduce it correctly.

63. Der Sohn dankt dem Vater.
64. Sie ist schöner als ihre Schwester.
65. Sein Freund ist ein reicherer Mann als mein Freund.
66. Es ist ein schönes hohes Gebäude.
67. Der Student wird eine Reise machen.
68. Der Junge steckt die Hand in die Tasche.

63. The son thanks his father.
64. She is more beautiful than her sister.
65. His friend is a richer man than my friend.
66. It is a beautiful high building.
67. The student will take a trip.
68. The boy is putting his hand in his pocket.

II. Pattern Practice. Repeat the model sentence. Then substitute the following items in the equivalent part of the model sentence. Repeat the entire sentence with each substitute item.

a. Der Sohn dankt dem Vater.

1. Der Junge
2. Das Kind
3. Das Mädchen
4. Die Tochter
5. Der Mann
6. Der Student
7. Die Frau
8. Die Studentin

b. Sie ist schöner als ihre Schwester.
1. ihre Freundin
2. meine Tante
3. ihre Kusine
4. meine Kusine
5. seine Tochter
6. unsere Freundin

c. Sein Freund ist ein reicherer Mann als mein Freund.
1. Sein Vater, mein Vater
2. Ihr Bruder, mein Bruder
3. Unser Onkel, sein Onkel
4. mein Vetter, sein Vetter
5. Unser Lehrer, ihr Lehrer
6. Sein Sohn, ihr Sohn

d. Es ist ein schönes hohes Gebäude.
1. Die Schule
2. Unsere Schule
3. Ihre Schule
4. Seine Schule

e. Der Student wird eine Reise machen.
1. Der Junge
2. Der Lehrer
3. Die Studentin
4. Sie
5. Das Kind
6. Das Mädchen
7. Meine Tante
8. Der Professor

f. Der Junge steckt die Hand in die Tasche.
1. Der Mann
2. Der Schüler
3. Der Student
4. Er
5. Das Kind
6. Das Mädchen
7. Die Studentin
8. Die Frau

C. STRUCTURE

1. A few verbs, such as **danken** (*to thank*), **helfen** (*to help*), **antworten** (*to answer*), require their object to be in the dative:

a. Der Sohn **dankt dem Vater.**
The son thanks his father.

b. Ich **helfe ihm.**
I am helping him.

c. Er **antwortet Ihnen.**
He is answering you.

2. The names of cities, states, continents, and most countries are neuter nouns and are usually employed without the article, as in English:

(**das**) **Berlin**	*Berlin*	(**das**) **Frankreich**	*France*
(**das**) **Deutschland**	*Germany*	(**das**) **Italien**	*Italy*
(**das**) **England**	*England*	(**das**) **Österreich**	*Austria*
(**das**) **Europa**	*Europe*	(**das**) **Spanien**	*Spain*

3. Some names of countries are feminine or plural nouns, which are always used with the definite article:

die Schweiz   *Switzerland*
die Vereinigten Staaten   *the United States*

Note: **Die Vereinigten Staaten** requires a plural verb when used as a subject.

4. **Nach** (*to*) indicates direction with neuter and plural geographical names:

   a. Wir reisen **nach Deutschland.**
   We are traveling to Germany.

   b. Unsere Freunde reisen **nach den Vereinigten Staaten.**
   Our friends are traveling to the United States.

   In plus article is used with feminine geographical names:

   c. Reisen Sie **in die Schweiz?**
   Are you traveling to Switzerland?

5. The comparative form of adjectives is formed by adding the suffix **-er** to the stem. If the adjective is a monosyllable whose stem vowel is **a, o,** or **u,** the vowel is umlauted:

   Er ist **älter** als sie.
   He is older than she.
   Sie ist **schöner** als ihre Schwester.
   She is more beautiful than her sister.

6. The comparative form of the adjective is inflected when it precedes the noun it modifies:

   Sein Freund ist ein **reicherer** Mann als mein Freund.
   His friend is a richer man than my friend.

   Note: The comparative form of the adjective is often used in an absolute sense, without reference to any other person or thing:

   Er ist ein **älterer** Mann.
   He is an elderly man.
   He is a rather old man.

7. The adjective **hoch** has two forms. When a vowel follows, the stem is **hoh-,** otherwise the stem is **hoch-:**

   a. Das Haus ist zu **hoch.**
   The house is too high.
   b. Es ist ein schönes **hohes** Gebäude.
   It is a beautiful high building.

   Note: When two or more descriptive adjectives precede a noun, both have the same ending: ein **schönes hohes** Gebäude.

8. The present tense of **werden** plus the infinitive of the main verb form the future tense:

> Der Student **wird** eine Reise **machen.**
> *The student will take a trip.*

The future of **machen** (*to make, to do*):

ich **werde . . . machen**	*I will do, make*
du **wirst . . . machen**	*you will do, make*
er, sie, es **wird . . . machen**	*he, she, it will do, make*
wir **werden . . . machen**	*we will do, make*
ihr **werdet . . . machen**	*you will do, make*
sie **werden . . . machen**	*they will do, make*
Sie **werden . . . machen**	*you will do, make*

9. The definite article rather than the possessive adjective is used for articles of clothing or parts of the body when ownership is clear from the context:

> Der Junge steckt **die** Hand in **die** Tasche.
> *The boy is putting his hand in his pocket.*

Note: With nouns of relationship, the definite article may be used in place of the possessive adjective:

> Der Sohn dankt **dem** Vater.
> *The son thanks his father.*

D. EXERCISES

Write the following sentences in German and be able to express them orally.

1. They will take a trip to Italy.
2. She has a newer house than I.
3. The sister is thanking her brothers.
4. The child is putting her hand in her pocket.
5. Their house is as high as the school.
6. Isn't she coming to Austria?
7. I am helping my parents now.
8. Is Berlin as big as Paris?
9. They are traveling to Switzerland, but not to Germany.
10. The poorer brother is younger.
11. The other building is high, but this building is higher.
12. The pupils will begin the lesson.
13. Is he answering me?
14. The younger children are helping the older child.

15. Is the little boy playing in that big cold room?
16. Don't thank him.
17. The pupils (*f.*) are helping the teachers.
18. Are you taking a trip to France?
19. Spain is larger than Switzerland.
20. Is she a rather young woman?
21. She is answering her father.
22. We will buy the old books.
23. The United States is big and beautiful.
24. Is she putting the letters in her pocket?
25. He will go home now.
26. My two brothers are smaller than I.

E. COMPREHENDING AND SPEAKING

I. Repeat the following after your instructor (or the speaker) and study thoroughly.

EINE GEOGRAPHIELEKTION

Seit Herrn Hausers Besuch denkt Peter nur noch an Europa.[1]
Herr Schmidt gibt seinem Sohn einen Atlas.

„Hier ist eine Karte[2] Europas!"

„Wo wohnt Herr Hauser, Vater?"

5   „In München. Findest du München auf der Karte?"

Peter sucht lange, aber er findet München nicht. Der Vater muß
ihm helfen: „Sieh, mal,[3] Peter, hier ist England! Und hier sind
Spanien, Italien und die Schweiz. Die Schweiz liegt zwischen Österreich, Deutschland, Frankreich und Italien. München liegt hier, nahe
10 bei der Grenze der Schweiz."[4]

Peter dankt seinem Vater für die Lektion. Er schaut in den Atlas
und vergleicht[5] die Länder[6] Europas mit den Vereinigten Staaten.
„Österreich und die Schweiz sind kleine Länder", meint[7] er, „sie sind
viel kleiner als Deutschland oder Frankreich. Aber die Vereinigten
15 Staaten sind größer als ganz[8] Europa."

Mit dem Finger macht Peter eine Reise durch Europa und besucht
alle größeren Städte.

[1]**Seit Herrn Hausers Besuch denkt Peter nur noch an Europa.**	Since Mr. Hauser's visit Peter thinks of nothing but Europe.	[4]**nahe bei der Grenze der Schweiz**	near the Swiss border
[2]**die Karte, -n**	the map	[5]**vergleichen**	to compare
[3]**sieh mal!**	look!	[6]**das Land, ⸚er**	the country
		[7]**meinen**	to say
		[8]**ganz Europa**	all of Europe

II. Beantworten Sie die folgenden Fragen auf deutsch!

1. Seit wann denkt Peter nur noch an Europa?
2. Was gibt Herr Schmidt seinem Sohn?
3. Findet Peter München auf der Karte?
4. Was muß der Vater schließlich tun?
5. Wo liegt die Schweiz?
6. Ist Europa größer als die Vereinigten Staaten?

UNIT 10

A. UNITS OF SPEECH AND VOCABULARY

I. Study and Practice Aloud.

Das tut mir leid.	I'm sorry.
Das tut ihm leid.	He's sorry.
Zuerst besuchen wir Köln, dann besuchen wir Heidelberg.	First we visit Cologne; then we visit Heidelberg.
Wohin gehen Sie?	Where are you going (to)?
aufs Land	to the country
auf dem Lande	in the country
für mich	for me
ohne ihn	without him
an den Fluß	to the river
an den Rhein	to the Rhine
an den See	to the lake
an die See	to the ocean, to the sea(shore)
am Fluß	at the river, on the river
am Rhein	at the Rhine, on the Rhine
an der See	at the sea(shore)

bleiben	to remain, to stay	**ißt**	eats
		laufen	to run
fahren	to drive, to ride	**läuft**	runs
fährt	drives, rides	**lesen**	to read
gibt	gives	**liest**	reads

(*77*)

sehen	to see	die See, -n	the ocean, sea
sieht	sees	die Universität,	the university
der Fluß, des	the river	-en	
Flusses, die		etwas	something
Flüsse		durch + *acc.*	through
das Land, ⸚er	the country	für + *acc.*	for
Heidelberg	Heidelberg	ohne + *acc.*	without
Köln	Cologne	dann	then
München	Munich	nur	only
die Nordsee	the North Sea	oder	or
die Ostsee	the Baltic Sea	zuerst	first
der Rhein	the Rhine	wohin?	where (to)?
der See, -n	the lake		

II. Oral Practice. Repeat the pattern sentence. Then substitute the items listed below. Repeat the entire sentence with each substitute item, changing the verb where necessary.

a. Das tut mir leid.

1. ihm
2. meinem Bruder
3. seinem Vater
4. ihrer Mutter
5. ihr
6. meinen Eltern
7. ihnen
8. uns

b. Zuerst besuchen wir Köln, dann besuchen wir Heidelberg.

1. Heidelberg, München
2. München, Köln
3. Köln, Berlin
4. Berlin, Heidelberg
5. Berlin, München
6. München, Berlin

c. Wohin gehen Sie?

1. wir
2. Ihre Freunde
3. sie (*pl.*)
4. seine Freundin
5. sie (*sing.*)
6. das Mädchen
7. das Kind
8. der Student

d. Er fährt aufs Land.

1. Mein Vater
2. Sein Vetter
3. Ihr Onkel
4. Seine Tante
5. Meine Schwester
6. Ihre Kusine
7. Seine Mutter
8. Sie (*sing.*)

e. Sie wohnt auf dem Lande.

1. Die Studentin
2. Die Verkäuferin
3. Die Schülerin
4. Sein Onkel
5. Mein Professor
6. Er

f. Er kauft es für mich.

1. ihn
2. sie (*sing.*)
3. uns
4. nur für mich

5. nur für ihn
6. nur für Sie

7. nur für uns
8. nur für sie

g. Sie geht ohne ihn.
1. mich
2. Sie (*pl.*)
3. uns
4. ihre Schwester

5. ihren Bruder
6. meinen Vetter
7. ihren Vater
8. seine Mutter

h. Sie fahren durch Deutschland.
1. Europa
2. Frankreich
3. Heidelberg

4. Berlin
5. das Land

i. Sieht sie den See oder den Fluß?
1. den Fluß oder die See
2. das Mädchen oder den Jungen

3. ihren Bruder oder ihre Schwester
4. die Universität oder die Schule

j. Er gibt es mir.
1. Ihnen
2. uns
3. seinem Bruder

4. meinem Vater
5. ihrem Onkel
6. ihm

III. Oral Practice. Repeat the pattern sentence. Then substitute the items listed below in the appropriate places. Repeat the entire sentence with each substitute item, changing the verb where necessary.

a. Er läuft an den Fluß.
1. Das Kind _____
2. Es _____
3. _____ See.
4. Die Frau _____

5. Sie _____
6. Wir _____
7. Die Kinder _____
8. Sie _____

b. Sie fahren an die See.
1. Wir _____
2. Sie (*pl.*) _____
3. _____ die Nordsee.
4. Der Student _____
5. Der Lehrer _____

6. _____ die Ostsee.
7. Der Mann _____
8. _____ den Rhein.
9. Die Frau _____
10. Sie (*sing.*) _____

c. Die Stadt liegt am Fluß.
1. Unsere Stadt _____
2. Diese Stadt _____
3. _____ am Rhein.

4. Die Städte _____
5. Köln _____
6. Es _____

d. Bleibt er an der See?
1. _____ Ihr Bruder _____
2. _____ Ihre Tante _____
3. _____ an der Ostsee?
4. _____ sie _____

5. _____ wir _____
6. _____ an der Nordsee?
7. _____ Sie _____
8. _____ Ihre Freunde _____

c. **Sie ißt etwas.**

1. Er _____	6. Sie (*sing.*) _____
2. Das Kind _____	7. Wir _____
3. Der Junge _____	8. Er und sie _____
4. _____ liest _____	9. Seine Freunde _____
5. Die Frau _____	10. Die Kinder _____

B. MODEL SENTENCES

I. Study each sentence until you can reproduce it correctly.

69. **Wohin läuft der Junge?**
70. **Seine Eltern fahren an den Rhein.**
71. **Sie wohnen an der See.**
72. **Sie besucht die Stadt Köln und die Universität Heidelberg.**
73. **Hans ist der jüngste Sohn.**
74. **Meine Schwester ist älter als ich, aber mein Bruder ist am ältesten.**
75. **Er schreibt besser als ich, aber sie schreibt am besten.**

69. Where is the boy running (to)?
70. His parents are driving to the Rhine.
71. They live at the seashore.
72. She is visiting the city of Cologne and the University of Heidelberg.
73. Hans is the youngest son.
74. My sister is older than I, but my brother is (the) oldest.
75. He writes better than I, but she writes best.

II. Pattern Drill. Repeat the model sentence. Then substitute the following items in the equivalent part of the model sentence. Repeat the entire sentence with each substitute item.

a. **Wohin läuft der Junge?**

1. er	4. das Kind
2. Ihr Bruder	5. das Mädchen
3. sein Vetter	6. der Schüler

b. **Seine Eltern fahren an den Rhein.**

1. den Fluß	4. die Nordsee
2. den See	5. die Ostsee
3. die See	6. die Nordsee und die Ostsee

c. **Sie wohnen an der See.**

1. an der Ostsee	4. am Fluß
2. an der Nordsee	5. am Rhein
3. am See	

d. Sie besucht die Stadt Köln und die Universität Heidelberg.
1. die Stadt Köln, die Universität Köln
2. die Stadt Heidelberg, die Universität Heidelberg
3. die Stadt Heidelberg, die Universität Köln
4. die Stadt Berlin, die Universität Berlin
5. die Stadt München, die Universität München

e. Hans ist der jüngste Sohn.
1. Verkäufer
2. Schüler
3. Bruder
4. Student
5. Vetter

f. Meine Schwester ist älter als ich, aber mein Bruder ist am ältesten.
1. Mein Bruder, meine Schwester, ich
2. Mein Onkel, meine Tante, mein Vater
3. Marie, Klara, Grete
4. Sein Haus, ihr Haus, unser Haus

g. Er schreibt besser als ich, aber sie schreibt am besten.
1. sie, ich, er
2. mein Vetter, mein Onkel, meine Tante
3. sie, er, ihr Bruder
4. Karl, Richard, Marie

C. STRUCTURE

1. Wohin? (*where? where to?*) is used to inquire after a goal, **wo?** (*where?*) about a location:

a. Wohin gehen Sie?
Where are you going?

b. Wohin läuft der Junge?
Where is the boy running (to)?

c. Wo wohnen Sie?
Where do you live?

d. Wo ist der Tisch?
Where is the table?

2. An (*at, to*) indicates location near or motion toward a body of water:

a. Die Stadt liegt **am Fluß.**
The city is situated on the river.

b. Sie wohnen **an der See.**
They live at the seashore.

c. Er läuft **an den Fluß.**
He is running to the river.

d. Seine Eltern fahren **an den Rhein.**
His parents are driving to the Rhine.

3. A geographical name stands unchanged immediately after a common noun:

> Sie besucht **die Stadt Köln** und **die Universität Heidelberg.**
> *She is visiting the city of Cologne and the University of Heidelberg.*

4. Some common prepositions always require the accusative case. Among them are **durch** (*through*), **für** (*for*), **ohne** (*without*):

   a. Er kauft es **für mich.**
      He is buying it for me.
   b. Sie fahren **durch das Land.**
      They are driving through the country.
   c. Er geht **ohne ihn.**
      He is going without him.

5. The superlative of a descriptive adjective is formed by adding **-st** and the appropriate strong or weak adjective endings. Superlatives are almost always inflected. If the comparative takes umlaut, the superlative also takes umlaut:

POSITIVE	COMPARATIVE	SUPERLATIVE
der junge Sohn	der jüng**er**e Sohn	der jüng**ste** Sohn
the young son	*the younger son*	*the youngest son*

If the stem of the adjective ends in **-d, -t,** or a vowel other than **-e,** then **-est** is added in the superlative:

sein alter Freund	sein älterer Freund	sein ält**est**er Freund
his old friend	*his older friend*	*his oldest friend*
das neue Haus	das neuere Haus	das neu**est**e Haus
the new house	*the newer house*	*the newest house*

6. Some adjectives have irregular comparative and superlative forms:

gut	**besser**	**der, die, das beste**
good	*better*	*the best*
groß	**größer**	**der, die, das größte**
big	*bigger*	*the biggest*
hoch	**höher**	**der, die, das höchste**
high	*higher*	*the highest*

7. The predicate form of the superlative consists of **am** plus the superlative with the ending **-en:**

> Meine Schwester ist älter als ich, aber mein Bruder ist **am ältesten.**
> *My sister is older than I, but my brother is (the) oldest.*

8. The comparative form of the adverb is identical with the adjective:

> Er schreibt **besser** als ich.
> *He writes better than I.*

The superlative form of the adverb corresponds to that of the predicate adjective (paragraph 7):

> Sie schreibt **am besten.**
> *She writes best.*

9. Certain verbs have irregular forms in the second and third persons singular of the present tense. Some verbs change **e** to **i,** like **geben** (*to give*) and **essen** (*to eat*).

The present tense of **geben:**

ich gebe	*I give*
du **gibst**	*you give*
er, sie, es **gibt**	*he, she, it gives*
wir geben	*we give*
ihr gebt	*you give*
sie geben	*they give*
Sie geben	*you give*

The present tense of **essen** (*to eat*):

ich esse	*I eat*
du **ißt**	*you eat*
er, sie, es **ißt**	*he, she, it eats*
wir essen	*we eat*
ihr eßt	*you eat*
sie essen	*they eat*
Sie essen	*you eat*

Other verbs change **e** to **ie,** like **lesen** (*to read*) and **sehen** (*to see*). The present tense of **sehen:**

ich sehe	*I see*
du **siehst**	*you see*
er, sie, es **sieht**	*he, she, it sees*
wir sehen	*we see*
ihr seht	*you see*
sie sehen	*they see*
Sie sehen	*you see*

Some verbs with stem vowel **a** or **au** umlaut the stem vowel. The present tense of **fahren** (*to drive, ride*):

ich fahre	*I drive, ride*
du **fährst**	*you drive, ride*
er, sie, es **fährt**	*he, she, it drives, rides*
wir fahren	*we drive, ride*
ihr fahrt	*you drive, ride*
sie fahren	*they drive, ride*
Sie fahren	*you drive, ride*

The present tense of **laufen** (*to run*):

ich laufe	*I run*
du **läufst**	*you run*
er, sie, es **läuft**	*he, she, it runs*
wir laufen	*we run*
ihr lauft	*you run*
sie laufen	*they run*
Sie laufen	*you run*

D. EXERCISES

Write the following sentences in German and be able to express them orally.

1. My cousin (*f.*) lives in the city of Munich.
2. Is your girl friend taking a trip to the seashore?
3. Where are your parents going?
4. The pupil is writing the lesson for the teacher.
5. His friends live in Cologne on the Rhine.
6. The oldest son is smallest.
7. She is eating without her brother.
8. She is the youngest girl here.
9. Their daughter is traveling through the country.
10. Where is the child running to?
11. First we are driving to the North Sea and then to the Baltic Sea.
12. Where is he putting the letter?
13. My aunt is coming without her children.
14. Is the school the highest building in town?
15. I will travel through Switzerland and Austria.
16. Is the Rhine the biggest river in Germany?
17. He is visiting friends at the lake.
18. The best car is not the newest car.
19. Go without me.

20. The new pupil (*f.*) understands the teacher best.
21. His brother is doing the work for me.
22. Hans is young, Karl is younger, but Hermann is youngest.
23. Our best friend is giving us his books.
24. Where is your uncle going now?
25. Are you visiting the University of Cologne?
26. Which room is warmest?

E. COMPREHENDING AND SPEAKING

I. Repeat the following after your instructor (or the speaker) and study thoroughly.

BEIM AUTOMECHANIKER

Peter bringt sein Auto zum Automechaniker Meier.

„Was fehlt Ihrem Auto?"[1] fragt Herr Meier.

„Ich bin nicht sicher.[2] Der Motor hustet.[3] Auch fährt der Wagen langsamer als früher.[4] Aber es ist eine kleinere Sache, glaube ich."[5]

5 „Wir wollen mal sehen",[6] sagt Herr Meier und öffnet die Motorhaube.[7] Mit seinen Werkzeugen[8] dreht er an größeren und kleineren Schrauben.[9] „Bitte starten Sie den Motor!" sagt er zu Peter.

Peter dreht den Schlüssel,[10] und der Motor springt an.[11] Zuerst läuft er schnell und regelmäßig,[12] aber dann wird er immer langsamer,
10 und schließlich stoppt er.

„Haben Sie noch genug Benzin?"[13] fragt Herr Meier.

Peter schaut auf die Benzinuhr:[14] „Nur noch wenig", sagt er.

„Dann müssen wir zuerst den Tank füllen."

Peter holt[15] zwanzig Liter Benzin. Unterdessen prüft Herr Meier
15 die Zündkerzen.[16]

„Sehen Sie diese Zündkerzen!" sagt er, „eine ist schmutziger[17] als die andere! Kein Wunder, daß Ihr Wagen hustet!"

[1]**Was fehlt Ihrem Auto?**	What's wrong with your car?	[9]**die Schraube, -n**	the screw
[2]**Ich bin nicht sicher.**	I'm not sure.	[10]**der Schlüssel, -**	the key
[3]**husten**	to cough	[11]**springt an**	starts
[4]**langsamer als früher**	slower than before	[12]**regelmäßig**	regularly
[5]**es ist eine kleinere Sache**	it's a rather small matter	[13]**das Benzin**	the gasoline
[6]**wir wollen mal sehen**	let's have a look	[14]**die Benzinuhr, -en**	the gas gauge
[7]**die Motorhaube, -n**	the hood	[15]**holen**	to get
[8]**das Werkzeug, -e**	the tool	[16]**Unterdessen prüft Herr Meier die Zündkerzen.**	In the meantime Mr. Meier checks the spark plugs
		[17]**schmutzig**	dirty

II. Beantworten Sie die folgenden Fragen auf deutsch!

1. Wem bringt Peter sein Auto?
2. Was fragt Herr Meier?
3. Wie läuft der Motor?
4. Was macht Herr Meier mit seinen Werkzeugen?
5. Hat es noch viel Benzin im Tank?
6. Warum hustet der Motor von Peters Auto?

REVIEW UNIT 2

A. *Supply the proper form of the word in parentheses in the place indicated.*

1. (wer) _____ geben Sie die Bücher?
2. (hoch) Sind diese Häuser _____?
3. (ihr) Er fährt sein Auto und sie fährt _____.
4. (alt) Richard ist _____ als Hans, aber Robert ist am _____.
5. (wenig) Ich sehe _____ Leute hier.
6. (essen) Was _____ der Junge jetzt?
7. (klein) Österreich ist ein _____ Land.
8. (wer) _____ besucht Ihr Vetter?
9. (laufen) Wohin _____ du jetzt, mein Kind?
10. (mein) Ihr Bruder ist älter als _____.
11. (gut) Die Schülerin liest _____.
12. (fahren) Wann _____ du nach Heidelberg, Hans?
13. (hoch) Ist dieses Haus _____ als das andere?
14. (müssen) Ich _____ meine Aufgaben machen.
15. (neu) Ihre _____ Hüte sind schön.
16. (reden) Er _____ jetzt mit ihr.
17. (sein) Er bringt es für _____ Mutter.
18. (werden) Herr Schmidt _____ alt.
19. (warm) Mein Zimmer ist_____ als sein Zimmer.
20. (wer) _____ Auto ist es?
21. (geben) Die Mutter _____ dem Kind Geld.
22. (groß) Der Rhein ist ein _____Fluß.
23. (viel) Mein Vater trinkt _____ Wasser.

24. (sehen) Die Frau _____ ihre Tochter.
25. (alt) Marie ist das _____ Mädchen im Zimmer.
26. (müssen) Richard, du _____ hier bleiben!
27. (jung) Das _____ Mädchen heißt Klara Schmidt.
28. (wer) _____ steht am Fenster?
29. (alt) Er kommt aus dem _____ Hause.
30. (antworten) Der Junge _____ seiner Tante.
31. (schön) Sie hat einen _____ Hut als ihre Schwester.
32. (neu) Die Mutter des _____ Schülers ist hier.
33. (lesen) Was _____ Ihre Kusine jetzt?
34. (gut) Wir reden mit _____ Freunden.
35. (müssen) Trude _____ das Buch lesen.
36. (groß) Hans ist _____ als Marie.
37. (ihr) Klara geht ohne _____ Bruder.
38. (reich) Er hat zwei _____ Onkel.
39. (werden) Wann _____ du nach Hause gehen, Marie?
40. (neu) Er hat ein _____ Haus als sie.
41. (hoch) Es ist das _____ Gebäude in der Stadt.
42. (fahren) Morgen _____ ich nach Berlin.

B. *Change the following sentences to plural.*

1. Das Kind liest die Aufgabe.
2. Wie heißt die Verkäuferin?
3. Das Auto ist schön.
4. Was sieht der Student?
5. Wo ist das Kino?
6. Der Junge schreibt gut.
7. Wohin läuft Ihre Kusine?
8. Sein Vetter kommt morgen.
9. Wann fährt der Verkäufer nach Europa?
10. Die Frau steht dort.
11. Wo ist das Restaurant?
12. Die Familie ist groß.

C. *Expand the following sentences to include the words in parentheses in their proper places.*

1. (zu Hause) Wir müssen bleiben.
2. (gerne) Er trinkt Wasser.
3. (einen Brief) Ich werde ihr schreiben.
4. (nach England) Sie wird reisen.
5. (gerne) Die Schüler lesen Bücher.

D. *Complete the following sentences by adding* **wo?** *or* **wohin?** *as appropriate.*

1. _____ wohnt er?
2. _____ laufen Sie?
3. _____ legt er die Bücher?
4. _____ steht sie jetzt?
5. _____ bringt er die Kinder?
6. _____ bleiben Ihre Freunde?

E. *Supply one word, if necessary, to complete the meaning of each sentence.*

1. Er schreibt so gut _____ sie.
2. Bleiben Sie _____ der See?
3. Sie werden die Stadt _____ Köln sehen.
4. Sie macht eine Reise _____ Spanien.
5. Das tut uns _____.
6. Fahren Sie morgen _____ Land?
7. Wir wohnen in den _____ Staaten.
8. Sechs und sieben ist _____.
9. Ich habe _____. Bringen Sie mir ein Glas Wasser!
10. Wann fährt er _____ die Schweiz?
11. Er besucht die Universität _____ München.
12. Heidelberg ist nicht _____ groß wie Berlin.
13. Wir müssen essen, denn wir haben _____.
14. Seine Familie ist jetzt _____ der Stadt.

F. *Supply the proper form of the definite article in the place indicated. Use contractions wherever possible.*

1. Er legt das Buch auf _____ Tisch.
2. Der Verkäufer dankt _____ Mann.
3. Die Stadt liegt an _____ Fluß.
4. Ich gehe an _____ Tür.
5. Was lesen Sie in _____ Buch?
6. Geht sie an _____ Fenster?
7. Die Jungen helfen _____ Frauen.
8. Die Leute kommen in _____ Haus.
9. Seine Hand liegt auf _____ Brief.
10. Die Mädchen sitzen hinter _____ Frauen.
11. Unsere Eltern sitzen vor _____ Lehrer.
12. Ich antworte _____ Frau.

G. *Change the following statements to commands.*

1. Wir fahren nach Hause.
2. Sie lesen das Buch.

3. Sie stecken den Brief in die Tasche.
4. Wir geben ihm den Hut.

H. *Change the following sentences to future.*
   1. Die Frau besucht ihren Onkel.
   2. Ich schreibe ihr nicht.
   3. Die Kinder lernen nicht gerne.
   4. Die Studentin versteht den Herrn.
   5. Wir gehen ins Kino.

I. *Using the following outline, compose a short paragraph in German about your family.*
Ich heiße Hans Braun. Mein Vater heißt Robert und meine Mutter heißt Grete. Ich habe einen Bruder. Er heißt Willi. Eine Schwester heißt Lotte und die andere heißt Trude. Die drei Kinder gehen in die Schule, und ich studiere auf der Universität. Mein Vater arbeitet und meine Mutter bleibt zu Hause.

J. *Write a short paragraph in German about your uncle. Include the following details:*
   1. State what his name is.
   2. Tell whether he is your father's brother or your mother's brother.
   3. Say that he has been living at your house for some time.
   4. Tell whether he likes to play with your brother(s) and/or sister(s) and whether they like to play with him.
   5. State that he is going home now.

K. *Write a short paragraph in German stating that you are in town and are hungry. You don't go into a big restaurant, because you don't have much money. You go to a small one, eat, drink, and return home.*

L. *Write a short paragraph in German stating that you have been corresponding for some time with a friend in Germany. Tell us his name and where he lives. You are planning a trip to Europe to visit him. Name the other countries you plan to visit.*

UNIT 11

A. UNITS OF SPEECH AND VOCABULARY

I. Study and Practice Aloud.

Sie können gehen	you can go, you are able to go
wir sollen lernen	we are (supposed) to learn
sie wollen laufen	they want to run
am Samstag	on Saturday
am nächsten Tag	(on) the next day
im Juli	in July
im Frühling	in the spring
nächsten Monat	next month
den ganzen Nachmittag	the whole afternoon (long), all afternoon long
die ganze Nacht	the whole night (long), all night long
den ganzen Sommer	the whole summer (long), all summer long

der Abend, -e	the evening	der Mittwoch	Wednesday
die Nacht, ⸚e	the night	der Donnerstag	Thursday
der Vormittag, -e	the morning	der Freitag	Friday
der Nachmittag, -e	the afternoon	der Samstag	Saturday
		der Sonnabend	Saturday
der Sonntag	Sunday	der Monat, -e	the month
der Montag	Monday	der Januar	January
der Dienstag	Tuesday	der Februar	February

(91)

der März	March	der Winter, -	winter
der April	April	**Wien**	Vienna
der Mai	May	**können**	can, to be able
der Juni	June		(to)
der Juli	July	**sollen**	to be (to), to be
der August	August		supposed (to)
der September	September	**wollen**	to want (to)
der Oktober	October	**ganz**	entire, whole, all
der November	November		of
der Dezember	December	**nächster,**	next
der Frühling, -e	spring	**nächste,**	
der Sommer, -	summer	**nächstes**	
der Herbst, -e	autumn, fall		

II. Oral Practice. Repeat the pattern. Then substitute the items listed below. Repeat the entire sentence with each substitute item, making any necessary changes.

a. Sie können gehen.

1. fahren
2. laufen
3. reisen
4. bleiben
5. lesen
6. schreiben

b. Wir sollen lernen.

1. schreiben
2. lesen
3. essen
4. trinken
5. kommen
6. bleiben

c. Sie wollen laufen.

1. spielen
2. essen
3. trinken
4. schreiben
5. lesen
6. gehen

d. Am Samstag kommt er.

1. Sonntag
2. Montag
3. Dienstag
4. Mittwoch
5. Donnerstag
6. Freitag
7. Sonnabend
8. nächsten Tag
9. nächsten Vormittag
10. nächsten Nachmittag
11. nächsten Abend

e. Im Juli reisen wir.

1. August
2. September
3. Oktober
4. November
5. Dezember
6. Januar
7. Februar
8. März
9. April
10. Mai
11. Juni
12. Frühling
13. Sommer
14. Herbst
15. Winter

f. Nächsten Monat kommt er.

1. Sonnabend
2. Sonntag
3. Montag
4. Dienstag
5. Mittwoch
6. Donnerstag
7. Freitag
8. Samstag

g. Den ganzen Nachmittag bleibt er hier.

1. Vormittag
2. Abend
3. Tag
4. Monat
5. Sommer
6. Herbst
7. Winter
8. Frühling
9. Nacht

B. MODEL SENTENCES

I. Study each sentence until you can reproduce it correctly.

76. **Er will ganz Deutschland sehen.**
77. **Wollen Sie nach Hause?**
78. **Sie soll ihn morgen sehen.**
79. **Der Sommer ist warm.**

76. He wants to see all of Germany.
77. Do you want to go home?
78. She is to see him tomorrow.
79. Summer is warm.

II. Pattern Practice. Repeat the model sentence. Then substitute the items listed below in the appropriate places and make any other necessary changes. Repeat the entire sentence with each substitute item.

a. Er will ganz Deutschland sehen.

1. Frankreich
2. Italien
3. Spanien
4. Berlin
5. Österreich
6. Europa

b. Wollen Sie nach Hause?

1. in die Stadt
2. in die Schule
3. ins Zimmer
4. an den Rhein
5. an die See
6. aufs Land

c. Sie soll ihn morgen sehen.

1. _____ uns _____
2. _____ besuchen.
3. Er _____
4. _____ helfen.
5. _____ schreiben.
6. _____ mir _____

d. Der Sommer ist warm.

1. _____ schön.
2. _____ Frühling _____
3. _____ Herbst _____
4. _____ Winter _____
5. _____ kalt.
6. _____ nicht warm.

C. STRUCTURE

1. Nouns denoting seasons, months, days, or parts of days are normally used with the definite article:

a. Der Sommer ist warm.
Summer is warm.
b. Wir reisen **im Juli.**
We are traveling in July.
c. Er kommt **am Samstag.**
He is coming on Saturday.

2. Definite time is expressed by the accusative case:

Er kommt **nächsten Monat.**
He is coming next month.

3. Duration of time is expressed by the accusative case:

Er bleibt **den ganzen Nachmittag** hier.
He is staying here the whole afternoon.

4. The adjective **ganz** (*all of, the whole of*) is usually uninflected before neuter geographical names:

Er will **ganz Deutschland** sehen.
He wants to see all of Germany.

In other contexts it is inflected, as in the example of paragraph 3, above.

5. Present indicative of **können** (*can, to be able*):

ich **kann**	*I can, am able*
du **kannst**	*you can, are able*
er, sie, es **kann**	*he, she, it can, is able*
wir **können**	*we can, are able*
ihr **könnt**	*you can, are able*
sie **können**	*they can, are able*
Sie **können**	*you can, are able*

6. Present indicative of **sollen** (*to be to, to be supposed to*):

ich **soll**	*I am to, am supposed to*
du **sollst**	*you are to, are supposed to*
er, sie, es **soll**	*he, she, it is to, is supposed to*
wir **sollen**	*we are to, are supposed to*
ihr **sollt**	*you are to, are supposed to*
sie **sollen**	*they are to, are supposed to*
Sie **sollen**	*you are to, are supposed to*

7. Present indicative of **wollen** (*to want* [*to*]):

ich **will**	*I want* (*to*)
du **willst**	*you want* (*to*)
er, sie, es **will**	*he, she, it wants* (*to*)
wir **wollen**	*we want* (*to*)
ihr **wollt**	*you want* (*to*)
sie **wollen**	*they want* (*to*)
Sie **wollen**	*you want* (*to*)

8. Können (*can, to be able*), **müssen** (*must, to have to*), **sollen** (*to be to, to be supposed to*), and **wollen** (*to want* [*to*]) are modal auxiliary verbs, which may be used without the infinitive of a verb of motion if direction is indicated by an adverb or a prepositional phrase. The verb of motion is then understood:

a. Wollen Sie **nach Hause** (gehen)?
   Do you want to go home?
b. Mein Vetter Franz und meine Kusine Anna **müssen nach Hause** (gehen).
   My cousin Franz and my cousin Anna have to go home.

Note: An infinitive dependent on a modal auxiliary is never preceded by **zu:**

a. Er **will** ganz Berlin **sehen.**
   He wants to see all of Berlin.
b. Sie **soll** ihn morgen **sehen.**
   She is to see him tomorrow.

D. EXERCISES

Write the following sentences in German and be able to express them orally.

1. The students learn German on Tuesday and Thursday.
2. July is a warm month.
3. Can the child read well?
4. Next month we'll travel through the whole country.
5. My friends live at the seashore all year long.
6. Do you like to travel in January?
7. I want to go to the movies on Wednesday.
8. Must he go home now?
9. We will be able to go in June.
10. Heidelberg is supposed to be beautiful in the spring.
11. She stays home on Saturday.

12. Is September warm?
13. I can read all evening long.
14. He is to visit his parents tomorrow.
15. Where is the boy to go now?
16. On Friday she teaches English.
17. My aunt wants to read that book.
18. Vienna is beautiful in the summer.
19. She works the whole afternoon.
20. My cousin wants to see all of Europe.
21. The salesgirl is taking a trip next Sunday.
22. The pupils will study the whole morning.
23. My cousin (*f.*) will go to school next month.
24. Autumn in Switzerland is beautiful.

E. COMPREHENDING AND SPEAKING

I. Repeat the following after your instructor (or the speaker) and study thoroughly.

EINE AUTOREISE NACH NEW YORK

Peter und Walter fahren am Montag in Walters Auto nach New York, um ihre Europareise vorzubereiten.[1]

Im Auto sprechen sie von ihren Reiseplänen.[2]

Peter liest ein Buch mit dem Titel „Reisen in Europa". „Ich lese
5 seit dem Herbst nur noch deutsche Bücher", sagt er.

„Wann wollen wir unsere Reise machen?" fragt Walter.

„Im Frühling ist das Wetter in ganz Europa warm, und es sind nicht so viele Touristen dort. Aber wir haben leider nur zwei Wochen Ferien."[3]

10 „Wir müssen im Sommer gehen. Auch im Juni, Juli und August sollen Deutschland und die anderen Länder Europas schön sein."

„Können wir den ganzen Sommer dort bleiben?"

„Ich glaube nicht. Wir haben zu wenig Geld, um während des ganzen Sommers zu reisen."

[1]**um ihre Europareise vorzubereiten**	in order to prepare their trip to Europe	[3]**wir haben leider nur zwei Wochen Ferien**	unfortunately we have only two weeks vacation
[2]**sprechen sie von ihren Reiseplänen**	they talk about their travel plans		

15   „Wir wollen in New York Herrn Wagner besuchen!"

„Wer ist Herr Wagner?"

„Er ist ein Freund meines Vetters Karl. Er arbeitet in einem Reisebüro und kann uns sicher[4] helfen."

II. Beantworten Sie die folgenden Fragen auf deutsch!

1. Wann fahren Peter und Walter nach New York?
2. Warum fahren sie nach New York?
3. Wo sprechen sie von ihren Reiseplänen?
4. Was liest Peter nur noch seit dem Herbst?
5. Wie ist das Wetter im Frühling in Europa?
6. Warum müssen die beiden im Sommer nach Europa reisen?
7. Wie soll Deutschland im Sommer sein?
8. Warum können Peter und Walter nicht den ganzen Sommer bleiben?
9. Wen wollen sie in New York besuchen?

[4]**sicher**   certainly

UNIT 12

A. UNITS OF SPEECH AND VOCABULARY

I. Study and Practice Aloud.

Wir hören Radio.	We are listening to the radio.
Was tut er?	What is he doing?
Dürfen wir es tun?	May we do it?
Ich habe keine Zeit.	I have no time.
in der Kirche	in church, at church
in die Kirche	to church
nach der Kirche	after church
nach der Schule	after school
vor einem Monat	a month ago
vor einer Stunde	an hour ago

der Arzt, ⸚e	the physician, doctor	**der Vogel, ⸚**	the bird	
		die Woche, -n	the week	
der Baum, ⸚e	the tree	**die Zeit, -en**	the time	
die Kirche, -n	the church	**dürfen**	may, to be permitted to	
die Lehrerin, -nen	the teacher (*f.*)			
		hören	to hear, to listen to	
der Professor, -en	the professor			
		mögen	to like, to care (to)	
das Radio, -s	the radio			
der Stuhl, ⸚e	the chair	**studieren**	to study (*at a university*)	
die Stunde, -n	the hour, class			

(*98*)

tun	to do	**spät**	late
tut	does, is doing	**gestern**	yesterday
war	was	**vorgestern**	the day before
waren	were		yesterday
interessant	interesting	**immer**	always
langsam	slow, slowly	**oft**	often
schnell	quick, quickly,	**sehr**	very
	fast		

II. Oral Practice. Repeat the pattern. Then substitute the items listed below. Repeat the entire sentence with each substitute item, changing the verb where necessary.

a. Wir hören Radio.

1. Die Schüler
2. Sie (*pl.*)
3. Der Schüler
4. Er
5. Die Studentin
6. Sie (*sing.*)
7. Die Frau
8. Ich

b. Was tut er?

1. der Professor
2. die Lehrerin
3. sie (*sing.*)
4. die Lehrerinnen
5. die Professoren
6. sie (*pl.*)

c. Dürfen wir es tun?

1. Sie
2. die Kinder
3. die Jungen
4. die Mädchen
5. die Schüler
6. die Schülerinnen

d. Ich habe keine Zeit.

1. Wir
2. Der Professor
3. Er
4. Die Lehrerin
5. Sie (*sing.*)
6. Die Studentin

e. Die Lehrerin ist in der Kirche.

1. Sie (*sing.*)
2. Der Arzt
3. Der Professor
4. Er
5. Die Ärzte
6. Wir
7. Die Professoren
8. Die Lehrerinnen

f. Der Arzt geht in die Kirche.

1. Er
2. Der Professor
3. Die Lehrerin
4. Die Lehrerinnen
5. Die Professoren
6. Die Ärzte

g. Nach der Kirche geht der Professor nach Hause.

1. die Lehrerin
2. der Arzt
3. die Ärzte
4. die Professoren
5. die Lehrerinnen
6. sie (*pl.*)

h. Nach der Schule fahren die Lehrerinnen nach Hause.
    1. die Lehrer   4. die Lehrer und die Lehrerinnen
    2. die Schüler   5. sie (*pl.*)
    3. die Schülerinnen   6. die Kinder

i. Er war vor einem Monat hier.
    1. vor einem Jahr   4. vor einer Stunde
    2. vor zwei Jahren   5. vor einer Woche
    3. vor zwei Monaten   6. vor drei Wochen

j. Sie studiert in Berlin.
    1. Heidelberg   5. Spanien
    2. Deutschland   6. Italien
    3. Europa   7. England
    4. Frankreich   8. Österreich

III. Oral Practice. Repeat the pattern sentence. Then substitute the items listed below in the appropriate places. Repeat the entire sentence with each substitute item, changing the verb where necessary.

a. Der Vogel sitzt auf dem Baum.
    1. Der kleine Vogel _____   3. _____ den Bäumen.
    2. Die Vögel _____   4. Die kleinen Vögel _____

b. Die Deutschstunde ist interessant.
    1. _____ oft interessant.   4. _____ oft sehr _____
    2. _____ immer _____   5. _____ immer sehr _____
    3. _____ sehr _____   6. _____ sehr gut.

c. Sie mögen die Lehrerin.
    1. _____ diese _____   3. _____ die Lehrerinnen.
    2. Wir _____   4. _____ diese _____

d. Fährt er langsam?
    1. _____ schnell?   4. _____ langsam?
    2. _____ die Frau _____ꞓ   5. _____ oft _____?
    3. _____ Sie _____?   6. _____ immer _____?

e. Er kommt spät.
    1. Wir _____   3. Die Kinder _____
    2. _____ später.   4. Sie (*pl.*) _____

f. Gestern war Samstag.
    1. _____ Sonntag.   5. _____ Mittwoch.
    2. _____ Montag.   6. _____ Donnerstag.
    3. _____ Dienstag.   7. _____ Freitag.
    4. Vorgestern _____   8. _____ Sonnabend.

B. MODEL SENTENCES

I. Study each sentence until you can reproduce it correctly.

80. **Er hat das Buch gelesen.**
81. **Ich habe in den Vereinigten Staaten studiert.**
82. **Vor einem Jahr ist sie durch Europa gereist.**
83. **Unsere Freunde sind alt geworden.**
84. **Heute mag der Junge nicht lernen.**
85. **Darf ich ins Kino gehen, Vater? — Ja, du darfst es.**
86. **Wir dürfen nicht reden.**

80. He (has) read the book.
81. I (have) studied in the United States.
82. She traveled through Europe a year ago.
83. Our friends have become old.
84. The boy doesn't care to study today.
85. May I go to the movies, father? — Yes, you may.
86. We mustn't talk.

II. Pattern Practice. Repeat the model sentence. Then substitute the items listed below in the equivalent part of the model sentence. Repeat the entire sentence with each substitute item.

a. **Er hat das Buch gelesen.**

1. Der Professor		5. Die Schülerin	
2. Die Lehrerin		6. Die Studentin	
3. Der Lehrer		7. Der Student	
4. Der Schüler		8. Der Junge	

b. **Ich habe in den Vereinigten Staaten studiert.**

1. Frankreich	4. Heidelberg
2. Österreich	5. Köln
3. Wien	6. Deutschland

c. **Vor einem Jahr ist sie durch Europa gereist.**

1. Österreich	4. England
2. Spanien	5. Frankreich
3. Italien	6. die Vereinigten Staaten

d. **Unsere Freunde sind alt geworden.**

1. Unsere Vettern	4. Ihre Schwestern
2. Seine Eltern	5. Seine Tanten
3. Meine Kusinen	6. Meine Brüder

e. **Heute mag der Junge nicht lernen.**

1. er	5. mein Bruder
2. das Mädchen	6. Ihre Schwester
3. die Schülerin	7. sein Sohn
4. sie (*sing.*)	8. ihr Kind

f. Darf ich ins Kino gehen, Vater? — Ja, du darfst es.
   1. ins Restaurant   4. an die See
   2. in die Stadt   5. an den Fluß
   3. aufs Land   6. nach Hause

g. Wir dürfen nicht reden.
   1. laufen   4. sitzen
   2. spielen   5. stehen
   3. bleiben   6. schreiben

C. STRUCTURE

1. The preposition **vor** plus the dative of a noun of time expresses the idea of *ago:*

vor einem Jahr   *a year ago*
vor einer Stunde   *an hour ago*

2. The past participle of most regular (or "weak") verbs is formed by prefixing **ge-** to the present stem and adding the suffix **-t:**

INFINITIVE		PAST PARTICIPLE	
sagen	*to say*	**gesagt**	*said*
reisen	*to travel*	**gereist**	*traveled*

Haben forms its past participle similarly:

haben	*to have*	**gehabt**	*had*

The following regular verbs form their past participles like **sagen:**

danken	*to thank*	**gedankt**	*thanked*
fragen	*to ask*	**gefragt**	*asked*
hören	*to hear*	**gehört**	*heard*
kaufen	*to buy*	**gekauft**	*bought*
legen	*to lay, put*	**gelegt**	*laid, put*
lehren	*to teach*	**gelehrt**	*taught*
lernen	*to learn*	**gelernt**	*learned*
machen	*to make*	**gemacht**	*made*
reisen	*to travel*	**gereist**	*traveled*
sollen	*to be (supposed) to*	**gesollt**	*been obliged to*
spielen	*to play*	**gespielt**	*played*
stecken	*to stick, put*	**gesteckt**	*stuck, put*
wohnen	*to dwell, live*	**gewohnt**	*dwelt, lived*
wollen	*will, to want (to)*	**gewollt**	*wanted (to)*

Some verbs also change their stem vowel. Among these are the following:

INFINITIVE		PAST PARTICIPLE	
bringen	*to bring*	**gebracht**	*brought*
dürfen	*may, to be permitted to*	**gedurft**	*permitted*
können	*can, to be able*	**gekonnt**	*been able*
mögen	*like, care to*	**gemocht**	*liked, cared to*
müssen	*must, to have to*	**gemußt**	*had to*

3. Verbs whose stems end in **-d** or **-t,** like **reden** (*to talk*) or **antworten** (*to answer*), add **e** before the suffix **-t** to facilitate pronunciation:

INFINITIVE		PAST PARTICIPLE	
reden	*to talk*	geredet	*talked*
antworten	*to answer*	geantwortet	*answered*

4. Verbs in **-ieren** form their past participle without the prefix **ge-:**

studieren	*to study*	**studiert**	*studied*

5. Irregular (or "strong") verbs form their past participles by prefixing **ge-** to the past-participle stem and adding the suffix **-en.** The past participle often has a different vowel from that of the present stem, as well as consonant irregularities. A list of irregular past participles follows for verbs learned up to this point:

INFINITIVE		PAST PARTICIPLE	
bleiben	*to remain*	**geblieben**	*remained*
essen	*to eat*	**gegessen**	*eaten*
finden	*to find*	**gefunden**	*found*
geben	*to give*	**gegeben**	*given*
gehen	*to go*	**gegangen**	*gone*
heißen	*to be called*	**geheißen**	*called*
helfen	*to help*	**geholfen**	*helped*
kommen	*to come*	**gekommen**	*come*
laufen	*to run*	**gelaufen**	*run*
lesen	*to read*	**gelesen**	*read*
liegen	*to lie*	**gelegen**	*lain*
schreiben	*to write*	**geschrieben**	*written*
sehen	*to see*	**gesehen**	*seen*
sein	*to be*	**gewesen**	*been*
sitzen	*to sit*	**gesessen**	*sat*
stehen	*to stand*	**gestanden**	*stood*

trinken	*to drink*	**getrunken**	*drunk*
tun	*to do*	**getan**	*done*
werden	*to become*	**geworden**	*become*

6. The compound past of most verbs consists of the present tense of the auxiliary verb **haben** (*to have*) and the past participle. In a main clause, the past participle (like the infinitive) stands last:

   a. Er **hat** das Buch **gelesen.**
   He read the book.
   He has read the book.

   b. Ich **habe** in den Vereinigten Staaten **studiert.**
   I studied in the United States.
   I have studied in the United States.

   The compound past is generally used in conversation to express a past action. It may be equivalent to an English simple past or a present perfect.

   Note: The above sentences could also mean:

   a. *He did read the book.*
   b. *I did study in the United States.*

7. Some intransitive verbs require **sein** (*to be*) as their auxiliary in the compound past:

   a. Vor einem Jahr **ist** sie durch Europa **gereist.**
   She traveled through Europe a year ago.

   b. Unsere Freunde **sind** alt **geworden.**
   Our friends have become old.

   Verbs requiring **sein** in the compound past include verbs of motion, such as **reisen** (*to travel*), **fahren** (*to ride*), **kommen** (*to come*), **gehen** (*to go*), **laufen** (*to run*); verbs indicating a change of state or condition, such as **werden** (*to become*), **wachsen** (*to grow*); and **sein** (*to be*) and **bleiben** (*to remain*).

8. Present tense of the modal auxiliary **mögen** (*to like, care to*):

ich **mag**	*I like, care (to)*
du **magst**	*you like, care (to)*
er, sie, es **mag**	*he, she, it likes, cares (to)*
wir **mögen**	*we like, care (to)*
ihr **mögt**	*you like, care (to)*
sie **mögen**	*they like, care (to)*
Sie **mögen**	*you like, care (to)*

9. Present tense of the modal auxiliary **dürfen** (*may, to be permitted to*):

ich **darf**	*I may, am permitted to*
du **darfst**	*you may, are permitted to*
er, sie, es **darf**	*he, she, it may, is permitted to*
wir **dürfen**	*we may, are permitted to*
ihr **dürft**	*you may, are permitted to*
sie **dürfen**	*they may, are permitted to*
Sie **dürfen**	*you may, are permitted to*

Note: When **dürfen** is used in the negative, it may mean *must not*:

Wir **dürfen nicht** reden.
We mustn't talk.

Note that **nicht** (*not*) usually precedes an infinitive.

10. A modal auxiliary may be used without a dependent infinitive when it refers to a previous statement. An indefinite neuter pronoun object, usually **es** (*it*) or **das** (*that*), completes such a reference:

a. Darf ich **ins Kino gehen,** Vater? — Ja, du darfst **es.**
May I go to the movies, father? — Yes, you may.

b. Muß er **den Brief lesen?** — Ja, **das** muß er.
Must he read the letter? — Yes, he must.

11. Present tense of **tun** (*to do*):

ich **tue**	*I do, am doing*
du **tust**	*you do, are doing*
er, sie, es **tut**	*he, she, it does, is doing*
wir **tun**	*we do, are doing*
ihr **tut**	*you do, are doing*
sie **tun**	*they do, are doing*
Sie **tun**	*you do, are doing*

D. EXERCISES

Write the following sentences in German and be able to express them orally.

1. The pupils (*f.*) are permitted to go home today.
2. He did see his brother a week ago.
3. The child answered her father.
4. My sister listened to the radio.
5. They ask what I am doing.
6. We don't care to go to the movies now.

7. Did those men study in England?
8. Two months ago the professor took a trip to Switzerland.
9. The pupils learned the lessons after school.
10. Don't you care to go to school today? — No, I don't care to.
11. You must not eat in this building.
12. What did your aunt eat?
13. My uncle has become old.
14. I brought them the letter an hour ago.
15. The girl ran out of the house.
16. Has my cousin been here?
17. What did the student want?
18. Did you stay at your sister's house the day before yesterday?
19. Are the children permitted to play there?
20. Where did you live three years ago?
21. We must not drink cold water.
22. Has your cousin (*f.*) talked with the doctors?
23. Her teacher wrote the letter yesterday.
24. May I read your book? — Yes, you may.

E. COMPREHENDING AND SPEAKING

I. Repeat the following after your instructor (or the speaker) and study thoroughly.

IM REISEBÜRO

Herr Wagner sitzt an einem Tisch im Reisebüro und schreibt.

,,Guten Tag, Herr Wagner", sagt Walter.

,,Ah, guten Tag, Walter. Ich habe Sie seit langer Zeit nicht mehr gesehen."[1]

5　　　,,Ich habe viel zu tun gehabt. Wir müssen viel lernen. Unsere Professoren wollen es so."

,,Oh ja, ich weiß,[2] wie es ist. Ich habe vor einigen Jahren auch studiert. Was kann ich jetzt für Sie tun?"

,,Herr Wagner, mein Freund Peter und ich möchten[3] dieses Jahr
10　gern nach Europa reisen. Wir haben allerdings[4] nicht viel Geld, aber viel Zeit. Sie sind schon oft in Europa gewesen. Vielleicht[5] können Sie uns helfen."

[1]**Ich habe Sie seit langer Zeit nicht mehr gesehen.**	I have not seen you for a long time.	[3]**möchten . . . gern**	would like very much to
		[4]**allerdings**	to be sure
[2]**ich weiß**	I know	[5]**vielleicht**	perhaps

„Na, wir wollen mal sehen", sagt Herr Wagner freundlich.[6] „Ich
habe zwei Jahre in Deutschland studiert und habe auch nicht viel
15 Geld gehabt. Trotzdem[7] bin ich durch ganz Europa gereist und habe
viel erlebt.[8] Die zwei Jahre in Deutschland waren meine schönste
Zeit, aber ich bin auch in Italien, in Österreich und in der Schweiz
gereist."

Er beschreibt[9] den beiden Freunden die Länder und Städte
20 Europas.

„Ich habe in Heidelberg gewohnt und studiert. Sie müssen Heidelberg auf jeden Fall[10] besuchen. Ich habe dort einen Freund, und ich
werde ihm schreiben. Nun muß ich wieder arbeiten. Ich habe leider
keine Zeit mehr. Bitte kommen Sie während des Nachmittags wieder.
25 Nach fünf Uhr können wir dann über Deutschland und Ihre Reise-
pläne reden."

II. Beantworten Sie die folgenden Fragen auf deutsch!
1. Was tut Herr Wagner im Reisebüro?
2. Seit wann hat er Walter nicht mehr gesehen?
3. Warum muß Walter so viel lernen?
4. Warum weiß Herr Wagner, wie es ist?
5. Was für ein Problem haben Peter und Walter?
6. Kennt Herr Wagner Europa?
7. Warum kann er den beiden vielleicht helfen?
8. Wo hat Herr Wagner studiert?
9. Wann sollen die beiden wieder kommen?

[6]**freundlich**	amiably	[9]**beschreiben**	to describe
[7]**trotzdem**	nevertheless	[10]**auf jeden Fall**	in any case, by all
[8]**erleben**	to experience		means

UNIT 13

A. UNITS OF SPEECH AND VOCABULARY

I. Study and Practice Aloud.

Das ist mein Freund.	That's my friend.
Dies ist mein Nachbar.	This is my neighbor.
Ich kann Deutsch.	I know German.
Wir kennen die Lehrerin.	We know the teacher (*f.*).
Wir haben die Lehrerin gekannt.	We knew the teacher (*f.*).
Er weiß es.	He knows it.
Haben Sie das gewußt?	Did you know that?
nicht wahr?	isn't it? aren't they? doesn't he? etc.
vor dem Frühstück	before breakfast
nach dem Mittagessen	after lunch
während des Abendessens	during supper

das Essen	the meal, food	**der Nachbar, -n**	the neighbor
das Frühstück	the breakfast	**die Hauptstadt,**	the capital (city)
das Mittagessen	the lunch, dinner	**ˮe**	
		Englisch	English, the English language
das Abendessen	the dinner, supper		
das Eßzimmer, -	the dining room	**das**	that
das Schlafzimmer, -	the bedroom	**dies**	this
		kennen	to know
das Wohnzimmer, -	the living room	**gekannt** (*past. part.*)	known
die Küche, -n	the kitchen	**schlafen**	to sleep

(108)

schläft	sleeps	**kurz**	short
sprechen	to speak	**lang**	long
spricht	speaks	**zwanzig**	twenty
wissen	to know	**einund-**	twenty-one
gewußt (*past.*	known	**zwanzig**	
part.)		**dreißig**	thirty
zeigen	to show	**zweiund-**	thirty-two
erst	not until	**dreißig**	
früh	early	**vierzig**	forty
gewöhnlich	usual	**fünfzig**	fifty
hübsch	pretty	**fast**	almost

II. Oral Practice. Repeat the pattern. Then substitute the items listed below. Repeat the entire sentence with each substitute item, changing the verb where necessary.

a. Das ist mein Freund.

1. mein Nachbar
2. die Haupstadt
3. die Küche
4. das Eßzimmer
5. das Schlafzimmer
6. das Wohnzimmer
7. unser Haus
8. die Schule

b. Dies ist mein Nachbar.

1. mein Vetter
2. mein Freund
3. mein Lehrer
4. mein Bruder
5. meine Schwester
6. meine Tante

c. Wir kennen die Lehrerin.

1. Die Schüler
2. Die Schülerinnen
3. Die Nachbarn
4. Die Kinder
5. Die Mädchen
6. Die Jungen

d. Wir haben die Lehrerin gekannt.

1. Sie
2. Meine Eltern
3. Seine Brüder
4. Ihre Kusine
5. Die Frau
6. Das Kind

e. Er weiß es.

1. Der Junge
2. Das Kind
3. Das Mädchen
4. Die Schülerin
5. Der Schüler
6. Ich

f. Haben Sie das gewußt?

1. die Jungen
2. die Kinder
3. die Mädchen
4. Ihre Eltern
5. seine Freunde
6. unsere Nachbarn

g. Das ist sein Freund, nicht wahr?

1. Dies ist sein Nachbar
2. Wir kennen die Lehrerin
3. Wir haben die Lehrerin gekannt

   4. Er weiß es   6. Jetzt lernen wir Deutsch
   5. Sie haben das gewußt

h. **Kommt er vor dem Frühstück?**
   1. vor dem Mittagessen   5. nach dem Frühstück
   2. vor dem Abendessen   6. während des Frühstücks
   3. nach dem Abendessen   7. während des Mittagessens
   4. nach dem Mittagessen   8. während des Abendessens

i. **Er schläft.**
   1. Unser Nachbar   4. Seine Kinder
   2. Mein Bruder   5. Meine Eltern
   3. Sein Kind   6. Die Jungen

j. **Sie spricht.**
   1. Die Lehrerin   4. Seine Nachbarn
   2. Die Schülerin   5. Die Ärzte
   3. Ihr Nachbar   6. Die Professoren

k. **Er zeigt mir das Eßzimmer.**
   1. das Wohnzimmer   4. das Haus
   2. das Schlafzimmer   5. das Gebäude
   3. die Küche   6. die Schule

l. **Das Mädchen ist hübsch.**
   1. Seine Schwester   4. Die Frau
   2. Meine Kusine   5. Die Studentin
   3. Ihre Tante   6. Sie

m. **Er hat zwanzig Bücher.**
   1. 32   4. 21
   2. 40   5. 30
   3. 50   6. 48

n. **Warum ist er in der Küche?**
   1. im Wohnzimmer   4. in der Haupstadt
   2. im Eßzimmer   5. in der Stadt
   3. im Schlafzimmer   6. in der Kirche

III. Oral Practice. Repeat the pattern sentence. Then substitute the items listed below in the appropriate places. Repeat the entire sentence with each substitute item, changing the verb where necessary.

a. **Ich kann Deutsch.**
   1. Er _____   4. Ich _____
   2. Wir _____   5. Mein Onkel _____
   3. _____ Englisch.   6. Ihre Tante _____

b. **Gewöhnlich kommt sie früh.**
   1. _____ meine Freun-   2. _____ sein Freund _____
      din _____

3. _____ geht _____
4. _____ er _____
5. _____ wir _____
6. _____ erst nach dem Abendessen.

7. _____ erst nach dem Mittagessen.
8. _____ erst nach dem Frühstück.

c. **Die Aufgabe ist kurz.**

1. Der Brief _____
2. Die Briefe _____
3. Die Aufgaben _____
4. Die Tage _____

5. _____ lang.
6. Die Aufgaben _____
7. Die Aufgabe _____
8. Der Brief _____

B. MODEL SENTENCES

I. Study each sentence until you can reproduce it correctly.

87. **Es ist mein Vater.**
88. **Dies sind mein Brüder und das sind meine Nachbarn.**
89. **Wissen Sie, wann er kommt? — Ja, ich weiß es.**

87. It's my father.
88. These are my brothers and those are my neighbors.
89. Do you know when he is coming? — Yes, I know.

II. Pattern Practice. Repeat the model sentence. Then substitute the following items in the equivalent part of the model sentence. Repeat the entire sentence with each substitute item.

a. **Es ist mein Vater.**

1. Ihr Bruder
2. sein Onkel
3. unsere Tante

4. meine Kusine
5. seine Mutter
6. ihre Schwester

b. **Dies sind meine Brüder und das sind meine Nachbarn.**

1. meine Vettern, meine Onkel
2. ihre Vettern, ihre Schwestern
3. seine Kusinen, seine Schwestern

4. unsere Kusinen, unsere Freundinnen
5. meine Tanten, meine Freundinnen
6. seine Tanten, seine Schwestern

c. **Wissen Sie, wann er kommt? — Ja, ich weiß es.**

1. Ihr Freund
2. sein Onkel
3. ihre Freundin

4. unsere Kusine
5. meine Tante
6. die Kinder

C. STRUCTURE

1. The neuter indefinite pronouns **es** (*it*), **dies** (*this*), and **das** (*that*) are used with the verb **sein** (*to be*) and predicate nouns in identifications:

   a. **Es ist** mein Vater.
      It's my father.
   b. **Das ist** mein Freund.
      That's my friend.
   c. **Dies ist** mein Nachbar.
      This is my neighbor.

   Note: If the predicate noun is plural, a plural verb is used, but the pronoun remains singular (**es** is then equivalent to *they*, **dies** to *these*, and **das** to *those*).

2. **Kennen** means *to know* in the sense of *to be acquainted with* and is usually used with nouns or pronouns denoting persons:

   > Wir **kennen** die Lehrerin.
   > *We know the teacher.*

3. **Können** means *to know how* with subjects of study or skills:

   > Ich **kann** Deutsch.
   > *I know German.*
   > Ich **kann** lesen.
   > *I can read.*

4. **Wissen** means *to know* in the sense of *to have knowledge of* or *to know a fact*. It is usually followed by a clause or by a neuter indefinite pronoun object (**es, das**):

   > **Wissen Sie, wann er kommt?** — Ja, **ich weiß es.**
   > *Do you know when he is coming? — Yes, I know.*

5. The present tense of **wissen** (*to know*):

ich	**weiß**	*I know*
du	**weißt**	*you know*
er, sie, es	**weiß**	*he, she, it knows*
wir	**wissen**	*we know*
ihr	**wißt**	*you know*
sie	**wissen**	*they know*
Sie	**wissen**	*you know*

6. The phrase **nicht wahr?** (literally, *is it not true?*) makes a question out of a statement:

   a. Das ist sein Freund, **nicht wahr?**
   That's his friend, isn't it?
   b. Er weiß es, **nicht wahr?**
   He knows it, doesn't he?
   c. Sie haben das gewußt, **nicht wahr?**
   You knew that, didn't you?
   d. Jetzt lernen wir Deutsch, **nicht wahr?**
   We are studying German now, aren't we?

7. Two-digit numbers from 21 on are formed by putting the units digit first, followed by **und** and the tens digit, all written as one word:

   einundzwanzig *21*
   zweiunddreißig *32*

   Note: Cardinal numbers, except **ein** (*one*), are not inflected.

8. Regular verbs form the simple past tense by adding the past endings to the stem (**sag-**):

ich sag**te**	*I said, was saying, did say*
du sag**test**	*you said, were saying, did say*
er, sie, es sag**te**	*he, she, it said, was saying, did say*
wir sag**ten**	*we said, were saying, did say*
ihr sag**tet**	*you said, were saying, did say*
sie sag**ten**	*they said, were saying, did say*
Sie sag**ten**	*you said, were saying, did say*

9. The following regular verbs form their past tense like **sagen:**

begrüßen	*to greet*	**lernen**	*to learn, to study*
besuchen	*to visit*	**machen**	*to make, to do*
danken	*to thank*	**reisen**	*to travel*
fragen	*to ask*	**sollen**	*to be (supposed) to*
hören	*to hear, to listen to*	**spielen**	*to play*
kaufen	*to buy*	**stecken**	*to stick, to put*
legen	*to lay, to put*	**wohnen**	*to dwell, to live*
lehren	*to teach*	**wollen**	*will, to want*

10. Verbs whose stems end in **-d** or **-t,** like **reden** (*to talk*) or **antworten** (*to answer*), add **e** before the past endings to facilitate pronunciation:

reden	*to talk*	ich red**ete**	*I talked, was talking, did talk*

antworten   *to answer*   ich antwor**tete**   *I answered, was answering,*
                                                         did answer

11. Some verbs add the past endings and alter the stem:

bringen   *to bring*   ich **brachte**   *I brought, was bringing,*
                                                                  did bring

dürfen   *may, to be permitted to*   ich **durfte**   *I was permitted to*
haben   *to have*   ich **hatte**   *I had*
können   *can, to be able to*   ich **konnte**   *I could, was able to*
mögen   *to like, care to*   ich **mochte**   *I liked, cared to*
müssen   *must, to have to*   ich **mußte**   *I had to*
wissen   *to know*   ich **wußte**   *I knew*

12. The simple past tense is used primarily in connected narrative. In this
book, we will use it principally in the narrative portions of the E sections.
As you learned in Unit 12, the compound past is normally used in
conversation.[1] Note, however, that the past tense of **haben, sein, werden**
and modal auxiliaries is often preferred even in conversation.

D. EXERCISES

Write the following sentences in German and be able to express them orally.

1. I know why he is staying.
2. This is my cousin (*f.*).
3. He gave his uncle the money, didn't he?
4. Twenty-six students are in this room.
5. Those are her sisters.
6. His cousins knew German.
7. Who is speaking with your sister? — It's your uncle.
8. Is that your doctor?
9. You know our neighbors.
10. Your aunt has read this book, hasn't she?
11. My mother knows where we are.
12. You have talked with your teacher (*f.*), haven't you?
13. These are my best friends.
14. My mother knows your teachers.
15. Your father has come home, hasn't he?
16. Did he know that? — Yes, he knew it.
17. The children were playing in the living room, weren't they?

---

[1] There are also regional differences. The simple past is more general in Northern
Germany, the compound past in Southern Germany, Austria, and Switzerland.

18. Do your friends know English?
19. After breakfast they went to church, didn't they?
20. Did you know her younger brother?
21. They found fifty-one books there.
22. Did you know Mr. and Mrs. Meyer?
23. My father doesn't talk until after breakfast.
24. The pupils knew the lesson, didn't they?

E. COMPREHENDING AND SPEAKING

I. Repeat the following after your instructor (or the speaker) and study thoroughly.

IN NEW YORK

Walter kennt New York. Für Peter ist die Stadt neu. Walter zeigt seinem Freund die großen Gebäude und Kirchen der Stadt. Kurz nach fünf sind sie wieder im Reisebüro.

Herr Wagner begrüßt sie und sagt: „Ich habe gerade[1] am Tele-
5 phon mit meiner Frau gesprochen. Sie werden bei uns zu Abend essen, nicht wahr?"

„Danke, Herr Wagner, wir kommen gerne!"

Walter hat sein Auto vor das Haus gestellt.[2] Während der Fahrt[3] fragt Herr Wagner: „Haben Sie heute viel von New York gesehen?"

10 Peter antwortet: „Oh ja! Wir gingen zuerst in ein großes Museum und sahen dort viele alte Gemälde.[4] Dann besuchten wir den Zoo und spielten eine Weile mit den Affen.[5] Im Zoo trafen[6] wir auch einen Studenten. Er konnte nur Deutsch, und wir sprachen lange mit ihm. Um zwölf Uhr gingen wir in ein Restaurant und aßen zu Mittag.

15 Nach dem Mittagessen tranken wir Kaffee und schrieben unseren Familien eine Postkarte. Wir blieben bis drei Uhr. Nachher[7] zeigte mir Walter die schönsten Straßen New Yorks.

„Hier sind wir endlich zu Hause", ruft[8] Herr Wagner. Er begrüßt seine Frau und sagt: „Nelly, dies sind meine zwei Freunde. Du kennst

20 Walter schon. Das ist Peter."

„Guten Abend!" sagt Frau Wagner freundlich, „es freut mich, Sie kennenzulernen."[9]

[1]**gerade**	just	[6]**treffen**	to meet
[2]**stellen**	to put, park	[7]**nachher**	afterwards
[3]**die Fahrt, -en**	the trip	[8]**rufen**	to call
[4]**das Gemälde, -**	the painting	[9]**es freut mich, Sie**	I am glad to meet
[5]**der Affe, -n**	the monkey	**kennenzulernen**	you

II. Beantworten Sie die folgenden Fragen auf deutsch!

1. Was zeigt Walter seinem Freund in New York?
2. Wann sind sie wieder im Reisebüro?
3. Was sagt Walter zu ihnen?
4. Wo steht Walters Auto?
5. Was fragt Herr Wagner während der Fahrt?
6. Wen haben die beiden im Zoo getroffen?
7. Hat der Student Englisch gesprochen?
8. Wie lange sind die zwei Freunde im Restaurant geblieben?
9. Kennt Frau Wagner Peter schon?

UNIT 14

A. UNITS OF SPEECH AND VOCABULARY

I. Study and Practice Aloud.

Er ist ihr begegnet.	He met her.
gestern morgen	yesterday morning
gestern nachmittag	yesterday afternoon
gestern abend	yesterday evening
heute morgen	this morning
heute nachmittag	this afternoon
heute abend	this evening
morgen früh	tomorrow morning
morgen nachmittag	tomorrow afternoon
morgen abend	tomorrow evening
Freitag morgen	Friday morning
Sonntag nachmittag	Sunday afternoon
Dienstag abend	Tuesday evening
nicht mehr	no longer, no more, not . . . any more

der Apfel, ⸚	the apple	**bekommen**	to get, to receive
die Blume, -n	the flower	**fallen**	to fall
der Boden, ⸚	the ground, floor	**fällt**	falls
der Garten, ⸚	the garden	**nehmen**	to take
das Gras, ⸚er	the grass	**nimmt**	takes
begegnen	to meet (*by chance*)	**schicken**	to send
+ *dat.*		**tragen**	to carry, to wear

(*117*)

trägt	carries, wears	reif	ripe
wachsen	to grow	**rot**	red
wächst	grows	**also**	therefore, conse-
gelb	yellow		quently
grün	green	**mehr**	more
halb	half	**wieder**	again

II. Oral Practice. Repeat the pattern sentence. Then substitute the items below. Repeat the entire sentence with each substitute item.

a. Er ist ihr begegnet.
1. der Frau
2. dem Mann
3. ihm
4. den Kindern
5. ihnen
6. mir

b. Gestern morgen ist sie gekommen.
1. Gestern nachmittag
2. Gestern abend
3. Heute morgen
4. Heute nachmittag
5. Heute abend
6. Freitag morgen
7. Sonntag nachmittag
8. Dienstag abend

c. Besucht er ihn heute morgen?
1. heute nachmittag
2. heute abend
3. morgen früh
4. morgen nachmittag
5. morgen abend
6. Samstag morgen
7. Montag nachmittag
8. Mittwoch abend

d. Meine Freunde kommen wieder.
1. gehen
2. essen
3. trinken
4. reisen
5. spielen
6. sprechen

III. Oral Practice. Repeat the pattern sentence. Then substitute the items listed below in the appropriate places. Repeat the entire sentence with each substitute item, changing the verb where necessary.

a. Der Apfel ist nicht mehr gelb.
1. Die Äpfel _____
2. _____ grün.
3. Die Gärten _____
4. Der Garten _____

b. Der Apfel fällt ins Gras.
1. _____ auf den Boden.
2. Der reife Apfel _____
3. Die reifen Äpfel _____
4. _____ ins Gras.

c. Sie bekommen weiße Blumen.
1. _____ schicken _____
2. Ich _____
3. _____ gelbe _____
4. _____ bekomme _____
5. Sie bekommt _____
6. _____ rote _____
7. _____ schickt _____
8. Er _____

d. Wir tragen das Kind.

1. _____ das Buch.
2. Die Frau _____
3. _____ einen Hut.

4. _____ einen grünen Hut.
5. _____ einen roten Hut.
6. Das Mädchen _____

e. Also nimmt sie den Apfel.

1. _____ den reifen Apfel.
2. _____ ich _____
3. _____ die reifen Äpfel.

4. _____ die grünen Äpfel.
5. _____ das Mädchen _____
6. _____ der Junge _____

B. MODEL SENTENCES

I. Study each sentence until you can reproduce it correctly.

90. **Welche Städte in Europa haben Sie gesehen?**
91. **Welches sind die größten Städte in Europa?**
92. **Mein Onkel ist nicht Lehrer. Er ist Arzt.**
93. **Zeige mir dein Buch, Hans!**
94. **Lernt eure Aufgaben, Kinder!**
95. **Hat der Junge in die Schule gehen können?**
96. **Nein, er hat es nicht gekonnt.**

90. Which cities in Europe did you see?
91. Which are the biggest cities in Europe?
92. My uncle is not a teacher. He's a doctor.
93. Show me your book, Hans.
94. Learn your lessons, children.
95. Has the boy been able to go to school?
96. No, he hasn't been able to.

II. Pattern Practice. Repeat the model sentence. Then substitute the items listed below in the appropriate places. Repeat the entire sentence with each substitute item.

a. Welche Städte in Europa haben Sie gesehen?

1. _____ Länder _____?
2. _____ besucht?
3. Welche Freunde _____?

4. Welche Familien _____?
5. Welche Kirchen _____?
6. _____ gesehen?

b. Welches sind die größten Städte in Europa?

1. _____ Länder _____?
2. _____ Flüsse _____?
3. _____ Deutschland?

4. _____ Kirchen _____?
5. _____ Städte _____?
6. _____ in den Vereinigten Staaten?

c. Mein Onkel ist nicht Lehrer. Er ist Arzt.

1. _____ Professor _____
2. Mein Vetter _____
3. _____ Lehrer.

4. Sein Vater _____
5. _____ Arzt _____
6. Unser Freund _____

d. Zeige mir dein Buch, Hans!

1. _____ deine Blumen _____   4. _____ Klara!
2. _____ Trude!   5. _____ deinen Hut _____
3. _____ deine Freundin _____   6. _____ Richard!

e. Lernt euere Aufgaben, Kinder!

1. _____ Hans und Robert!   3. Macht _____
2. _____ die Aufgabe _____   4. _____ Klara und Trude!

f. Hat der Junge in die Schule gehen können?

1. _____ das Mädchen _____?   4. _____ in die Kirche _____?
2. _____ ins Kino _____?   5. _____ Ihre Mutter _____?
3. _____ das Kind _____?   6. _____ in die Stadt _____?

g. Nein, er hat es nicht gekonnt.

1. _____ der Junge _____   4. _____ die Frau _____
2. _____ das Kind _____   5. _____ der Mann _____
3. _____ das Mädchen _____   6. _____ der Arzt _____

C. STRUCTURE

1. **Morgen** (*morning*), **Vormittag** (*morning, forenoon*), **Nachmittag** (*afternoon*), **Abend** (*evening*), and **Nacht** (*night*) are not capitalized in adverbial combination with **gestern** (*yesterday*), **vorgestern** (*the day before yesterday*), **heute** (*today*), **morgen** (*tomorrow*), or names of days of the week:

gestern morgen	*yesterday morning*
heute nachmittag	*this afternoon*
morgen abend	*tomorrow evening*
Freitag morgen	*Friday morning*

2. **Welcher?** (*which?*), when used as an adjective, agrees in gender, number, and case with the noun it modifies:

   a. Welche Städte in Europa haben Sie gesehen?
   Which cities in Europe did you see?

   When the noun is in the predicate, the neuter indefinite pronoun form **welches?** (*which?*) is used regardless of the gender or number of the noun:

   b. Welches sind die größten Städte in Europa?
   Which are the biggest cities in Europe?

3. The indefinite article is not used before predicate nouns of vocation:

   Mein Onkel ist nicht **Lehrer.** Er ist **Arzt.**
   My uncle is not a teacher. He is a doctor.

4. Familiar imperative (or command) forms of regular verbs add **-e** to the present stem in the singular and **-t** in the plural. The pronoun is omitted, as in English. Imperative sentences usually end with an exclamation mark:

    a. Zeige[1] mir dein Buch, Hans!
    Show me your book, Hans.
    b. Lernt euere Aufgaben, Kinder!
    Learn your lessons, children.

5. When a compound-past form of a modal auxiliary is used with a dependent infinitive, the past participle of the auxiliary is replaced by the infinitive form:

    Hat der Junge in die Schule **gehen können** (in place of **gekonnt**)?
    Has the boy been able to go to school?

This construction is known as a "double infinitive." Note that the modal auxiliary is last, with the dependent infinitive of the main verb preceding it.

6. Without a dependent infinitive, modal auxiliary verbs use the regular past participle form beginning with **ge-** and ending in **-t:**

    Nein, er **hat** es nicht **gekonnt.**
    No, he was not able to.

Note: **Nicht** immediately precedes a past participle.

7. Most irregular verbs form their past tense by changing the stem vowel and then adding endings, as in the past tense of **kommen** (*to come*):

ich **kam**	*I came, did come, was coming*
du **kamst**	*you came, did come, were coming*
er, sie, es **kam**	*he, she, it came, did come, was coming*
wir **kamen**	*we came, did come, were coming*
ihr **kamt**	*you came, did come, were coming*
sie **kamen**	*they came, did come, were coming*
Sie **kamen**	*you came, did come, were coming*

8. The basic forms of irregular verbs, from which all other forms can be derived, are called the "principal parts": the infinitive, the third person singular of the simple past, and the past participle.

---

[1] In colloquial German, final **e** is often dropped: **Zeig** mir dein Buch, Hans!

Since changes in stem vowels are irregular and hard to predict, it is best to memorize the principal parts of an irregular verb as it occurs.

Following are the principal parts of most of the irregular verbs of Units 1-14, showing also vowel variations in the second and third persons singular of the present indicative and verbs conjugated with **sein** in the compound past:

INFINITIVE		SIMPLE PAST	PAST PART.	3RD SING. PRESENT
bleiben	*to remain*	blieb	ist geblieben	
essen	*to eat*	aß	gegessen	ißt
fahren	*to ride*	fuhr	ist gefahren	fährt
fallen	*to fall*	fiel	ist gefallen	fällt
finden	*to find*	fand	gefunden	
geben	*to give*	gab	gegeben	gibt
gehen	*to go*	ging	ist gegangen	
heißen	*to be called*	hieß	geheißen	
helfen	*to help*	half	geholfen	hilft
kommen	*to come*	kam	ist gekommen	
laufen	*to run*	lief	ist gelaufen	läuft
lesen	*to read*	las	gelesen	liest
liegen	*to lie*	lag	gelegen	
nehmen	*to take*	nahm	genommen	nimmt
schlafen	*to sleep*	schlief	geschlafen	schläft
schreiben	*to write*	schrieb	geschrieben	
sehen	*to see*	sah	gesehen	sieht
sein	*to be*	war	ist gewesen	ist
sitzen	*to sit*	saß	gesessen	
sprechen	*to speak*	sprach	gesprochen	spricht
stehen	*to stand*	stand	gestanden	
tragen	*to carry, to wear*	trug	getragen	trägt
trinken	*to drink*	trank	getrunken	
wachsen	*to grow*	wuchs	ist gewachsen	wächst
werden	*to become*	wurde	ist geworden	wird

D. EXERCISES

Write the following sentences in German and be able to express them orally.

1. Her aunt has always wanted to visit her.
2. Which was their house?

3. What did your brother eat this afternoon?
4. Answer me, Richard.
5. Was the child sitting on the floor?
6. We spoke with them Thursday evening.
7. His cousin (*f.*) is becoming a teacher.
8. Have the ripe apples fallen on the ground?
9. Which are your books?
10. My neighbor sent his wife flowers.
11. Why didn't you go home yesterday evening?
12. Isn't her cousin a professor? — No, he's a physician.
13. She wore her new hat Saturday evening.
14. Did your parents drive to town?
15. My mother has been able to go to church again.
16. He'll visit us tomorrow morning.
17. Tell me what your names are, children.
18. My friend took my books home Wednesday afternoon.
19. The boy ate the green apples.
20. Play in the garden, Marie and Trude.
21. Which lesson did you study this morning?
22. Send your mother red flowers, Robert.
23. Why did your father have to stay at home?
24. My younger sister was permitted to take a trip to Europe.

E. COMPREHENDING AND SPEAKING

I. Repeat the following after your instructor (or the speaker) and study thoroughly.

DAS TAGEBUCH[1]

Nach dem Abendessen gingen alle ins Wohnzimmer. Dort tranken sie Kaffee und sprachen über Europa.

„Bitte, Herr Wagner, erzählen[2] Sie uns von Ihren Studentenjahren in Heidelberg!" sagte Peter.

5 „Ja, das war eine herrliche[3] Zeit!" meinte Herr Wagner. „Bitte, Walter, geben Sie mir das Buch dort auf dem Tisch!"

Auf dem Tisch lag ein großes rotes Buch. Walter nahm es und brachte es Herrn Wagner.

[1]**das Tagebuch, ⸗er**	the diary	[3]**herrlich**	magnificent
[2]**erzählen**	to tell		

„Das ist mein altes Tagebuch", sagte Herr Wagner. „Ich habe es
10   heute nachmittag in meinem Schreibtisch[4] gefunden. Vor sieben
Jahren schrieb ich jeden Abend in das Buch, aber ich habe es seit
vielen Jahren nicht mehr getan."

Im Buch lagen viele Fotografien.

„Seht, hier in diesem Haus hatte ich ein Zimmer! Vor dem Haus
15   war ein grüner Garten. Dort wuchsen große Apfelbäume. Im Herbst
waren die Äpfel rot und reif. Ich ging jeden Tag in den Garten und
aß frische Äpfel."

„Welches war Ihr Zimmer?"

Herr Wagner zeigte auf ein großes Fenster: „Ich wohnte in
20   dieser Bude."

„Was ist eine Bude?"

„Ein Studentenzimmer heißt in der Studentensprache eine Bude.
Das Restaurant, wo wir aßen und tranken, hieß Mensa und die
Zimmervermieterin[5] Schlummermutter. Wir Studenten sprachen ein
25   spezielles Deutsch. Nur wenige Leute verstanden uns."

II. Beantworten Sie die folgenden Fragen auf deutsch!

1. Wohin gingen alle nach dem Abendessen?
2. Was sollte Herr Wagner erzählen?
3. Was mußte Walter ihm geben?
4. Welche Farbe hatte das Tagebuch?
5. Wann hatte Herr Wagner sein Tagebuch gefunden?
6. Was lag im Tagebuch?
7. Was konnten Walter und Peter auf der Fotografie sehen?
8. Was tat Herr Wagner im Garten vor dem Haus?
9. Was ist eine Schlummermutter?

[4]**der Schreibtisch, -e**   the desk   [5]**die Zimmervermieterin,**   the landlady
                                                        -nen

UNIT 15

A. UNITS OF SPEECH AND VOCABULARY

I. Study and Practice Aloud.

Sie wartet auf ihn.	She is waiting for him.
Ich esse lieber Kuchen.	I prefer to eat cake.
Er ißt am liebsten Eis.	He likes best to eat ice cream.
eine Flasche Milch	a bottle of milk
ein Glas Bier	a glass of beer
eine Tasse Tee	a cup of tea
ein Stück Käse	a piece of cheese
eine halbe Stunde	half an hour, a half hour
ein halbes Glas	half a glass
ein halber Apfel	half an apple
immer besser	better and better
immer mehr	more and more

das Bier, -e	the beer	**das Stück, -e**	the piece
das Eis	the ice	**die Tasse, -n**	the cup
die Flasche, -n	the bottle	**der Tee**	the tea
das Fleisch	the meat	**der Wein, -e**	the wine
das Gemüse, -	the vegetable	**sechzig**	sixty
der Kaffee	the coffee	**siebzig**	seventy
der Käse	the cheese	**achtzig**	eighty
der Kuchen, -	the cake	**neunzig**	ninety
die Milch	the milk	**glauben**	to believe

(*125*)

warten	to wait	**hoffen**	to hope
treffen (trifft)	**traf**	**getroffen**	to meet

II. Oral Practice. Repeat the Pattern. Then substitute the items listed below. Repeat the entire sentence with each substitute item, changing the verb where necessary.

a. **Sie wartet auf ihn.**
   1. ihren Vater
   2. den Arzt
   3. die Lehrerin
   4. ihre Freundinnen
   5. mich
   6. uns

b. **Ich esse lieber Kuchen.**
   1. Fleisch
   2. Käse
   3. Gemüse
   4. Eis
   5. ein Stück Käse
   6. ein Stück Kuchen

c. **Er ißt am liebsten Eis.**
   1. Käse
   2. Kuchen
   3. Gemüse
   4. Fleisch

d. **Er will eine Flasche Milch.**
   1. eine Flasche Bier
   2. eine Flasche Wein
   3. ein Glas Wein
   4. ein Glas Bier
   5. ein Glas Milch
   6. eine Tasse Milch
   7. eine Tasse Tee
   8. eine Tasse Kaffee
   9. ein Stück Kuchen
   10. ein Stück Käse
   11. ein Stück Fleisch
   12. eine halbe Flasche Bier
   13. eine halbe Tasse Tee
   14. ein halbes Glas Milch
   15. einen halben Apfel

e. **Ich glaube, er hat Eis.**
   1. Kaffee
   2. Tee
   3. ein Stück Kuchen
   4. ein Stück Käse
   5. einen halben Apfel
   6. eine halbe Flasche
   7. eine halbe Tasse
   8. ein halbes Glas

f. **Wir hoffen, es geht Ihnen gut.**
   1. ihm
   2. Ihrem Vater
   3. Ihrer Mutter
   4. ihr
   5. Ihren Eltern
   6. ihnen

III. Oral Practice. Repeat the pattern sentence. Then substitute the items listed below in the appropriate places. Repeat the entire sentence with each substitute item, changing the verb where necessary.

a. **Er hat eine halbe Stunde gewartet.**
   1. Ich _____
   2. _____ einen halben Tag _____
   3. Meine Tante _____
   4. Sie (*sing.*) _____
   5. _____ ein halbes Jahr _____
   6. Wir _____

b. **Wir treffen ihn.**
    1. _____ seinen Onkel.
    2. Meine Eltern _____
    3. Mein Vater _____
    4. Er _____
    5. _____ seine Mutter.
    6. _____ sie.
    7. Ich _____

c. **Sie haben sechzig Tassen.**
    1. _____ siebzig _____
    2. _____ achtzig _____
    3. _____ Flaschen.
    4. _____ neunzig _____

d. **Es wird immer besser.**
    1. _____ immer wärmer.
    2. _____ immer kälter.
    3. _____ immer schöner.
    4. Das Mädchen _____
    5. Der Garten _____
    6. _____ immer grüner.

e. **Das Kind will immer mehr.**
    1. _____ ißt _____
    2. _____ läuft _____
    3. _____ lernt _____
    4. Meine Kusine _____
    5. _____ liest _____
    6. _____ schreibt _____

B. MODEL SENTENCES

I. Study each sentence until you can reproduce it correctly.

  97. **Geh zu Bett, Karl!**
  98. **Gib ihr das Geld und laufe nach Hause, Hans!**
  99. **Kommt ins Zimmer und lest euere Bücher, Richard und Klara!**
100. **Er hatte eine halbe Stunde auf mich gewartet.**
101. **Ich war in der Stadt geblieben.**
102. **Sie werden wohl Ihren Freund getroffen haben.**
103. **Mein Vater wird wohl zu Hause sein.**
104. **Der Arzt trinkt gerne Milch, aber er trinkt lieber Kaffee.**

  97. Go to bed, Karl.
  98. Give her the money and run home, Hans.
  99. Come into the room and read your books, Richard and Klara.
100. He had waited half an hour for me.
101. I had stayed in town.
102. They probably met their friend.
103. My father is probably at home.
104. The doctor likes to drink milk, but he prefers to drink coffee.

II. Pattern Practice. Repeat the model sentence. Then substitute the items listed below in the appropriate places. Repeat the entire sentence with each substitute item.

a. **Geh zu Bett, Karl!**
    1. Komm _____!
    2. Bleibe dort, _____!
    3. Schreibe den Brief, _____!
    4. Warte einen Moment, _____!

b. Gib ihr das Geld und laufe nach Hause, Hans!

1. _____ das Buch _____   4. _____ den Brief _____
2. _____ ihm _____   5. _____ uns _____
3. _____ mir _____   6. _____ ihnen _____

c. Kommt ins Zimmer und lest euere Bücher, Richard und Klara!

1. _____ ins Wohn-   4. _____ und schreibt _____
   zimmer _____
2. _____ euere Auf-   5. _____ euere Briefe _____
   gaben _____
3. _____ und macht _____   6. Geht _____

d. Er hatte eine halbe Stunde auf mich gewartet.

1. Meine Mutter _____   4. Das Mädchen _____
2. Sie (*sing.*) _____   5. Ich _____
3. _____ ihn _____   6. _____ sie _____

e. Ich war in der Stadt geblieben.

1. Er _____   4. _____ gewesen.
2. Mein Onkel _____   5. Sie _____
3. Seine Freundin _____   6. Die Frau _____

f. Sie werden wohl ihren Freund getroffen haben.

1. _____ ihre Freunde _____   4. _____ besucht _____
2. _____ gesehen _____   5. _____ meinen Vater _____
3. _____ ihre Eltern _____   6. _____ gefunden _____

g. Mein Vater wird wohl zu Hause sein.

1. Ihr Vetter _____   4. _____ in der Küche _____.
2. _____ im Restaurant _____   5. _____ im Eßzimmer _____
3. _____ essen.   6. Meine Kusine _____

h. Der Arzt trinkt gerne Milch, aber er trinkt lieber Kaffee.

1. Mein Vater _____   4. _____ gerne Milch _____
2. _____ gerne Tee _____   5. Seine Freundin _____
3. Mein Bruder _____   6. _____ lieber Tee.

C. STRUCTURE

1. Irregular verbs with stem change **e** to **i** or **ie** in the second and third persons singular of the present indicative have the same change in the familiar singular imperative. Such verbs omit the **-e** ending:

geben	*to give*	**gib!**	*give!*

Verbs that have a similar change of stem vowel in the familiar singular imperative include the following:

essen	*to eat*	**iß!**	*eat!*

helfen	*to help*	**hilf!**	*help!*
lesen	*to read*	**lies!**	*read!*
nehmen	*to take*	**nimm!**	*take!*
sehen	*to see*	**sieh!**	*see!*
sprechen	*to speak*	**sprich!**	*speak!*

2. All other irregular verbs form the familiar singular imperative regularly:

gehen	*to go*	**geh(e)!**	*go!*
laufen	*to run*	**lauf(e)!**	*run!*
schlafen	*to sleep*	**schlaf(e)!**	*sleep!*

Note that these forms are used only for persons addressed with **du:**

a. Gehe zu Bett, mein Kind!
Go to bed, my child.

b. Gib ihr das Geld und **laufe** nach Hause, Hans!
Give her the money and run home, Hans.

3. The familiar plural imperative of irregular verbs is identical with that of the present indicative, omitting the pronoun:

Kommt ins Zimmer und **lest** euere Bücher, Richard und Klara!
Come into the room and read your books, Richard and Klara.

4. The past perfect tense consists of the past tense of the auxiliary verb **haben** (or **sein**) and the past participle:

a. Er **hatte** eine halbe Stunde auf mich **gewartet.**
He had waited half an hour for me.

b. Ich **war** in der Stadt **geblieben.**
I had stayed in town.

5. The future perfect tense consists of the future tense of **haben** (or **sein**) and the past participle. This tense is most often used to indicate past probability, especially when used with **wohl** (*probably*):

Sie **werden** (**wohl**) ihren Freund **getroffen haben.**
They probably met their friend.

6. The future tense, with **wohl** (*probably*), is often used to express present probability:

Mein Vater **wird** (**wohl**) zu Hause **sein.**
My father is probably at home.

7. The comparative and superlative forms of **gerne** (*gladly*) are **lieber** (*rather*) and **am liebsten** (*most gladly*), respectively. **Lieber** plus verb means *to prefer to*; **am liebsten** plus verb, *to like best to:*

a. Der Arzt **trinkt gerne** Milch, aber er **trinkt lieber** Kaffee.

The doctor likes to drink milk, but he prefers to drink coffee.

b. Er **ißt am liebsten** Eis.

He likes to eat ice cream best.

8. After nouns of measure, other nouns have the same case and follow directly:

a. Er will **eine Flasche Milch.**

He wants a bottle of milk.

b. Ich esse lieber **ein Stück Kuchen.**

I prefer to eat a piece of cake.

D. EXERCISES

Write the following sentences in German and be able to express them orally.

1. Take another piece of meat, Richard.
2. My cousin (*f.*) likes to wear yellow hats best.
3. Write your uncle a letter, children.
4. She went to school an hour ago.
5. Do the pupils (*f.*) like to speak German best?
6. His parents probably believed it.
7. They had drunk two cups of coffee.
8. His cousin (*f.*) prefers to travel to Switzerland.
9. We are getting older and older.
10. Eat more slowly, Trude.
11. His friends had waited for an hour.
12. We prefer to eat cheese.
13. The children probably went home at three o'clock.
14. The girl had brought him two bottles of milk.
15. His father became fifty years old in February.
16. Read the lesson, Marie.
17. The little boy ate a big piece of cake.
18. My friends had lived in that house half a year.
19. Bring me another cup of tea, mother.
20. They are probably sitting in the dining room.
21. Do you prefer to drink beer or wine?
22. Give me a glass of cold water.
23. The children are getting bigger and bigger.
24. Carry this chair into the dining room, Hans.
25. His aunt is probably eighty years old.

E. COMPREHENDING AND SPEAKING

I. Repeat the following after your instructor (or the speaker) and study thoroughly.

CAMPING

Peter, Hans und Walter gingen an einem Wochenende in einen Nationalpark. Hans besaß[1] ein großes grünes Zelt,[2] und die drei Jungen wollten für drei Tage wie Robinson leben.[3]

Sie fuhren mit dem Auto langsam auf einem Waldweg[4] und schau-
5   ten aufmerksam nach rechts und links,[5] um einen günstigen Platz[6] für ihr Zelt zu finden.

„Dort", rief Walter, „ich habe eine Waldwiese[7] gesehen!" Eine halbe Stunde später stand das Zelt auf der Waldwiese, und die drei Freunde sammelten Holz,[8] um ein Feuer zu machen.

10   Peter war der Koch.[9] „Was gibt es zu essen?"[10] fragte Hans.

„Es gibt gebratene[11] Knackwürste oder Spiegeleier.[12] Was wollt ihr lieber haben?"

„Ich esse am liebsten Knackwürste", sagte Walter.

Hans hatte Spiegeleier lieber. „Dann werde ich eben beides[13]
15   machen", sagte Peter.

Nach dem Abendessen saßen sie noch eine Weile um das Feuer, sangen Lieder und erzählten Geschichten.[14] Dann krochen[15] sie ins Zelt, um zu schlafen.

Spät in der Nacht weckte[16] Walter Peter: „Hast du es nicht
20   gehört? Es ist jemand vor dem Zelt!"[17]

Peter nahm seine Taschenlampe[18] und öffnete die Zelttür. „Ich sehe nichts", sagte er, „es wird wohl ein Hase[19] gewesen sein."

[1]besitzen	to own, possess	[11]braten	to roast
[2]das Zelt, -e	the tent	[12]das Spiegelei, -er	the fried egg
[3]wie Robinson leben	to live like Robinson Crusoe	[13]beides	both
[4]der Waldweg, -e	the wood path	[14]Geschichten erzählen	to tell stories
[5]schauten aufmerksam nach rechts und links	looked carefully to the right and left	[15]kriechen	to creep
		[16]wecken	to waken
		[17]es ist jemand vor dem Zelt	there is somebody in front of the tent
[6]günstiger Platz	good spot	[18]die Taschenlampe, -n	the flashlight
[7]die Waldwiese, -n	the clearing		
[8]Holz sammeln	to gather wood		
[9]der Koch, -̈e	the cook	[19]der Hase, -n	the rabbit
[10]Was gibt es zu essen?	What's for supper?		

II. Beantworten Sie die folgenden Fragen auf deutsch!

1. Wie wollten die drei Jungen über das Wochenende leben?
2. Was besaß Hans?
3. Warum fuhren sie langsam auf dem Waldweg?
4. Was hat Hans gesehen?
5. Warum sammelten die Freunde Holz?
6. Was kochte Peter?
7. Was machten sie nach dem Abendessen?
8. Wann weckte Walter Peter?
9. War jemand vor dem Zelt?

REVIEW UNIT 3

A. *Supply the proper form of the word in parentheses in the place indicated.*

1. (wollen) Ich _____ ihn morgen besuchen.
2. (schreiben) Er hat drei Briefe _____.
3. (ganz) Wir werden durch _____ Spanien fahren.
4. (bringen) Der Junge hat das Buch _____.
5. (geben) Richard, _____ mir die Tasse!
6. (mögen) Das Kind _____ kein Fleisch.
7. (89) Dieser Mann ist _____ Jahre alt.
8. (wollen) Wir haben Kaffee _____.
9. (dürfen) Ich _____ nicht hier bleiben.
10. (gehen) Seine Eltern sind nach Hause _____.
11. (wissen) Die Frau _____ nicht, wo ihr Sohn ist.
12. (tragen) _____ die Stühle ins Eßzimmer, Kinder!
13. (werden) Meine Tante ist alt _____.
14. (sollen) Hans, du _____ das nicht tun.
15. (machen) Die Schüler haben ihre Aufgaben _____.
16. (lesen) _____ die Aufgabe, Klara!
17. (studieren) Wo hat er _____?
18. (können) Jetzt _____ ich nicht essen.
19. (sprechen) _____ langsamer, Karl!
20. (tun) Was _____ Ihr Vetter heute?
21. (ganz) Er bleibt die _____ Woche hier.
22. (müssen) Wir haben viel lernen _____.
23. (laufen) _____ schneller, mein Kind!

(*133*)

24. (34) In diesem Garten sind _____ Bäume.
25. (antworten) Wir haben ihm nicht _____.

B. *Supply, where necessary to complete the sentence, an appropriate word in the place indicated.*

1. Am _____ gehen die Kinder nicht in die Schule.
2. Gestern _____ er hier gewesen.
3. War ihr Bruder _____ Lehrer?
4. Seine Kusinen kommen _____ Herbst.
5. Kann er das Buch lesen? — Ja, er kann _____.
6. Das ist Ihr Bruder, _____ _____?
7. Meine Kusine _____ wohl in der Küche sein.
8. Sein Vetter trinkt gerne Kaffee, aber er trinkt _____ Tee.
9. Den ganzen Nachmittag hatte sie auf ihren Freund _____.
10. Wir machen _____ August eine Reise nach Italien.
11. Bringen Sie mir ein Glas _____ Wasser!
12. Ihr Onkel wird wohl nach Hause gegangen _____.
13. Wann kommen sie? — _____ Dienstag.
14. Meine Schwester kann _____ Lehrerin werden.
15. Ich bin zwanzig Jahre alt. _____ zwei Jahren war ich achtzehn.
16. Das _____ meine Eltern.
17. Heute nachmittag ist er gekommen. _____ früh kommt seine Frau.
18. Wollen Sie eine Tasse _____ Kaffee?
19. Ich esse gerne Kuchen. Was essen Sie am _____?
20. Das Kind _____ schnell ins Haus gelaufen.

C. *Supply the appropriate form of* **kennen, können,** *or* **wissen** *as the sense of the sentence requires.*

1. _____ Ihre Mutter, wo Ihr Bruder ist?
2. Ich _____ diese Leute gut.
3. Mein Freund _____ Englisch und Deutsch.
4. Wir _____, warum sie kommt.
5. Die Kinder _____ die Aufgaben.
6. _____ Ihr Bruder meinen Onkel?

D. *Make the following statements commands.*

1. Du ißt das Fleisch.
2. Ihr gebt mir die Bücher.
3. Du fährst nach Hause.
4. Ihr antwortet mir.
5. Du trägst die Bücher für mich.
6. Ihr bleibt hier.

E. *Beantworten Sie die folgenden Fragen auf deutsch!*

1. Welcher Tag der Woche ist heute?
2. Welcher Tag der Woche war gestern?
3. An welchem Tag gehen Sie in die Kirche?
4. Wie heißt die Hauptstadt Österreichs?
5. Kommen Sie am Montag in dieses Zimmer?
6. Was lernen Sie hier?
7. Essen Sie lieber Fleisch oder (*or*) Gemüse?
8. Trinken Sie am liebsten Milch, Tee oder Kaffee?
9. Stehen Sie oder sitzen Sie jetzt?
10. Wie heißt Ihr Nachbar?

F. *Change the following to past time (Treat each sentence as an isolated conversational utterance).*

1. Die Mutter dankt ihren Töchtern.
2. Er kommt nicht nach Deutschland.
3. Ich stecke die Briefe in die Tasche.
4. Die Lehrer helfen den Schülern.
5. Wir beginnen die Aufgabe.
6. Mein Freund gibt mir seine Bücher.
7. Wohin bringt er das Geld?
8. Ich reise durch Europa.
9. Wir fahren an die Nordsee.
10. Er ißt ohne seine Freundin.
11. Seine Eltern wohnen in Köln.
12. Der Schüler schreibt die Aufgabe.
13. Er liest sein Buch.
14. Am Sonntag bleibt er hier.
15. Er sieht alles.
16. Wir arbeiten den ganzen Tag.
17. Er spielt mit den Kindern.
18. Lehrt sie Deutsch?
19. Die Bücher liegen auf dem Tisch.
20. Wo steht der Mann?

G. *Change the following narrative to past time.*

Am Freitag gehen Hans und Käthe zu einem Ball. Sie tanzen den ganzen Abend. Am Samstag hilft Hans seinem Vater im Laden. Am Abend geht er mit seiner Freundin ins Kino. Nach dem Kino haben sie Hunger und gehen in ein Restaurant. Nach dem Essen bringt er sie nach Hause.

H. *Write a brief paragraph in the narrative past in German, using the following outline.*

The pupils are going to school. One pupil meets his best friend on the street in front of the building. They greet one another and go in together. They enter the classroom. The teacher is not there yet. They put their books on the table and wait for the teacher to arrive. The teacher comes in and says "Good morning." The pupils greet the teacher, and the class begins.

UNIT 16

A. UNITS OF SPEECH AND VOCABULARY

I. Study and Practice Aloud.

Da kommt er.	There he comes.
ich würde singen	I would sing
sie würde gehen	she would go
würden Sie essen?	would you eat?
während er arbeitet	while he works
ob sie kommt	whether she is coming
bevor ich ging	before I went
bis sie kamen	until they came
entweder blau oder gelb	either blue or yellow
weder hell noch dunkel	neither light nor dark
nicht weiß, sondern schwarz	not white, but black
sowohl der Vater als auch die Mutter	both the father and the mother

alles	everything	**schwarz**	black
nichts	nothing	**schwer**	heavy, difficult
blau	blue	**weiß**	white
dunkel	dark	**da** *adv.*	there
hell	light (*in color*), bright	**da** *conj.*	because, since
		als	when, as
leicht	light (*in weight*), easy	**bevor** *conj.*	before
		ehe *conj.*	before

(*137*)

bis	until	sowohl ... als auch	both ... and
daß *conj.*	that	während	while
entweder ... oder	either ... or	weder ... noch	neither ... nor
nachdem *conj.*	after	weil	because, since
ob	whether	wenn	when, when-
obgleich	although		ever, if
sobald	as soon as	lachen	to laugh
sondern	but		

| schwimmen | schwamm | ist geschwommen | to swim |
| singen | sang | gesungen | to sing |

II. Oral Practice. Repeat the pattern sentence. Then substitute the items below. Repeat the entire sentence with each substitute item, changing the verb where necessary.

a. Da kommt er.

1. der Professor
2. die Studentin
3. sie (*sing.*)

4. die Kinder
5. die Ärzte
6. die Verkäuferinnen

b. Ich würde singen.

1. schreiben
2. lesen

3. laufen
4. schwimmen

c. Sie würde gehen.

1. schwimmen
2. singen
3. lachen

4. arbeiten
5. verstehen
6. schreiben

d. Sie würden essen.

1. singen
2. arbeiten
3. kommen

4. lachen
5. bleiben
6. schwimmen

e. Sie sehen alles.

1. essen
2. trinken

3. glauben
4. lesen

f. Er will nichts.

1. ißt
2. trinkt
3. tut

4. schreibt
5. liest
6. glaubt

g. Er singt, während er arbeitet.

1. wenn
2. sobald

3. weil
4. obgleich

h. Ich wartete, bis sie mich hörten.

1. mich verstanden
2. mir halfen

3. mich sahen
4. mich fanden

i. **Als ich kam, schwamm er schon.**
   1. sang   4. aß
   2. arbeitete ·   5. schrieb
   3. saß   6. las

III. Oral Practice. Repeat the pattern sentence. Then substitute the items below in the appropriate places. Repeat the entire sentence with each substitute item.

a. **Weiß er, ob sie kommt?**
   1. _____ arbeitet?   4. _____, daß _____?
   2. _____ schwimmt?   5. _____ schwimmt?
   3. _____ wartet?   6. _____ schläft?

b. **Sie kamen, nachdem wir gegessen hatten.**
   1. _____ getrunken _____   4. _____ gegessen _____
   2. _____ gesprochen _____   5. _____ getrunken _____
   3. _____, sobald _____   6. _____ gesungen _____

c. **Es ist entweder blau oder gelb.**
   1. _____ oder schwarz.   7. _____ blau _____ gelb.
   2. _____ weiß oder _____   8. _____ schwarz _____ blau.
   3. _____ dunkel oder hell.   9. _____ nicht _____ son-
                                         dern _____
   4. _____ weder _____   10. _____ weiß.
        noch _____
   5. _____ leicht _____ schwer.   11. _____ leicht _____ schwer.
   6. _____ weiß _____ schwarz.   12. _____ hell _____ dunkel.

d. **Sowohl der Vater als auch die Mutter sind hier.**
   1. _____ der Bruder _____ die Schwester _____
   2. _____ der Mann _____ seine Frau _____
   3. _____ die Eltern _____ die Kinder _____
   4. _____ die Schüler _____ die Lehrer _____

B. MODEL SENTENCES

I. Study each sentence until you can reproduce it correctly.

105. **Er arbeitet nicht schnell, aber gut.**
106. **Als ich nach Hause kam, war mein Vater nicht mehr da.**
107. **Wenn er in die Stadt ging, kaufte er viel.**
108. **Ich werde meinen Onkel sehen, wenn er uns besucht.**
109. **Da sie erst spät kommen kann, wird sie uns nicht sehen.**
110. **Da kommen sie.**
111. **Sie wußte, daß er ihr schreiben würde.**
112. **Ich glaube, er kommt morgen.**

105. He does not work quickly, but well.
106. When I came home, my father was no longer there.
107. Whenever he went to town, he bought much (a lot).
108. I'll see my uncle when he visits us.
109. Since she cannot come until late, she will not see us.
110. There they come.
111. She knew (that) he would write to her.
112. I believe he is coming tomorrow.

II. Pattern Drill. Repeat the model sentence. Then substitute the items listed below in the equivalent part of the model sentence. Repeat the whole sentence with each substitute item.

a. Er arbeitet nicht schnell, aber gut.
1. lernt
2. schwimmt
3. spricht
4. fährt
5. schreibt
6. redet

b. Als ich nach Hause kam, war mein Vater nicht mehr da.
1. meine Mutter
2. meine Schwester
3. mein Bruder
4. mein Onkel
5. meine Tante
6. meine Kusine

c. Wenn er die Stadt ging, kaufte er viel.
1. in die Kirche, sang
2. ins Kino, lachte
3. an die See, schwamm
4. ins Restaurant, aß

d. Ich werde meinen Onkel sehen, wenn er uns besucht.
1. Ihren Freund
2. seinen Vetter
3. den Arzt
4. den Professor

e. Da sie erst spät kommen kann, wird sie uns nicht sehen.
1. unsere Kusine
2. meine Tante
3. Ihre Freundin
4. die Studentin
5. die Frau
6. die Verkäuferin

f. Da kommen sie.
1. die Kinder
2. die Schüler
3. die Studentinnen
4. die Lehrer
5. die Schülerinnen
6. die Lehrerinnen

g. Sie wußte, daß er ihr schreiben würde.
1. mir
2. uns
3. Ihnen
4. ihrem Bruder
5. seiner Mutter
6. meinem Onkel

h. Ich glaube, er kommt morgen.
1. fährt
2. antwortet
3. reist
4. arbeitet
5. geht
6. bleibt

C. STRUCTURE

1. In main clauses, the finite (conjugated) verb is usually the second element. In normal word order, the first element is the subject; in inverted word order — with the subject after the verb — the first element may be an adverb, a prepositional phrase, an object or some other element (see page 30 paragraph 7).

2. Coordinating conjunctions (so-called because they connect expressions of equal value) do not affect word order, either normal or inverted:

a. Er hat zwei Bücher, **und** ich habe eins.
He has two books and I have one.
b. Er hat kein Geld, **denn** er ist arm.
He has no money, for he is poor.

The principal coordinating conjunctions are:

aber	*but*
denn	*for*
oder	*or*
sondern	*but*
entweder . . . oder	*either . . . or*
sowohl . . . als auch	*both . . . and*
weder . . . noch	*neither . . . nor*

3. Sondern (*but*) is used only after a negative and suggests *but rather* or *but on the contrary:*

a. Es ist nicht schwarz, **sondern** weiß.
It is not black but white.
b. Es ist nicht hell, **sondern** dunkel.
It is not light but dark.

Aber (*but*) is used when no negative precedes:

c. Sein Onkel hat wenig Geld, **aber** viele Freunde.
His uncle has little money, but many friends.

or following a negative when the elements preceding and following are not mutually exclusive:

d. Er arbeitet nicht schnell, **aber** gut.
He does not work quickly but well.

4. Subordinating conjunctions introduce subordinate (dependent) clauses, in which the finite verb is normally last. This word order is called "dependent word order":

a. Ich werde meinen Onkel sehen, **wenn er uns besucht.**
  I'll see my uncle when he visits us.

b. **Als ich nach Hause kam,** war mein Vater nicht mehr da.
  When I came home, my father was no longer there.

Note: In German subordinate clauses are always set off by commas.

5. The principal subordinating conjunctions are:

als	*when, as*
bevor, ehe	*before*
bis	*until*
da, weil	*because, since*
daß	*that*
nachdem	*after*
ob	*whether*
obgleich	*although*
sobald	*as soon as*
während	*while*
wenn	*when, whenever, if*

6. An indirect question becomes a subordinate clause:

Ich weiß nicht, **wann er kommt.**
I don't know when he is coming.

Other interrogative words that may introduce indirect questions are:

warum?	*why?*
was?	*what?*
welcher? welche? welches?	*which?*
wer?	*who?*
wo?	*where?*
wohin?	*where (to)?*

7. **Als** (*when, as*) is generally used for a single past action:

a. **Als ich nach Hause kam,** war mein Vater nicht mehr da.
  When I came home, my father was no longer there.

Wenn (*whenever, when, if*) is used for repeated action in any tense or for any future action:

b. **Wenn er in die Stadt ging,** kaufte er viel.
  Whenever he went to town, he bought a lot.

c. Ich werde meinen Onkel sehen, **wenn er uns besucht.**
  I'll see my uncle when (if) he visits us.

Note: The simple past tense is often preferred conversationally in sentences of more than one clause, especially time clauses, (*a* and *b*, above).

8. Distinguish between the adverb **da** (*there*) and the subordinating conjunction **da** (*because, since*):

   a. **Da** kommen sie. (adverb)
      There they come.
   b. **Da sie** erst spät kommen **kann,** wird sie uns nicht sehen.
      Since she cannot come until late, she will not see us.

   Note that in *b* the subordinate clause has dependent word order: the subject (**sie**) immediately follows **da** and the finite verb (**kann**) is last.

9. The subordinating conjunction **daß** (*that*), which normally requires dependent word order, may be omitted. This omission then requires normal word order in the clause:

   a. Ich glaube, **daß er** morgen **kommt.**
      I believe that he is coming tomorrow.
   b. Ich glaube, **er kommt** morgen.
      I believe he is coming tomorrow. (normal)

   Note: Do not confuse the conjunction **daß** (*that*) with the indefinite pronoun **das** (*that*) or the neuter article **das** (*the*).

D. EXERCISES

Write the following sentences in German and be able to express them orally.

 1. My sister usually drinks a glass of milk before she goes to bed.
 2. Her cousin (*f.*) knows when she is going to school again.
 3. Both his uncle and his aunt read German.
 4. Her car is not white but black.
 5. If they meet her, they will talk with her.
 6. Would you bring me a piece of cake?
 7. Her mother was reading a book while she was sitting at the table.
 8. When he eats lunch, he always drinks coffee.
 9. I'll ask him whether his aunt is at home.
10. My cousin always sings while he works.
11. Our parents know that we are here.
12. There come the teacher and the children.
13. My friends drink either milk or tea.
14. The doctor would not take the trip.
15. The little child ran until he fell.

16. He is not a professor but a student.
17. The salesgirl read the letter as soon as she saw it.
18. The pupils (*f*.) knew that they had to study their lessons.
19. Ask the little girl what she has in her hand.
20. Although my neighbor is old, he works a lot.
21. A year ago my best friend traveled to Germany because he wanted to
    see the Rhine.
22. My brother's girl friend is pretty, but she is very poor.
23. After my cousins had gone home, the neighbors came.
24. He knows neither my brother nor my sister.
25. When the teacher came into the room, the pupils were doing their
    lessons.

E. COMPREHENDING AND SPEAKING

I. Repeat the following after your instructor (or the speaker) and study thoroughly.

IM WARENHAUS[1]

Bevor die große Reise begann, wollten die zwei Studenten alles
kaufen, was sie für die Fahrt brauchten.[2]

,,Komm, wir gehen in dieses Warenhaus!" riet[3] Peter, ,,da können
wir sicher alles finden."

5   Sie fuhren auf der Rolltreppe[4] zum obersten Stockwerk,[5] wo sie
eine Abteilung für Reiseartikel[6] fanden.

,,Zuerst brauche ich einen großen Koffer",[7] meinte Walter, ,,aber
er muß leicht sein, da wir fliegen."[8]

Der Verkäufer zeigte ihnen gelbe, grüne und rote Koffer.

10   ,,Der rote Koffer scheint gut zu sein",[9] sagte Peter, ,,ich würde
ihn kaufen."[10]

,,Ich mag den roten nicht", sagte Walter. ,,Haben Sie den
gleichen[11] Koffer in schwarz oder braun?"

,,Warten Sie", sagte der Verkäufer, ,,vielleicht haben wir noch
15   einen schwarzen."

[1]**das Warenhaus, ⸗er**	department store	[7]**der Koffer, -**	suitcase
[2]**brauchen**	to need	[8]**fliegen**	to fly
[3]**raten**	to advise	[9]**scheint gut zu sein**	seems to be good
[4]**die Rolltreppe, -n**	escalator	[10]**ich würde ihn**	I'd buy it
[5]**das Stockwerk, -e**	floor	**kaufen**	
[6]**die Abteilung für**	travel articles de-	[11]**gleich**	same
Reiseartikel	partment		

Als er zurückkam, erklärte er:[12] „Es tut mir leid, aber Sie können nur entweder einen roten oder einen blauen Koffer bekommen. Wir haben weder schwarze noch braune."

„Dann nehme ich einen blauen", sagte Walter.

20 Nachdem Walter den Koffer bezahlt[13] hatte, gingen die beiden in die Fotoabteilung, weil Peter eine neue Kamera kaufen wollte.

„Wollen Sie mit Schwarzweißfilm oder Farbfilm[14] fotografieren?" fragte die Verkäuferin.

„Das ist schwer zu sagen", meinte Peter. „Am liebsten würde ich 25 sowohl schwarz-weiße als auch farbige Aufnahmen[15] machen."

„Dann würde ich Ihnen diese Kamera empfehlen.[16] Ich weiß, daß Sie mit dieser zufrieden[17] sein werden."

II. Beantworten Sie die folgenden Fragen auf deutsch!

1. Was wollten die Studenten vor der großen Reise noch tun?
2. Wo wollten sie alles kaufen?
3. Wie fuhren sie zum obersten Stockwerk?
4. Wie mußte Walters Koffer sein?
5. Was zeigte ihnen der Verkäufer?
6. Hatte der Verkäufer einen schwarzen Koffer?
7. Welchen Koffer kaufte Walter?
8. Warum gingen sie in die Fotoabteilung?
9. Was für[18] Aufnahmen würde Peter am liebster machen?

[12]erklären	to explain	[16]empfehlen	to recommend
[13]bezahlen	to pay for	[17]zufrieden	satisfied
[14]der Farbfilm, -e	color film	[18]was für	what kind of
[15]die Aufnahme, -n	snapshot		

UNIT 17

A. UNITS OF SPEECH AND VOCABULARY

I. Study and Practice Aloud.

Er fährt heute ab.	He's leaving today.
Ich rufe ihn an.	I'm calling him up.
Wir machen die Fenster auf.	We're opening the windows.
Sie steht früh auf.	She's getting up early.
Er geht jetzt fort.	He's going away now.
Er kommt morgen zurück.	He's coming back tomorrow.
Die Frau kommt ins Gebäude herein.	The woman is coming into the building.
Mein Bruder geht aus dem Zimmer hinaus.	My brother is going out of the room.
Das Haus gefällt mir.	I like the house.
Der wievielte ist heute?	What day of the month is today?
Heute ist der erste Februar.	Today is the first of February.

der Bleistift, -e	the pencil	der, die, das	
der Dampfer, -	the steamer, ship	zweite	the second
die Geschichte,		der, die, das	
-n	the story	dritte	the third
das Heft, -e	the notebook	der, die, das	
das Papier, -e	the paper	vierte	the fourth
der Zug, ̈e	the train	der, die, das	
der, die, das erste	the first	siebte	the seventh

der, die, das			
achte		the eighth	
der, die, das			
zwanzigste		the twentieth	

der, die, das			
einund-			
zwanzigste		the twenty-first	

abfahren (fährt ab)	fuhr ab	ist abgefahren	to leave, depart
anrufen	rief an	angerufen	to call up, telephone
aufmachen	machte auf	aufgemacht	to open
aufstehen	stand auf	ist aufgestanden	to get up, stand up
empfehlen (empfiehlt)	empfahl	empfohlen	to recommend
erzählen	erzählte	erzählt	to tell, narrate
entscheiden	entschied	entschieden	to decide
fortgehen	ging fort	ist fortgegangen	to go away
gefallen (gefällt)	gefiel	gefallen	to please
hereinkommen	kam herein	ist hereingekommen	to come in
hinausgehen	ging hinaus	ist hinausgegangen	to go out
zerreißen	zerriß	zerrissen	to tear to pieces
zurückkommen	kam zurück	ist zurückgekommen	to come back

II. Oral Practice. Repeat the pattern sentence. Then substitute the items below. Repeat the entire sentence with each substitute item, changing the verb where necessary.

a. Er fährt heute ab.
1. Der Arzt
2. Der Dampfer
3. Der Zug
4. Die Frau
5. Sie (*sing.*)
6. Ich

b. Ich rufe ihn an.
1. Seine Freundin
2. Sie (*sing.*)
3. Der Professor
4. Er
5. Seine Freunde
6. Sie (*pl.*)

c. Wir machen die Fenster auf.
1. Die Kinder
2. Sie (*pl.*)
3. Der Junge
4. Er
5. Die Studentin
6. Ich

d. Sie steht früh auf.
1. Meine Schwester
2. Mein Onkel
3. Er
4. Ich
5. Wir
6. Meine Eltern

e. Er geht jetzt fort.
1. Ihr Nachbar
2. Die Schülerin
3. Sie (*sing.*)
4. Wir
5. Ich
6. Die Verkäuferinnen

f. Er kommt morgen zurück.

1. Der Arzt
2. Die Lehrerin
3. Sie (*sing.*)
4. Ich
5. Unsere Vettern
6. Wir

g. Die Frau kommt ins Gebäude herein.

1. Das Kind
2. Das Mädchen
3. Die Lehrer
4. Wir
5. Der Verkäufer
6. Ich

h. Mein Bruder geht aus dem Zimmer hinaus.

1. Seine Kusine
2. Ich
3. Ihre Schwestern
4. Die Schüler
5. Sie (*pl.*)
6. Wir

i. Das Haus gefällt mir.

1. uns
2. ihnen
3. unseren Freunden
4. meiner Mutter
5. ihr
6. ihm

j. Der wievielte ist heute? — Heute ist der erste Februar.

1. der einundzwanzigste Februar
2. der zwanzigste Juli
3. der achte Juni
4. der dritte März
5. der siebte März
6. der vierte Oktober
7. der zweite Oktober
8. der dreißigste Mai

k. Der Bleistift ist gelb.

1. weiß
2. schwarz
3. blau
4. grün
5. rot
6. neu

l. Er erzählt eine Geschichte.

1. Der Herr
2. Die Frau
3. Sie (*sing.*)
4. Die Eltern
5. Wir
6. Ich

m. Sie empfiehlt diesen Dampfer.

1. Die Lehrerin
2. Der Arzt
3. Er
4. Die Professoren
5. Wir
6. Ich

III. Oral Practice. Repeat the pattern sentence. Then substitute the items listed below in the appropriate places. Repeat the entire sentence with each substitute item.

a. Er entscheidet alles.

1. Sie _____
2. _____ hat _____ entschieden.
3. _____ nichts _____
4. Die Frau _____
5. Sie _____
6. Ich habe _____

b. Sie zerreißen das Papier.

1. Die Jungen _____
2. Er zerreißt _____
3. _____ das Heft.
4. _____ hat _____ zerrissen.
5. Ich habe _____
6. Wir haben _____

B. MODEL SENTENCES

I. Study each sentence until you can reproduce it correctly.

113. **Schreibt er mit dem Bleistift? — Ja, er schreibt damit.**
114. **Was legt sie auf die Tische? — Sie legt die Hefte darauf.**
115. **Heute ist der neunzehnte Februar und morgen ist der zwanzigste Februar.**
116. **Wir fahren nicht ab, bevor die Kinder zurückkommen.**
117. **Er kam ins Zimmer herein, während sie hinausging.**
118. **Bitte kommen Sie herein!**
119. **Obgleich er früh aufgestanden war, ist er spät zurückgekommen.**
120. **Dieses Fenster ist schwer aufzumachen.**
121. **Haben Sie alles verstanden?**

113. Is he writing with the pencil? — Yes, he's writing with it.
114. What's she putting on the tables? — She's putting the notebooks on them.
115. Today is the nineteenth of February and tomorrow is the twentieth of February.
116. We're not leaving before the children come back.
117. He was coming into the living room while she was going out.
118. Please come in.
119. Although he had gotten up early, he came back late.
120. This window is hard to open.
121. Did you understand everything?

II. Pattern Practice. Repeat the model sentence. Then substitute the following items in the equivalent part of the model sentence. Repeat the entire sentence with each substitute item, changing the verb where necessary.

a. Schreibt er mit dem Bleistift? — Ja, er schreibt damit.

1. der Schüler
2. die Schülerin
3. sie (*sing.*)
4. die Studentin
5. die Lehrerin
6. der Professor

b. Was legt sie auf die Tische? — Sie legt die Hefte darauf.

1. auf die Stühle?
2. auf die Bücher?
3. auf die Papiere?
4. auf die Aufgaben?

c. Heute ist der neunzehnte Februar und morgen ist der zwanzigste Februar.

1. April
2. Dezember
3. Mai
4. Januar.
5. Juni
6. November

d. Wir fahren nicht ab, bevor die Kinder zurückkommen.

1. die Schüler
2. die Schülerinnen
3. unsere Eltern
4. unsere Freunde
5. unsere Freundinnen
6. unsere Vettern

e. Er kam ins Wohnzimmer herein, während sie hinausging.

1. ins Eßzimmer
2. ins Restaurant
3. ins Kino
4. ins Gebäude
5. in die Schule
6. in die Küche

f. Bitte kommen Sie herein!

1. stehen _____ auf
2. gehen _____ hinaus
3. kommen _____ zurück
4. gehen _____ fort

g. Obgleich er früh aufgestanden war, ist er spät zurückgekommen.

1. mein Freund
2. sein Vetter
3. ihr Onkel
4. der Arzt
5. der Mann
6. der Junge

h. Dieses Fenster ist schwer aufzumachen.

1. Mein Fenster
2. Die Fenster
3. Diese Tür
4. Diese Türen

i. Haben Sie alles verstanden?

1. nichts
2. etwas
3. es
4. das

C. STRUCTURE

1. As objects of a preposition, personal pronouns referring to inanimate objects are usually replaced by **da-** (or **dar-**), which is combined with the preposition. (If the preposition begins with a consonant, it is combined with **da-**; if it begins with a vowel, it is combined with **dar-**.):

    a. Schreibt er **mit dem Bleistift?** — Ja, er schreibt **damit.** (instead of **mit ihm**)

    Is he writing with the pencil? — Yes, he is writing with it.

    b. Was legt sie **auf die Tische?** — Sie legt die Hefte **darauf.** (instead of **auf sie**)

    What is she putting on the tables? — She is putting the notebooks on them.

Note: A **da**-compound has the same form whether the noun it replaces is singular or plural.

2. Ordinal numbers up to and including **neunzehnte** (*nineteenth*) are formed by adding **-t** to the corresponding cardinal number and the appropriate adjective endings. From **zwanzigste** on, **-st** plus adjective ending is added:

Heute ist der **neunzehnte** Februar und morgen ist der **zwanzigste** Februar.
Today is the nineteenth of February and tomorrow is the twentieth of February.

The forms **erste** (*first*), **dritte** (*third*), **siebte** (*seventh*), **achte** (*eighth*) are irregular.

3. Verbs with separable prefixes consist usually of an adverb or a preposition and a simple verb (**abfahren, hereinkommen**).[1] The prefix is placed at the end of a main clause when the verb is in the present or simple past tense. In subordinate clauses, however, the prefix precedes the verb and is attached to it:

a. Wir **fahren** nicht **ab,** bevor die Kinder **zurückkommen.**
   We are not leaving before the children come back.
b. Er **kam** ins Wohnzimmer **herein,** während sie **hinausging.**
   He was coming into the living room while she was going out.
c. Sie **steht** früh **auf.**
   She gets up early.
d. Ich glaube, daß sie früh **aufsteht.**
   I believe that she gets up early.

Note 1: **Nicht** immediately precedes a separated prefix in a main clause.

Note 2: **Hin** (*hence, from here*) and **her** (*hither,* [*to*] *here*) are frequently prefixed to other adverbial elements to indicate direction with relation to the speaker.

4. The separable prefix stands at the end of an imperative:

Bitte **kommen Sie herein!**
Please come in.

5. The past participle of a verb with separable prefix is formed by attaching the prefix to the past participle of the root verb:

aufstehen	*to get up*	ist **aufgestanden**
aufmachen	*to open*	**aufgemacht**

Obgleich er früh **aufgestanden** war, ist er spät **zurückgekommen.**
Although he had gotten up early, he came back late.

---

[1] Normally infinitives are written or printed: **abfahren, hereinkommen.** In glossaries, however, a hyphen is often used to indicate that the prefix is separable: **ab-fahren, herein-kommen.**

6. In verbs with separable prefixes, **zu** (*to*) is inserted between the prefix and the infinitive, and all three parts are written as one word:

> Dieses Fenster ist schwer **aufzumachen.**
> *This window is hard to open.*

7. Inseparable prefixes cannot be separated from the verb. The principal inseparable prefixes are **be-, emp-, ent-, er-, ge-, ver-, zer-.**

Note the following examples:

a. Er **entscheidet** alles.
   He decides everything.
b. Wir haben das Papier **zerrissen.**
   We tore the paper to pieces.
c. Ich weiß, daß er eine Geschichte **erzählt.**
   I know that he's telling a story.
d. Ich glaube, daß Sie alles **verstanden** haben.
   I believe you understood everything.

Note that the past participles of verbs with inseparable prefixes never add **ge-.**

8. The principal parts of the verbs with inseparable prefixes introduced before this lesson are:

begegnen	*to meet*	**begegnete**	**ist begegnet**
begrüßen	*to greet*	**begrüßte**	**begrüßt**
beginnen	*to begin*	**begann**	**begonnen**
bekommen	*to get, to receive*	**bekam**	**bekommen**
besuchen	*to visit*	**besuchte**	**besucht**
verstehen	*to understand*	**verstand**	**verstanden**

D. EXERCISES

Write the following sentences in German and be able to express them orally.
1. Our windows are not easy to open.
2. Yesterday was the ninth of August.
3. As soon as her friend had gone away, she received the letter.
4. Please go out of the living room, children.
5. The little girl has torn the paper to pieces.
6. Tell me something, Peter.
7. Did your cousins (*f.*) meet you in town today?
8. Tomorrow will be the eleventh of July.
9. Do you like my new car?

10. Come in now, children.
11. His uncle did not know whether he would come back again.
12. Please open the windows.
13. The day before yesterday was the sixteenth of November.
14. My parents are not going away until we call them up.
15. Her teacher (*f.*) recommended a good book to her.
16. While he was opening the door, his mother was going out of the room.
17. The little girl was standing near the table, and the little boy was sitting in front of it.
18. Her aunt likes the red flowers.
19. Please call me up tomorow, Mr. Schmidt.
20. The pupils have already gone away.
21. What are the students putting on the tables? — They are putting their books on them.
22. After the ship had left, our friend (*f.*) came back home.
23. He did not like my hat.
24. They have already called us up.
25. What are you putting on the table? — I'm putting a notebook on it.

E. COMPREHENDING AND SPEAKING

I. Repeat the following after your instructor (or the speaker) and study thoroughly.

REISEVORBEREITUNGEN[1]

„Der wievielte ist heute?" fragte Peter eines Tages.

„Heute ist der zweite Mai", entgegnete Walter. „Wir müssen bald mit den Reisevorbereitungen beginnen, da wir schon am fünften Juni abreisen."

5   „Gut! Ich werde Herrn Wagner sofort[2] anrufen, um die Flugkarten[3] zu bestellen."[4]

Nach einer Weile kam Peter zurück: „Wir können erst[5] am sechsten Juni fliegen, da für den fünften alle Plätze schon besetzt sind.[6] Ist dir das recht?"[7]

10   „Ja, mir ist das recht", entschied Walter. „Um wieviel Uhr fliegen wir ab?"

[1]**die Reisevorbereitungen**		[6]**da . . . alle Plätze**	because . . . all seats
	travel preparations	**schon besetzt**	are already taken
[2]**sofort**	at once	**sind**	
[3]**die Flugkarte, -n**	plane ticket	[7]**Ist dir das recht?**	Is that all right with
[4]**bestellen**	to order		you?
[5]**erst**	only		

„Sehr früh am Morgen, um acht Uhr dreißig.“

„Da müssen wir aber früh aufstehen. Ich stehe nicht gern früh auf.“

15   „Das macht nichts.[8] Wir können dafür im Flugzeug schlafen.“

Peter nahm ein großes Heft und riß eine Seite heraus:[9] „Ich schreibe alles auf, damit wir nichts vergessen.“[10]

Walter machte seinen neuen Koffer auf. Peter lachte: „Willst du schon packen? Dazu hast du noch Zeit.[11] Aber ich empfehle dir, den

20   Atlas aufzumachen und einen Reiseplan für Deutschland vorzube-reiten. Mach deinen Koffer nur wieder zu!“[12]

II. Beantworten Sie die folgenden Fragen auf deutsch!

1. Warum müssen Peter und Walter mit den Reisevorbereitungen be-ginnen?
2. Was wollte Peter sofort tun?
3. Warum konnten sie erst am sechsten Juni reisen?
4. Warum war es Walter nicht recht, daß das Flugzeug um acht Uhr dreißig abflog?
5. Was riß Peter aus dem Heft?
6. Warum tat er es?
7. Warum lachte Peter?
8. Was empfahl er Walter?
9. Was sollte Peter wieder zumachen?

[8]**Das macht nichts.**	That does not mat-ter.	[11]**Dazu hast du noch Zeit.**	You still have plen-ty of time for that.
[9]**herausreißen**	to tear out		
[10]**vergessen**	to forget	[12]**zu-machen**	to close

UNIT 18

A. UNITS OF SPEECH AND VOCABULARY

I. Study and Practice Aloud.

sie folgen mir	they are following me
sie ist ihr gefolgt	she followed her
Wieviel kostet es?	How much does it cost?
mit dem Zug	by train
mit der Straßenbahn	by streetcar
die meisten Leute	most people
alles Fremde	everything strange, foreign
nichts Graues	nothing gray
etwas Schönes	something beautiful
ein deutsches Flugzeug	a German airplane
ein englischer Autobus	an English bus

der Amerikaner, -	the American	**der Autobus,**	the bus
die Amerika-	the American	**-busse**	
nerin, -nen	girl, woman	**das Flugzeug, -e**	the airplane
der Deutsche,	the German	**der Reisende,**	the traveler
-n, -n		**-n, -n**	
ein Deutscher	a German	**ein Reisender**	a traveler
die Deutsche, -n	the German girl, woman	**die Straßenbahn,**	the streetcar
		-en	
der Engländer, -	the Englishman	**amerikanisch**	American
die Engländerin,	the English-	**deutsch**	German
-nen	woman	**englisch**	English

(*155*)

fremd	strange, foreign	**braun**	brown
angenehm	pleasant	**grau**	gray
billig	cheap, inexpen-	**heiß**	hot
	sive	**wieviel?**	how much?
teuer	dear, expensive	**folgen** + *dat.*	to follow
schlecht	bad, evil	**(ist)**	
		kosten	to cost

ankommen	**kam an**	**ist angekommen**	to arrive

II. Oral Practice. Repeat the pattern sentence. Then substitute the items listed below. Repeat the entire sentence with each substitute item, changing the verb where necessary.

a. Sie folgen mir.

1. Die Leute
2. Die Reisenden
3. Die Amerikaner
4. Die Amerikanerin
5. Die Engländerin
6. Die Deutsche

b. Sie ist ihr gefolgt.

1. Ihre Tochter
2. Ihre Schwester
3. Ihre Mutter
4. Seine Kusine
5. Seine Tante
6. Seine Freundin

c. Wieviel kostet es?

1. das
2. dies
3. der Hut
4. das Auto
5. das Buch
6. das Radio

d. Wir fahren mit dem Zug.

1. dem Autobus
2. dem Flugzeug
3. dem Dampfer
4. der Straßenbahn

e. Die meisten Leute gefallen uns.

1. Amerikaner
2. Deutschen
3. Engländer
4. Engländerinnen
5. Amerikanerinnen
6. Reisenden
7. Straßenbahnen
8. Flugzeuge

III. Oral Practice. Repeat the pattern sentence. Then substitute the items listed below in the places indicated. Repeat the entire sentence with each substitute item.

a. Sie kauft alles Billige.

1. _____ Teuere.
2. _____ Braune.
3. _____ nichts Graues.
4. _____ Schlechtes.
5. _____ liest _____
6. _____ etwas _____
7. _____ Englisches.
8. _____ Angenehmes.

b. Es ist ein deutsches Flugzeug.

1. _____ amerikanisches _____
2. _____ fremdes _____
3. _____ graues _____
4. _____ brauner Autobus.
5. _____ deutscher _____
6. _____ englischer _____

c. **Sie kommen jetzt an.**
   1. Die Leute _____
   2. Die Reisenden _____
   3. Ein Deutscher und ein Engländer _____
   4. _____ eine Amerikanerin _____
   5. _____ eine Engländerin _____
   6. _____ eine Deutsche _____

B. MODEL SENTENCES

I. Study each sentence until you can reproduce it correctly.

122. **Womit schreibt die Schülerin?**
123. **Worüber sprechen die Mädchen?**
124. **Ich habe die folgenden Bücher gelesen.**
125. **Das ist ein oft gelesenes Buch.**
126. **Der Deutsche kauft einen englischen Hut.**
127. **Die Kleine hat ihre Aufgabe gemacht.**
128. **Ein Reisender stand und die anderen Reisenden saßen.**
129. **Das Neue ist nicht immer besser als das Alte.**

122. With what is the student writing?
123. What are the girls talking about?
124. I have read the following books.
125. That is a frequently read book.
126. The German is buying an English hat.
127. The little girl did her lesson.
128. One traveler was standing and the other travelers were sitting.
129. The new is not always better than the old.

II. Pattern Practice. Repeat the model sentence. Then substitute the items listed below in the equivalent part of the model sentence. Repeat the entire sentence with each substitute item.

a. **Womit schreibt die Schülerin?**
   1. die Studentin   4. die Deutsche
   2. die Engländerin   5. der Deutsche
   3. die Amerikanerin   6. der Reisende
b. **Worüber sprechen die Mädchen?**
   1. die Deutschen   4. die Studenten
   2. die Engländer   5. die Verkäufer
   3. die Schüler   6. die Ärzte
c. **Ich habe die folgenden Bücher gelesen.**
   1. gekauft   2. gesehen

     3. gezeigt   5. empfohlen
     4. bekommen   6. genommen

d. Das ist ein oft gelesenes Buch.

     1. Dies _____   4. _____ liest _____
     2. Es _____   5. _____ nimmt _____
     3. Er hat _____   6. _____ bringt _____

e. Der Deutsche kauft einen englischen Hut.

     1. Die Deutsche _____   4. _____ deutschen _____
     2. Die Amerikanerin _____   5. _____ englischen _____
     3. _____ trägt _____   6. _____ amerikanischen _____

f. Die Kleine hat ihre Aufgabe gemacht.

     1. _____ gelesen.   4. _____ genommen.
     2. _____ zu Mittag gegessen.   5. _____ ein Buch _____
     3. _____ einen Apfel _____   6. _____ gebracht.

g. Ein Reisender stand und die anderen Reisenden saßen.

     1. _____ saß _____ standen.   4. _____ aß _____ tranken.
     2. _____ schrieb _____ lasen.   5. _____ trank _____ aßen.
     3. _____ las _____ schrieben.   6. _____ fuhr ab _____ blieben.

h. Das Neue ist nicht immer besser als das Alte.

     1. _____ angenehmer _____   4. Das Alte _____ das Neue.
     2. _____ teuerer _____   5. _____ schöner _____
     3. _____ oft _____   6. _____ angenehmer _____

C. STRUCTURE

1. As the object of a preposition, **was?** (*what?*) is usually replaced by **wo-** (or **wor-**), which is combined with the preposition. (If the preposition begins with a consonant, it is combined with **wo-**; if it begins with a vowel, it is combined with **wor-**):

    a. Womit schreibt die Studentin? (instead of **mit was**)
       With what is the student (f.) *writing?*
    b. Worüber sprechen die Mädchen? (instead of **über was**)
       What are the girls talking about?

2. The present participle of most verbs is formed by adding **-d** to the infinitive. The present participle is most often used as an adjective and is inflected with weak or strong endings like other descriptive adjectives (See Units 7 and 8):

       Ich habe die **folgenden** Bücher gelesen.
       I have read the following books.

3. Past participles are also used as descriptive adjectives, with weak or strong endings:

> Das ist ein oft **gelesenes** Buch.
> *That is a frequently read book.*

4. A descriptive adjective may be used as a noun, with weak or strong adjective endings. Such adjective-nouns are capitalized:

    a. **Der Deutsche** kauft einen englischen Hut.
    The German is buying an English hat.
    b. **Die Kleine** hat ihre Aufgabe gemacht.
    The little girl did her lesson.
    c. **Ein Reisender** stand und **die anderen Reisenden** saßen.
    One traveler was standing and the other travelers were sitting.

Masculine forms are used for male beings and feminine forms for female beings. Note that German does not require supplementary words like English *one, man, boy, woman,* or *girl* (See sentence b, above).

Note: Adjectives of nationality are not capitalized in German:

> ein **englischer** Hut   *an English hat*

5. The neuter form of a descriptive adjective may be used as a noun (capitalized!) to denote an abstraction:

> **Das Neue** ist nicht immer besser als **das Alte.**
> *The new is not always better than the old.*

6. Adjectives modified by **alles** (*everything*), **etwas** (*something*) or **nichts** (*nothing*) are considered nouns and have neuter singular endings:

> Sie kauft **nichts Billiges.**
> *She buys nothing cheap.*

Adjective-nouns after **etwas** or **nichts** have strong endings; after **alles,** weak endings:

> **etwas Schönes**   *something beautiful*
> **alles Billige**   *everything cheap*

D. EXERCISES

Write the following sentences in German and be able to produce them orally.

1. What are we waiting for?
2. That is found money.
3. On the following Saturday they went to the movies.

Einsteigende Passagiere

4. Most Englishmen travel by train.
5. The rich are supposed to help the poor.
6. We had followed the two Germans.
7. Did the boy follow his sister?
8. What is your cousin (*f.*) talking about?
9. The good is often cheaper than the bad.
10. We had met our friends on the street.
11. They arrived by ship.
12. Please bring me something interesting.
13. The old do not like to travel by airplane.
14. Do you see the sleeping children?
15. His daughter is buying something new.
16. Their uncle will arrive the following day.
17. One traveler was going by steamer and the other by plane.
18. What are the notebooks lying on?
19. The small one (*m.*) was older than the big one (*m.*).
20. Do you find spoken German easy?
21. The stranger will meet us in town.
22. The Englishwoman is traveling by car.
23. The aunt gave the child something nice.

E. COMPREHENDING AND SPEAKING

I. Repeat the following after your instructor (or the speaker) and study thoroughly.

AM FLUGHAFEN[1]

Früh am Morgen des sechsten Juni fuhren Walter und Peter nach New York, um ihre Europareise anzutreten.[2]

Sie kamen schon um sieben Uhr am Flughafen an. So hatten sie viel Zeit, um den Betrieb[3] auf dem Flughafen zu beobachten.[4]

5   Nachdem sie ihre Koffer abgegeben[5] hatten, gingen sie auf die Terrasse. Von dort konnten sie alle Flugzeuge sehen.

Der Betrieb auf dem Flughafen war etwas Neues für die beiden.

,,Sieh dort! Ein deutsches Flugzeug!"

Ein großes blaues Flugzeug fuhr langsam heran.[6] Nun stand es
10   still. Zwei Männer brachten die Rampe ans Flugzeug. Die Passagiere begannen auszusteigen.[7]

[1]**der Flughafen, ∸**	airport	[5]**ab-geben**	to check
[2]**um ... anzutreten**	in order to set out on	[6]**fuhr langsam heran**	came up slowly
[3]**der Betrieb**	intense activity	[7]**aus-steigen**	to get out
[4]**beobachten**	to observe		

„Wieviele Leute können wohl in diesem Flugzeug reisen?" fragte Walter.

„Ich würde sagen, ungefähr hundertundfünfzig",[8] antwortete
15   Peter.

Die Reisenden kamen jetzt zum Flughafengebäude. „Woher[9] kommen wohl diese Leute?" fragte Walter.

„Es sind meistens[10] Fremde", sagte sein Freund, „viele werden wohl Deutsche oder Engländer sein."

20   Das Wetter war heiß, aber angenehm. „Wir werden einen schönen Flug[11] haben", meinte Walter.

Jetzt sagte eine Stimme im Lautsprecher:[12] „Reisende für Flug siebenundsiebzig! Ihr Flugzeug ist startbereit.[13] Bitte gehen Sie zum Ausgang!"[14]

25   „Das ist für uns!" sagte Peter und ging schnell zur Tür. Walter folgte ihm.

Ein deutscher Reisender rief ihnen lachend nach: „Alles Gute, meine Herren!"

II. Beantworten Sie die folgenden Fragen auf deutsch!

1. Wann fuhren Walter und Peter nach New York?
2. Warum hatten sie viel Zeit?
3. Was wollten sie in dieser Zeit tun?
4. Wohin gingen sie?
5. Was konnten sie von dort sehen?
6. Was war etwas Neues für sie?
7. Was für ein Flugzeug fuhr heran?
8. Wohin gingen die Reisenden?
9. Was sagte die Stimme im Lautsprecher?

[8]**ungefähr hundertundfünfzig**	approximately one hundred and fifty	[11]**der Flug, ⸚e**	flight
		[12]**der Lautsprecher, -**	loudspeaker
[9]**woher**	from where	[13]**startbereit**	ready to start
[10]**meistens**	mostly	[14]**der Ausgang, ⸚e**	exit

UNIT 19

A. UNITS OF SPEECH AND VOCABULARY

I. Study and Practice Aloud.

Sie bittet um die Rechnung.	She is asking for the bill.
Er stellt mir eine Frage.	He's asking me a question.
Wir steigen in das Auto ein.	We are getting in the car.
Es ist Viertel vor eins.	It is a quarter of one.
Es ist Viertel nach sechs.	It is a quarter after six.
Ich gehe auch dahin.	I am also going there.
eine Weile	a (little) while

Amerika	America	**das Paket, -e**	the package
der Enkel, -	the grandson, grandchild	**die Rechnung, -en**	the bill
die Geschwister *pl.*	the brothers and sisters	**das Schiff, -e**	the ship
die Großmutter, ⸚	the grandmother	**die Speisekarte, -n**	the menu
der Großvater, ⸚	the grandfather	**das Viertel, -**	the quarter
der Neffe, -n, -n	the nephew	**die Weile**	the while
die Nichte, -n	the niece	**die Zigarette, -n**	the cigarette
der Verwandte, -n, -n	the relative	**dahin**	(to) there, thither
ein Verwandter	a relative	**hinten**	behind, in back
die Frage, -n	the question	**vorne**	forward, up front

(*163*)

alle *pl.*	all		**plaudern**	to chat
betrachten	to consider, look		**rauchen**	to smoke
	at		**stellen**	to put
lächeln	to smile			

bitten (um + *acc.*)	**bat**	**gebeten**	to ask (for), request
einsteigen (in + *acc.*)	**stieg ein**	**ist eingestiegen**	to get in, on
verlassen (verläßt)	**verließ**	**verlassen**	to leave (behind)

II. Oral Practice. Repeat the pattern sentence. Then substitute the items listed below in the appropriate places. Repeat the entire sentence with each substitute item, changing the verb where necessary.

a. Sie bittet um die Rechnung.
  1. _____ das Paket.   4. Er _____
  2. _____ die Speisekarte.   5. _____ Paket _____
  3. _____ hat _____ gebeten. 6. _____ Rechnung _____

b. Er stellt mir eine Frage.
  1. Mein Verwandter _____   4. _____ ihm _____
  2. Meine Verwandten _____   5. Alle seine Verwandten _____
  3. _____ Fragen.   6. _____ ihr _____

c. Wir steigen in das Auto ein.
  1. _____ den Zug _____
  2. Mein Verwandter _____
  3. _____ ist _____ eingestiegen.
  4. _____ die Straßenbahn _____
  5. Meine Verwandten _____
  6. _____ den Autobus _____

d. Es ist Viertel vor eins.
  1. _____ 5.   4. _____ 11.
  2. _____ 8.   5. _____ 7.
  3. _____ 2.   6. _____ 4.

e. Es ist Viertel nach sechs.
  1. _____ 4.   4. _____ 10.
  2. _____ 9.   5. _____ 3.
  3. _____ 12.   6. _____ 1.

f. Ich gehe auch dahin.
  1. Sein Enkel _____   4. Ihr Großvater _____
  2. Seine Nichte _____   5. Ihr Neffe _____
  3. Meine Großmutter _____   6. Unsere Eltern _____

g. Seine Großmutter sitzt hinten.
  1. Sein Großvater _____   3. Meine Nichte _____
  2. Mein Neffe _____   4. _____ vorne.

5. Sein Enkel _____
6. Ihre Nichte _____

7. _____ steht _____
8. Meine Großmutter _____

h. Sie betrachten das Paket.
  1. _____ die Rechnung.
  2. _____ die Speisekarte.

  3. _____ das Schiff.
  4. _____ das Haus.

i. Sie haben eine Weile geraucht.
  1. _____ gearbeitet.
  2. _____ gestanden.

  3. _____ gesprochen.
  4. _____ gelesen.

j. Sie rauchen Zigaretten.
  1. Die Amerikaner _____
  2. Die Studenten _____

  3. _____ keine _____
  4. _____ viele _____

k. Sie lächeln.
  1. Alle _____
  2. Meine Verwandten _____
  3. Sein Enkel _____
  4. Ihre Nichte _____
  5. Seine Enkel _____

  6. _____ plaudern.
  7. Alle _____
  8. Die Geschwister _____
  9. Ihre Geschwister _____
  10. Meine Geschwister _____

l. Er verläßt Amerika.
  1. Mein Verwandter _____
  2. Seine Nichte _____
  3. Wir _____
  4. _____ das Schiff.

  5. _____ haben _____ verlassen.
  6. Die Reisenden _____
  7. Der Reisende _____
  8. Die Amerikanerin _____

B. MODEL SENTENCES

I. Study each sentence until you can produce it correctly.

130. **Kennen Sie den Mann, der im Wohnzimmer sitzt?**
131. **Hier ist das Buch, das Sie wollen.**
132. **Ich sehe das Kind, dem ich das Heft gegeben habe.**
133. **Die Frau, der er hilft, ist sehr alt.**
134. **Die Mädchen, die hier waren, sind jetzt fortgegangen.**
135. **Die Armen, denen sie das Geld gibt, danken ihr.**
136. **Der Junge, dessen Schwester in meiner Klasse ist, heißt Richard.**
137. **Wir besuchten die Studentin, deren Vater wir kannten.**
138. **Viele Leute, deren Kinder in der Stadt wohnen, wohnen auf dem Lande.**
139. **Der Bleistift, womit er schreibt, ist gelb.**

130. Do you know the man who is sitting in the living room?
131. Here is the book (that) you want.
132. I see the child to whom I gave the notebook.
133. The woman (whom) he is helping is very old.

134. The girls who were here have now gone away.
135. The poor people to whom she is giving the money thank her.
136. The boy whose sister is in my class is called Richard.
137. We visited the student (*f.*) whose father we knew.
138. Many people whose children live in town live in the country.
139. The pencil with which he is writing is yellow.

II. Pattern Practice. Repeat the model sentence. Then substitute the items listed below in the appropriate places. Repeat the entire sentence with each substitute item, changing the verb where necessary.

a. **Kennen Sie den Mann, der im Wohnzimmer sitzt?**

1. den Jungen	4. den Professor
2. den Schüler	5. den Studenten
3. den Lehrer	6. den Reisenden

b. **Hier ist das Buch, das Sie wollen.**

1. das Heft	3. das Papier
2. das Paket	4. das Wasser

c. **Ich sehe das Kind, dem ich das Heft gegeben habe.**

1. das Mädchen	4. den Studenten
2. den Jungen	5. den Lehrer
3. den Schüler	6. den Professor

d. **Die Frau, der er hilft, ist sehr alt.**

1. Die Lehrerin	4. Die Kusine
2. Die Tante	5. Die Mutter
3. Die Großmutter	6. Die Verkäuferin

e. **Die Mädchen, die hier waren, sind jetzt fortgegangen.**

1. Die Jungen	4. Die Verwandten
2. Die Kinder	5. Die Leute
3. Die Enkel	6. Die Reisenden

f. **Die Armen, denen sie das Geld gibt, danken ihr.**

1. Die Alten	4. Die Enkel
2. Die Freunde	5. Die Nichten
3. Die Verwandten	6. Die Neffen

g. **Der Junge, dessen Schwester in meiner Klasse ist, heißt Richard.**

1. _____ Kusine _____	4. Der Student _____
2. Der Schüler _____	5. _____ Kusine _____
3. _____ Freundin _____	6. _____ Schwester _____

h. **Wir besuchten die Studentin, deren Vater wir kannten.**

1. _____ Onkel _____	4. _____ Bruder _____
2. _____ Vetter _____	5. _____ die Lehrerin _____
3. _____ die Frau _____	6. _____ Vater _____

i. **Viele Leute, deren Kinder in der Stadt wohnen, wohnen auf dem Lande.**

1. _____ auf dem Lande _____ in der Stadt.
2. Viele Eltern _____
3. _____ in der Stadt _____ auf dem Lande.
4. Unsere Verwandten _____

j. **Der Bleistift, womit er schreibt, ist gelb.**

1. _____ rot.
2. _____ ich _____
3. _____ grün.

4. _____ die Schülerin _____
5. _____ blau.
6. _____ der Schüler _____

C. STRUCTURE

1. The relative pronoun has the following forms:

	MASCULINE	NEUTER	FEMININE	PLURAL
NOM.	der (welcher)	das (welches)	die (welche)	die (welche)
GEN.	dessen	dessen	deren	deren
DAT.	dem (welchem)	dem (welchem)	der (welcher)	denen (welchen)
ACC.	den (welchen)	das (welches)	die (welche)	die (welche)

Note: The forms of the relative pronoun **der, die, das** are identical with those of the definite article, except for the four genitive forms and the dative plural.

2. The relative pronoun has the same gender and number as the antecedent, the noun in the main clause for which it stands. The case of the relative pronoun, however, depends on its function in the relative clause (subject, object, possessive):

a. Kennen Sie **den Mann, der** im Wohnzimmer sitzt?
   Do you know the man who is sitting in the living room?
b. Hier ist **das Buch, das** Sie wollen.
   Here is the book (that) you want.
c. Ich sehe **das Kind, dem** ich das Heft gegeben habe.
   I see the child (to) whom I gave the notebook.
d. **Die Frau, der** er hilft, ist sehr alt.
   The woman (whom) he is helping is very old.
e. **Die Mädchen, die** hier waren, sind jetzt fortgegangen.
   The girls who were here have now gone away.
f. **Die Armen, denen** sie das Geld gibt, danken ihr.
   The poor people to whom she is giving the money thank her.

Note: Contrary to English, the relative pronoun may not be omitted in

German. Relative clauses, like all subordinate clauses, are set off by commas, and the finite verb is last in the clause.

3. **Welcher, welche, welches** may be used instead of **der, die, das** in all cases but the genitive. The sentences in paragraph 2, above, may be rewritten as follows, with no change of meaning:

   a. Kennen Sie **den Mann, welcher** im Wohnzimmer sitzt?
   b. Hier ist **das Buch, welches** Sie wollen.
   c. Ich sehe **das Kind, welchem** ich das Heft gegeben habe.
   d. **Die Frau, welcher** er hilft, ist sehr alt.
   e. **Die Mädchen, welche** hier waren, sind fortgegangen.
   f. **Die Armen, welchen** sie das Geld gibt, danken ihr.

Note: Both **der** and **welcher** may refer to either persons or things. **Der** is generally preferred over **welcher,** especially in informal usage.

4. In the genitive, only **dessen** and **deren** (*whose*) may be used:

   a. **Der Junge, dessen** Schwester in meiner Klasse ist, heißt Richard.
      The boy whose sister is in my class is called Richard.
   b. Wir besuchten **die Studentin, deren** Vater wir kannten.
      We visited the student (f.) whose father we knew.
   c. **Viele Leute, deren** Kinder in der Stadt wohnen, wohnen auf dem Lande.
      Many people whose children live in town live in the country.

5. A **wo-** (or **wor-**) compound may replace a preposition plus relative pronoun in the dative or accusative case, when the pronoun represents an inanimate object:

      Der Bleistift, mit dem er schreibt, ist gelb.
      Der Bleistift, womit er schreibt, ist gelb.
      The pencil with which he is writing is yellow.

D. EXERCISES

Write the following sentences in German and be able to express them orally.

1. He is taking the glass of water that is standing on the table.
2. The parents whose children were playing in the dining room were chatting in the living room.
3. The friend to whom she wrote a letter called her up.
4. The day before yesterday I saw the salesgirl whose sister was here this afternoon.
5. His brothers and sisters were laughing while he was singing.

6. The table on which had laid the packages was small.
7. All the relatives that were in the room asked her questions.
8. His grandchildren like best to go to the movies.
9. Her grandmother, at whose house she lives, knows no English.
10. My nephew was looking at the package his grandfather had given him.
11. Their parents prefer to eat in a restaurant that is not too expensive.
12. Your mother is probably chatting with her nieces.
13. It was cold in the room in which his grandchild was sitting.
14. The man who is smoking a cigarette is his cousin.
15. The friends he was waiting for had already gone.
16. She is getting into the car, which her father bought for her a month ago.
17. My relatives probably smoked all the cigarettes.
18. Where is the little girl whose uncle taught us German?
19. Today I saw the man I helped yesterday.
20. The book the student (*f.*) was reading was very interesting.
21. What is your sister doing with the flowers her friend sent her?
22. The ship on which he is traveling will arrive tomorrow evening.
23. This morning I chatted with the salesman whose wife you know.
24. Can you give me the books I asked for?

E. COMPREHENDING AND SPEAKING

I. Repeat the following after your instructor (or the speaker) and study thoroughly.

FLUG NACH DEUTSCHLAND

Peter und Walter fanden in der Kabine des Flugzeugs, das vor dem Flughafengebäude auf sie wartete, zwei freie Plätze neben einem Fenster. Die freundliche Stewardeß zeigte ihnen, wo sie ihre Mäntel[1] und Kameras hinlegen[2] konnten. Im Lautsprecher, der über ihnen hing, ertönte[3] plötzlich eine Stimme:

5

„Meine Damen und Herren! Hier spricht Otto Kramer, Ihr Flugkapitän.[4] Ich heiße Sie an Bord unseres Flugzeuges willkommen![5] Wir fliegen in wenigen Minuten ab. Bitte schnallen Sie sich fest und rauchen Sie nicht mehr!"[6]

[1]**der Mantel, ∸**	coat	[5]**Ich heiße Sie an**	Welcome aboard!
[2]**hin-legen**	to put	**Bord . . .**	
[3]**ertönen**	to sound	**willkommen.**	
[4]**Hier spricht . . .**	This is . . . your	[6]**schnallen Sie sich**	fasten your seatbelts
Ihr	pilot speaking.	**fest und**	and no more
Flugkapitän.		**rauchen Sie**	smoking!
		nicht mehr!	

„Jetzt sind wir in der Luft."

10　　Das Flugzeug begann zu zittern.[7] Langsam rollte[8] es gegen das
Ende der Startbahn.[9] Dort heulten alle Motoren auf.[10] Das Flugzeug
fuhr immer schneller. Walter stieß Peter an:[11] „Jetzt sind wir in der
Luft!"[12]

　　Die Flughafengebäude wurden immer kleiner. Schon waren sie
15　in den Wolken,[13] die ihnen die Sicht verdeckten.[14] Aber plötzlich war
über ihnen wieder der blaue Himmel. Im Lautsprecher konnte man
wieder Kapitän Kramers Stimme hören: „Wir sind jetzt auf zwanzig-
tausend Meter Höhe und fliegen gegen Nordosten. In sechs Stunden
werden wir Irland überfliegen und in zwei weiteren[15] Stunden in
20　Frankfurt landen. Sie dürfen jetzt Ihre Sicherheitsgurten[16] lösen und
rauchen."

　　Die Stewardeß brachte eine Speisekarte, aber Walter wollte
nichts essen, sondern bat um ein Glas Wasser.

　　Die Freunde schauten zum Fenster hinaus und sahen durch die
25　Wolken das Meer und einmal, ganz weit unten,[17] einen großen weißen
Dampfer.

II. Beantworten Sie die folgenden Fragen auf deutsch!

1. Wo fanden Peter und Walter zwei freie Plätze?
2. Wer zeigte ihnen, wo sie ihre Mäntel und Kameras hinlegen konnten?
3. Was sagte Kapitän Kramer zu den Passagieren?
4. Wohin rollte das Flugzeug?
5. In welchem Moment stieß Walter Peter an?
6. Wie hoch flog das Flugzeug?
7. Wann sollte es landen?
8. Was wollte Walter von der Stewardeß?
9. Was sahen die Freunde durch die Wolken?

[7]**zittern**	to vibrate	[14]**die Ihnen die**	that made it im-
[8]**rollen**	to roll	**Sicht**	possible for them
[9]**die Startbahn,**	runway	**verdeckten**	to see anything
-en		[15]**weiter**	more
[10]**auf-heulen**	to roar	[16]**die**	
[11]**an-stoßen**	to give a push	**Sicherheitsgurte,**	
[12]**die Luft, ⸚e**	air	**-n**	seat belt
[13]**die Wolke, -n**	cloud	[17]**ganz weit unten**	far, far below

UNIT 20

A. UNITS OF SPEECH AND VOCABULARY

I. Study and Practice Aloud.

Es ist halb neun (Uhr).	It's half past eight (o'clock).
Es ist zehn (Minuten) vor eins.	It's ten minutes of one.
Es ist fünf (Minuten) nach acht.	It's five minutes after eight.
Sie kommen Punkt zwölf (Uhr).	They are coming at twelve o'clock sharp.
Sie reicht ihm die Hand.	She is shaking hands with him.
Wir wünschen Ihnen glückliche Reise.	We wish you a pleasant trip.
Er nimmt von seinen Freunden Abschied.	He is taking leave of his friends.
acht Uhr morgens	eight A.M., eight o'clock in the morning.
morgens	in the morning(s), A.M.
nachmittags	in the afternoon(s), P.M.
abends	in the evening(s), P.M.
nachts	at night
montags	on Monday(s)

der Abschied, -e	the farewell, departure	**der Bekannte, -n, -n**	the acquaintance
der Beamte, -n, -n	the official	**ein Bekannter**	an acquaintance
		das Beste	the best (thing)
ein Beamter	an official	**das Gepäck**	the baggage

(*172*)

die **Minute, -n**	the minute	**mehrere**	several
die **Sache, -n**	the thing	**glücklich**	happy
das **Schlimmste**	the worst (thing)	**schlimm**	bad
beide	both	**von** + *dat.*	from, of
einander	one another	**reichen**	to extend, hand
einige	some	**wünschen**	to wish

| **halten (hält)** | **hielt** | **gehalten** | to hold |
| **verlieren** | **verlor** | **verloren** | to lose |

II. Oral Practice. Repeat the pattern sentence. Then substitute the items below in the appropriate places. Repeat the entire sentence with each substitute item, changing the verb where necessary.

a. **Es ist halb neun.**

1. 2:30	8. 5:50
2. 6:30	9. 7:35
3. 10:30	10. 8:05
4. 3:30	11. 9:20
5. 12:50	12. 2:30
6. 3:42	13. 11:25
7. 10:40	14. 1:10

b. **Sie kommen Punkt zwölf Uhr.**

| 1. Die Beamten | 3. Ein Beamter |
| 2. Mehrere Beamte | 4. Der Beamte |

c. **Sie reicht ihm die Hand.**

1. Der Beamte _____	4. _____ einander _____
2. Ein Beamter _____	5. Sie (*pl.*) _____
3. Die Beamten _____	6. Wir _____

d. **Wir wünschen Ihnen glückliche Reise.**

1. _____ einander _____	4. Mehrere Freunde _____
2. Sie (*pl.*) _____	5. Beide Freundinnen _____
3. Einige Verwandte _____	6. Die Beamten _____

e. **Er nimmt von seinen Freunden Abschied.**

1. Der Beamte _____	4. _____ beiden _____
2. Mein Bekannter _____	5. _____ einigen _____
3. _____ mehreren _____	6. Sein Verwandter _____

f. **Es ist acht Uhr morgens.**

1. 10 A.M.	5. 2 P.M.
2. 7 A.M.	6. 1 P.M.
3. 4 A.M.	7. 9 P.M.
4. 3 P.M.	8. 11 P.M.

g. Morgens arbeite ich.

1. _____ schlafe _____

2. _____ er.

3. Nachmittags _____

4. _____ spielt _____

5. _____ sie (*sing.*).

6. _____ lernt _____

7. Abends _____

8. _____ wir.

9. _____ lesen _____

10. Nachts _____

11. _____ schlafen _____

12. _____ die meisten Leute.

h. Montags geht er ins Kino.

1. Freitags

2. Donnerstags

3. Samstags

4. Dienstags

5. Sonntags

6. Mittwochs

7. Sonnabends

i. Er hält das Gepäck.

1. Der Beamte

2. Sein Bekannter

3. Mein Freund

4. Ihr Verwandter

j. Das ist das Beste.

1. Dies _____

2. Es _____

3. _____ schlimm.

4. _____ das Schlimmste.

5. Dies _____

6. Das _____

k. Er verliert seine Sachen.

1. Mein Onkel _____

2. _____ hat _____ verloren.

3. Sein Bekannter _____

4. Unser Vetter _____

5. Ihr Nachbar _____

6. _____ nicht _____

B. MODEL SENTENCES

I. Study each sentence until you can reproduce it correctly.

140. Er kommt um halb sieben.

141. Er wollte alles, was sie hatten.

142. Das ist das Schlimmste, was wir tun können.

143. Es ging ihm besser, was ihn sehr glücklich machte.

144. Wir haben viele gute Freunde.

145. Kennen Sie ihren Bruder? Der ist mein bester Freund.

146. Sie ist mit ihrer Schwester und deren Sohn gekommen.

147. Sie weiß, daß er ins Kino hat gehen dürfen.

140. He is coming at half past six.

141. He wanted everything (that) they had.

142. That's the worst thing we can do.

143. He was feeling better, (a fact) which made him very happy.

144. We have many good friends.

145. Do you know her brother? *He* is my best friend.
146. She came with her sister and the latter's son.
147. She knows that he was permitted to go to the movies.

II. Pattern Practice. Repeat the model sentence. Then substitute the items listed below in the appropriate places. Repeat the entire sentence with each substitute item.

a. **Er kommt um halb sieben.**
   1. geht
   2. ißt
   3. beginnt
   4. fährt

b. **Er wollte alles, was sie hatten.**
   1. _____ nichts _____
   2. _____ etwas _____
   3. Das Mädchen _____
   4. _____ nichts _____
   5. Er _____
   6. Wir _____

c. **Das ist das Schlimmste, was wir tun können.**
   1. _____ Sie _____
   2. Es _____
   3. _____ das Beste _____
   4. Dies _____
   5. Es _____
   6. _____ wir _____

d. **Es ging ihm besser, was ihn sehr glücklich machte.**
   1. Er bekam viel Geld, _____
   2. Er besuchte seine Eltern, _____
   3. Er traf seine Freunde, _____
   4. Die Kinder kamen früh nach Hause, _____

e. **Wir haben viele gute Freunde.**
   1. wenige
   2. einige
   3. mehrere
   4. manche

f. **Kennen Sie ihren Bruder? — Der ist mein bester Freund.**
   1. Vetter
   2. Onkel
   3. Vater
   4. Lehrer
   5. Arzt

g. **Sie ist mit ihrer Schwester und deren Sohn gekommen.**
   1. ihrer Nichte
   2. ihrer Tochter
   3. ihrer Kusine
   4. ihrer Freundin

h. **Sie weiß, daß er ins Kino hat gehen dürfen.**
   1. dahin
   2. in die Schule
   3. ins Restaurant
   4. nach Hause
   5. an die See
   6. aufs Land

C. STRUCTURE

1. Genitives of nouns denoting days or parts of a day are used adverbially (not capitalized) to indicate habitual or repeated occurrence:

morgens	*in the morning(s)*
nachmittags	*in the afternoon(s)*
abends	*in the evening(s)*
nachts	*at night*
montags	*on Monday(s)*

Morgens, nachmittags, and **abends** are frequently added to clock time for clarity:

acht Uhr **morgens**   *eight A.M., eight o'clock in the morning.*

2. In expressing the half hour, German looks to the next hour. Most time expressions are preceded by **um** (*at*), except when **Punkt** (*exactly*) is used:

um halb sieben	*at half past six*
um fünf Uhr	*at five o'clock*
um Viertel vor elf	*at a quarter of eleven*
um fünf Minuten nach acht	*at five minutes after eight*

But:

Sie kommen **Punkt zwölf (Uhr).**
They are coming at twelve (o'clock) sharp.

3. **Was** is used as the relative pronoun:

a. when the antecedent is a neuter pronoun, such as **alles** (*everything*), **etwas** (*something*), **nichts** (*nothing*), **viel(es)** (*much, many things*):

Er wollte **alles, was** sie hatten.
He wanted everything (that) they had.

b. when the antecedent is a neuter superlative adjective used as a noun:

Das ist **das Schlimmste, was** wir tun können.
That's the worst thing we can do.

c. when the antecedent is a whole clause:

Es ging ihm besser, was ihn sehr glücklich machte.
He was feeling better, (a fact) which made him very happy.

4. Indefinite numerical adjectives, such as **einige** (*some, a few*), **manche** (*some*), **mehrere** (*several*), **viele** (*many*), **wenige** (*few*), take strong endings, as do descriptive adjectives following them:

Wir haben **viele gute** Freunde.
We have many good friends.

Alle (*all*), **beide** (*both*), and **keine** (*no*) are treated like **der**-words and are followed by descriptive adjectives with weak endings:

> Wir haben **keine guten** Freunde.
> *We haven't any good friends.*

5. The demonstrative pronoun **der, die, das** (*that one, he, she, that*) has the same forms as the relative pronoun **der, die, das.** It is frequently used as an emphatic substitute for **er, sie, es** (*he, she, it*):

> Kennen Sie **ihren Bruder? Der** ist mein bester Freund.
> *Do you know her brother? He is my best friend.*

The genitive demonstrative forms **dessen** and **deren** are used instead of the possessives **sein** (*his*) and **ihr** (*her, their*) to avoid ambiguity, often in the sense of *the latter's.* Compare:

> Sie ist mit **ihrer Schwester** und **deren** Sohn gekommen.
> *She came with her sister and the latter's son.*

> Sie ist mit **ihrer Schwester** und **ihrem** Sohn gekommen.
> *She came with her sister and her (own) son.*

6. A double infinitive stands last in any clause, main or subordinate. In subordinate clauses, the finite verb precedes the double infinitive:

> Sie weiß, daß er dahin **hat gehen dürfen.**
> *She knows that he was permitted to go there.*

D. EXERCISES

Write the following sentences in German and be able to express them orally.
1. Not all new buildings are beautiful.
2. Some pupils went away at five minutes after three.
3. Several young people were shaking hands with one another.
4. The younger children eat at 6:30 A.M.
5. She visited her aunts every week, which pleased them very much.
6. Her cousin (*f.*) has few good books.
7. This is not the worst thing he did.
8. It was five o'clock sharp.
9. My sisters are playing with their children and the latter's friends.
10. Several old people were standing there.
11. Does your girl friend study her lessons in the evenings?
12. The salesgirls stayed at home on Monday because they had to work on Saturday.

13. The official lost everything he had in his pocket.
14. Some officials came into the building at 8:45 A.M.
15. Who visits your grandfather on Sundays?
16. He found something he liked.
17. Both young men are waiting for their relatives.
18. It was ten minutes of seven when we got up.
19. Would you bring me a cup of tea at half past four?
20. Did you see his girl friend? *She* is not very pretty.
21. I don't know why the little girl has not wanted to go to school.
22. The little child wanted everything he saw.

E. COMPREHENDING AND SPEAKING

I. Repeat the following after your instructor (or the speaker) and study thoroughly.

ERSTE EINDRÜCKE[1]

Es war Punkt vier Uhr nachmittags, als das große Flugzeug in Frankfurt landete. Beide Studenten nahmen Abschied von der Stewardeß und von den anderen Reisenden. Dann gingen sie zum Flughafengebäude, um ihr Gepäck abzuholen.[2]

5   Sie fanden ihre Koffer und trugen sie zu einem großen Tisch, wo ein Zollbeamter[3] auf sie wartete und fragte: „Haben Sie etwas zu verzollen?[4] Alkohol? Parfüm? Tabak?" Als die beiden den Kopf schüttelten,[5] zeigte[6] er auf einen der Koffer.

     „Bitte öffnen Sie diesen Koffer. Ich will alles sehen, was darin
10 ist."

     Walter fand den Schlüssel[7] zum Koffer nicht und suchte in allen Taschen.

     „Das ist das Dümmste, was mir passieren[8] konnte", meinte er ärgerlich.[9] Der Zollbeamte schaute ihm mißtrauisch zu.[10] Endlich fand
15 Walter den Schlüssel und öffnete den Koffer.

     „Alles in Ordnung!"[11] sagte der Beamte, als er nichts als Hemden[12]

[1]**erste Eindrücke**	first impressions	[7]**der Schlüssel, -**	key
[2]**um ... abzuholen**	in order to get	[8]**passieren**	to happen
[3]**der Zollbeamte, -**	customs official	[9]**ärgerlich**	angrily
[4]**Haben Sie etwas zu verzollen?**	Do you have anything to declare?	[10]**schaute ihm mißtrauisch zu**	looked at him suspiciously
[5]**den Kopf schütteln**	to shake one's head	[11]**Alles in Ordnung!**	Everything is okay.
[6]**zeigen (auf)**	to point (to)	[12]**nichts als Hemden**	nothing but shirts

Frankfurt am Main

Fritz Henle from Monkmeyer

und Bücher im Koffer sah. „Ich habe Sie nicht belästigen wollen,[13] aber ich habe meine Pflicht tun müssen."[14]

Er war nun sehr freundlich geworden, fragte sie, wohin sie reisen
20   wollten und gab ihnen mehrere gute Ratschläge.[15]

II. Beantworten Sie die folgenden Fragen auf deutsch!

1. Wann landete das Flugzeug in Frankfurt?
2. Von wem nahmen die Studenten Abschied?
3. Wer wartete an einem großen Tisch auf sie?
4. Was fragte der Zollbeamte?
5. Hatten Peter und Walter etwas zu verzollen?
6. Was wollte der Zollbeamte sehen?
7. Warum schaute er Walter mißtrauisch zu?
8. Was sah er in Walters Koffer?
9. Wie war er nun geworden?

[13]**Ich habe Sie nicht belästigen wollen.** I did not mean to bother you.

[14]**Ich habe meine Pflicht tun müssen.** I had to do my duty.

[15]**mehrere gute Ratschläge** much good advice

REVIEW UNIT 4

A. *Supply the proper form of the word in parentheses in the place indicated.*

1. (gelb) Wir haben keine _____ Tassen.
2. (zurückkommen) Mein Bruder ist schon _____.
3. (alt) Der _____ spielt mit seinem Enkel.
4. (warten) Der Kellner hilft den _____ Gästen.
5. (interessant) Bringen Sie mir etwas _____!
6. (einsteigen) Der Reisende war in den Zug _____.
7. (jung) Beide _____ Männer sind hier.
8. (singen) Hören Sie die _____ Vögel?
9. (gut) Wir wünschen Ihnen alles _____.
10. (rot) Sind alle _____ Äpfel reif?
11. (fallen) Der _____ Baum liegt auf dem Boden.
12. (neu) Der Verkäufer verkauft wenige _____ Autos.
13. (kalt) Er ißt nichts _____.
14. (erzählen) Das ist eine oft _____ Geschichte.
15. (klein) Mein Bruder spricht mit dem _____.
16. (arm) Einige _____ Männer sitzen da.
17. (2:30) Er geht um _____ _____ Uhr fort.

B. *Supply an appropriate word in each space.*

1. Mein Bruder steht sehr früh _____.
2. Ich wünsche ihm _____ Reise.
3. Wir fahren gerne _____ dem Autobus.
4. Sein Auto ist _____ blau oder schwarz.

5. Ich werde meinen Vater _____ mehr Geld bitten.
6. Jeden Tag ruft er seine Freundin _____.
7. Ihr Onkel ist weder jung _____ alt.
8. _____ wartet er? — Er wartet auf den Zug.
9. Das Buch ist nicht gelb, _____ rot.
10. Sitzt Hans vorne oder_____?
11. Ich kenne _____ seine Tante als auch seinen Onkel.
12. Kommt der Zug um zehn Uhr morgens oder _____ an?
13. Die Studentin, _____ Bruder ich kenne, heißt Trude.
14. Wir kaufen alles, _____ wir brauchen.

C. *Combine each pair of sentences into one sentence, putting the connecting word in the place indicated, and making necessary changes in word order.*

1. (Da) Hans hat seinen Freund nicht getroffen. Er ist nach Hause gegangen.
2. Sie ist sehr reich. (aber) Sie wohnt in einem kleinen Hause.
3. Der Schüler begegnete seinem Lehrer. (als) Er ging in die Schule.
4. Der Gast bestellte etwas zu essen. (denn) Er hatte Hunger.
5. (Wenn) Ich lese zuviel. Die Augen tun mir weh.
6. Wir wissen nicht. (ob) Er hat Geschwister.
7. Wir schreiben ihr. (daß) Wir kommen in acht Tagen zu ihr.

D. *Combine each pair of sentences into one sentence, making the second part a relative clause.*

1. Die Reisenden fahren zum Dampfer. Er soll um zwölf Uhr abfahren.
2. Der Mann sieht seine Freunde. Er wird von ihnen Abschied nehmen.
3. Ich sehe den Zahnarzt. Seine Tante ist unsere Nachbarin.
4. Das ist unser Professor. Vor einer Stunde haben wir ihn begrüßt.
5. Hier ist der Stuhl. Ich habe mein Heft darauf gelegt.

E. *Change the sentences as indicated.*

1. (compound past) Er macht alle Fenster auf.
2. (compound past) Die Großmutter erzählt den Enkeln eine Geschichte.
3. (compound past) Er weiß, daß er seine Aufgaben machen kann.
4. (future) Wann kommen Ihre Verwandten zurück?
5. (future) Er empfiehlt mich.
6. (future) Sie geht um zwei Uhr aus dem Gebäude hinaus.
7. (present) Die Reisenden sind heute angekommen.
8. (present) Die Verkäuferin hat den Laden verlassen.
9. (command) Sie steigen in das Auto ein.

F. *Select from the list below an appropriate word to complete the sense of each sentence in the space indicated. Do not use a word more than once.*

aber	das	dessen	morgen	wenn
als	daß	gute	morgens	weil
beide	den	hat	neuen	welcher
da	denen	herein	obwohl	welches
darum	denn	hinein	sondern	worum
darunter	deren	ist	sowohl	worunter

1. Der neue Gast ist um acht Uhr _____ angekommen.
2. _____ er zu uns kam, spielte er immer mit den Kindern.
3. Meine Kusine ist nicht alt, _____ jung.
4. _____ kommen meine Bekannten.
5. Sie war müde, _____ sie nicht geschlafen hatte.
6. Ich sagte, _____ er nicht zu Hause war.
7. Was liegt unter dem Tisch? — Ein Buch liegt _____.
8. Die Schüler kommen ins Zimmer _____.
9. Die Soldaten, _____ er folgte, gingen fort.
10. Ich sah ihn vor zehn Minuten, _____ er hinausging.
11. Er schreibt wenig, _____ er bekommt viele Briefe.
12. Ich gebe Ihnen den Bleistift, _____ Sie bitten.
13. Das Mädchen, _____ Vater Arzt ist, redet mit Marie.
14. Manche _____ Bücher liegen auf dem Tisch.

G. *Beantworten Sie die folgenden Fragen auf deutsch!*

1. Um wieviel Uhr sind Sie heute aufgestanden?
2. Wieviel Uhr ist es jetzt?
3. Kommen Sie morgens oder nachmittags in dieses Zimmer?
4. Womit fahren Sie zur Schule?
5. Wieviel ist neunzehn und einunddreißig?
6. Um wieviel Uhr verlassen Sie dieses Zimmer?
7. Der wievielte ist heute?
8. Der wievielte war gestern?
9. Der wievielte ist morgen?
10. In welcher Jahreszeit schwimmen die meisten Leute am liebsten?

H. *Write a paragraph in German describing seeing someone off on a trip. Tell what time you got up, had breakfast, left the house, and arrived at the ship or airplane. Relate what the friends and relatives did, how they took leave, and how you went home.*

I. *Write a paragraph in German describing your activities on a typical school day including answers to the following questions.*

1. Um wieviel Uhr stehen Sie morgens auf?
2. Wann frühstücken Sie?
3. Was trinken Sie?
4. Was machen Sie am Vormittag? Am Nachmittag? Am Abend?
5. Wann essen Sie zu Mittag? zu Abend?
6. Um wieviel Uhr gehen Sie zu Bett?

UNIT 21

A. UNITS OF SPEECH AND VOCABULARY

I. Study and Practice Aloud.

Er geht zur Mutter; er geht zu ihr.	He's going to his mother's (house); he's going to her (house).
Sie fährt zum Postamt.	She's driving to the post office.
Es ist ein Gast im Zimmer.	There is a guest in the room.
Es sind heute hundert Gäste im Hotel.	There are a hundred guests in the hotel today.
Es gibt jetzt viel Regen.	There is a lot of rain now.
Die Uhr hat eben eins geschlagen.	The clock just struck one.
Ich trete in das Hotel ein.	I am entering the hotel.
Man tut so etwas nicht.	Such things are not done. (One doesn't do such things.)
Es ist	There is ....
Es sind	There are ....
Es gibt	There is, there are ....

der Gast, ̈e	the guest	**der Preis, -e**	the prize
das Heer, -e	the army	**der Regen**	the rain
das Hotel, -s	the hotel	**der Schnee**	the snow
die Mannschaft, -en	the team	**der Soldat, -en, -en**	the soldier
der Offizier, -e	the officer	**das Spiel, -e**	the game
das Postamt, ̈er	the post office	**die Uhr, -en**	the clock, watch

man	one, they, people	eben	just
hundert	a hundred, (one) hundred	**erstens**	in the first place
gesund	healthy, in good health, well	**zweitens**	in the second place
krank	sick	**drittens**	in the third place
müde	tired	**zu** + *dat.*	to
		verkaufen	to sell

eintreten (tritt ein)	**trat ein**	**ist eingetreten**	to enter
gewinnen	**gewann**	**gewonnen**	to win
schlagen (schlägt)	**schlug**	**geschlagen**	to strike, beat

II. Oral Practice. Repeat the pattern sentence. Then substitute the items listed below in the appropriate places. Repeat the entire sentence with each substitute item, changing the verb where necessary.

a. Er geht zur Mutter; er geht zu ihr.

1. Der Soldat
2. Der Offizier
3. Unser Gast
4. Mein Freund
5. Mein Vetter
6. Der Student

b. Sie fährt zum Postamt.

1. Die Verkäuferin
2. Der Offizier
3. Der Soldat
4. Die Soldaten
5. Die Offiziere
6. Die Gäste

c. Es ist ein Gast im Zimmer.

1. Soldat
2. Offizier
3. Mann
4. Stuhl
5. Tisch
6. Buch

d. Es sind heute hundert Gäste im Hotel.

1. Reisende
2. Leute
3. Deutsche
4. Engländer
5. Amerikaner
6. Männer

e. Es gibt jetzt viel Regen.

1. _____ im April _____
2. _____ im Frühling _____
3. _____ heute _____
4. _____ Schnee.
5. _____ im Januar _____
6. _____ im Winter _____

f. Die Uhr hat eben eins geschlagen.

1. _____ 11 _____
2. _____ 7 _____
3. _____ 4 _____
4. _____ schlägt _____
5. _____ 6.
6. _____ 9.
7. _____ 2.
8. _____ 12.

g. Ich trete ins Hotel ein.

1. Er _____
2. Die Lehrerin _____

3. _____ das Gebäude _____   5. Die Soldaten _____
4. Der Soldat _____   6. _____ den Laden _____

h. Man tut so etwas nicht.
   1. _____ sagt _____   3. _____ ißt _____
   2. _____ schreibt _____   4. _____ macht _____

i. Die Mannschaft gewinnt das Spiel.
   1. _____ den Preis.   4. Er _____
   2. _____ hat _____ gewonnen. 5. Wir haben _____
   3. Sie (*sing.*) _____   6. Unsere Verwandten _____

j. Erstens bin ich müde und zweitens habe ich kein Geld.
   1. _____ ist er _____   5. _____ ihr Vater _____
       hat er _____
   2. _____ ist mein Vetter _____ 6. _____ nicht gesund _____
   3. _____ krank _____   7. _____ unser Verwandter _____
   4. _____ sein Onkel _____   8. _____ unser Gast _____

k. Wir verkaufen Uhren.
   1. Die Verkäufer _____   4. _____ ihre Uhr.
   2. Die Verkäuferin _____   5. Die Frau _____
   3. Sie (*sing.*) _____   6. Die Studentin _____

B. MODEL SENTENCES

I. Study each sentence until you can reproduce it correctly.
148. Es gibt viele große Städte in Deutschland.
149. Man spricht Deutsch in Österreich.
150. Er lebe hoch!

148. There are many large cities in Germany.
149. They speak German in Austria.
150. Long may he live!

II. Pattern Practice. Repeat the model sentence. Then substitute the items below in the appropriate places. Repeat the entire sentence with each substitute item.

a. Es gibt viele große Städte in Deutschland.
   1. _____ Frankreich.   4. _____ den Vereinigten Staaten.
   2. _____ England.   5. _____ einige _____
   3. _____ Europa.   6. _____ der Schweiz.

b. Man spricht Deutsch in Österreich.
   1. Deutschland   4. München
   2. der Schweiz   5. Köln
   3. Berlin   6. Heidelberg

c. Er lebe hoch!
   1. Unser Großvater   3. Unsere Tante
   2. Unsere Großmutter   4. Unser Onkel

C. STRUCTURE

1. The ordinal adverbs **erstens** (*in the first place*), **zweitens** (*in the second place*), **drittens** (*in the third place*), and so on, are formed by adding **-ens** to the stem of the ordinal numbers (**der**) **erste** (*the first*), (**der**) **zweite** (*the second*), (**der**) **dritte** (*the third*), and so on.

2. The preposition **zu** (*to*) is used after verbs of motion with nouns or pronouns referring to persons:

> Er geht **zur Mutter;** er geht **zu ihr.**
> *He's going to his mother's (house); he's going to her (house).*

Note that **zur** is the contraction for **zu + der.**

3. **Zu** may also be used after verbs of motion with other nouns:

> Sie fährt **zum Postamt.**
> *She's driving to the post office.*

Note that **zum** is the contraction for **zu + dem.**

4. **Es ist** (*there is*) and **es sind** (*there are*) are used to indicate facts or situations:

a. Es ist ein Gast im Zimmer.
There is a guest in the room.
b. Es sind heute hundert Gäste im Hotel.
There are a hundred guests in the hotel today.

Note that the noun following **es ist** or **es sind** is in the nominative case. **Es ist** is used before a singular noun, **es sind** before a plural noun.

5. **Es gibt** (*there is, there are*) is used for general statements indicating existence and in descriptions of weather conditions:

a. Es gibt viele große Städte in Deutschland.
There are many large cities in Germany.
b. Es gibt jetzt viel Regen.
There is a lot of rain now.

Note that the noun following **es gibt** is an accusative direct object; therefore, the verb (**gibt**) does not change, whether the following noun is singular or plural.

6. The pronoun **man** (*one*) is an indefinite subject referring to people in general. It is frequently equivalent to *they* or *people:*

a. Man tut so etwas nicht.
One doesn't do such things.

b. Man spricht Deutsch in Österreich.
They speak German in Austria.

An active construction with **man** is equivalent to a passive construction in English. The above sentences may also mean:

a. *Such things are not done.*
b. *German is spoken in Austria.*

7. The present subjunctive I of **sagen** (*to say*):

ich sag**e**	wir sag**en**
du sag**est**	ihr sag**et**
er, sie, es sag**e**	sie sag**en**
	Sie sag**en**

The present subjunctive I of almost all other verbs is formed by adding the subjunctive endings to the infinitive stem. The present subjunctive I of **nehmen** (*to take*) is:

ich nehm**e**	wir nehm**en**
du nehm**est**	ihr nehm**et**
er, sie, es nehm**e**	sie nehm**en**
	Sie nehm**en**

The infinitive, the third person singular present indicative, and the third person singular present subjunctive I of typical strong verbs follow:

nehmen	*to take*	er **nimmt**	er **nehme**
lesen	*to read*	er **liest**	er **lese**
fallen	*to fall*	er **fällt**	er **falle**
laufen	*to run*	er **läuft**	er **laufe**
können	*to be able*	er **kann**	er **könne**
müssen	*to have to*	er **muß**	er **müsse**
wollen	*to want*	er **will**	er **wolle**

8. The only verb which is irregular in the present subjunctive I is **sein** (*to be*):

ich **sei**	wir **seien**
du **seist**	ihr **seiet**
er, sie, es **sei**	sie **seien**
	Sie **seien**

9. The present subjunctive I expresses realizable wishes:

Er **lebe** hoch!
Long may he live!

D. EXERCISES

Write the following sentences in German and be able to express them orally.

1. They say the new official will arrive next week.
2. Was there much snow in the winter?
3. We drove to church on Sunday.
4. English is spoken here.
5. In the first place it is too late, in the second place we're tired, and in the third place it isn't interesting.
6. Are your parents well again?
7. There was little rain in the summer.
8. We'll go to our uncle's later.
9. People say this country is very beautiful.
10. Were there steamships a hundred years ago?
11. I rode to school by streetcar.
12. Our relatives came to our house two months ago.
13. There are many children in town today.
14. Please bring these packages to the post office.
15. Her friends and relatives said: "Long may she live!"
16. Your acquaintances have gone to their cousin's (*f.*) house.
17. There is only one table in the kitchen.
18. They say that he is not well.
19. There are many countries in which English is spoken.
20. People believe the team will depart next Saturday.
21. You must come to our house.
22. There were many people on the street yesterday.
23. Many clocks are sold in this store.
24. There is only one Berlin.

E. COMPREHENDING AND SPEAKING

I. Repeat the following after your instructor (or the speaker) and study thoroughly.

EINE ALTE STADT

Peter und Walter hatten genug Zeit, um sich Frankfurt anzusehen.[1] Walter hatte schon im Flugzeug in einem Buch über Frankfurt gelesen, und nun begann er, seinem Freund einen Vortrag zu halten.[2] „Frankfurt ist eine sehr alte Stadt", fing er an.[3] „In ihrer be-

[1]um sich Frankfurt anzusehen	to look Frankfurt over	[2]einen Vortrag halten	to give a lecture
		[3]an-fangen	to begin

German Information Center

Frankfurt: Im Zentrum der Stadt

Frankfurt: Goethes Studierzimmer

5   rühmten[4] Kathedrale krönte[5] man im Mittelalter[6] die deutschen
Kaiser. Johann Wolfgang von Goethe, der größte deutsche Dichter,[7]
wurde hier geboren.[8] Heute hat die Stadt ungefähr 800 000 Einwohner[9]
und ist eines der wichtigsten Verkehrs- und Handelszentren[10] der
Bundesrepublik[11] Deutschland."

10   „Es lebe der Herr Professor!"[12] lachte Peter. „Gott sei Dank[13]
war dein Vortrag so kurz. Nun wollen wir aber in die Stadt gehen und
alle berühmten Häuser sehen!"

Zuerst suchten die beiden ein einfaches[14] Hotel und fragten den
Wirt,[15] wo das Goethehaus sei. Der Wirt zeigte ihnen auf der Karte
15   den Weg,[16] und bald standen sie vor einem kleineren Haus, das auf
einer Tafel[17] Goethes Namen trug.

„Du, das sieht aber neu aus", sagte Peter enttäuscht.[18]

„Es gibt nicht mehr viele alte Häuser in Frankfurt", entgegnete[19]
Walter. „Der Krieg[20] hat ungefähr achtzig Prozent der Stadt zerstört.[21]
20   Die meisten ‚alten' Häuser sind rekonstruiert."

„Sind Sie Amerikaner?" fragte ein Herr, der neben ihnen stand.
„Dann wollen Sie vielleicht die Paulskirche[22] dort drüben sehen. Dort
tagte[23] das erste deutsche Parlament, und 1963 hat Präsident Kennedy
in dieser Kirche eine berühmte Rede gehalten.[24]

II. Beantworten Sie die folgenden Fragen auf deutsch!

1. Warum hielt Walter einen Vortrag?
2. Was machte man im Mittelalter in der Kathedrale von Frankfurt?
3. Wer war Goethe?
4. Wie viele Einwohner hat Frankfurt heute?
5. Ist Frankfurt eine wichtige Stadt?
6. Was wollten die zwei Studenten in der Stadt sehen?
7. Wie sah das Goethehaus aus?
8. Warum war Peter enttäuscht?
9. Wann hat Präsident Kennedy in der Paulskirche eine Rede gehalten?

[4]berühmt	famous	[13]Gott sei Dank	Thank God
[5]krönen	to crown	[14]einfach	modest
[6]im Mittelalter	in the Middle Ages	[15]der Wirt, -e	innkeeper
[7]der Dichter, -	poet	[16]der Weg, -e	way
[8]wurde . . .		[17]die Tafel, -n	plaque
geboren	was . . . born	[18]enttäuscht	disappointed
[9]der Einwohner, -	inhabitant	[19]entgegnen	to reply
[10]eines der	one of the most im-	[20]der Krieg, -e	war
wichtigsten	portant centers of	[21]zerstören	to destroy
Verkehrs- und	traffic and com-	[22]die Paulskirche	St. Paul's Church
Handelszentren	merce	[23]tagen	to meet
[11]die		[24]eine Rede halten	to deliver a speech
Bundesrepublik	Federal Republic		
[12]Es lebe der Herr	Long live the pro-		
Professor!	fessor!		

UNIT 22

A. UNITS OF SPEECH AND VOCABULARY

I. Study and Practice Aloud.

Der Arm tut mir weh.	My arm hurts.
Die Augen tun ihm weh.	His eyes hurt.
Es regnet.	It's raining.
Die Sonne scheint.	The sun is shining.
Es scheint richtig zu sein.	It seems to be right.
Ich denke an ihn.	I'm thinking of him.
Er hat aufgehört zu lesen.	He has stopped reading.
acht Tage	a week

der Arm, -e	the arm	der Kugel-	the ball-point
das Auge, -n	the eye	schreiber, -	pen
der Fuß, ⸚e	the foot	der Rat	the advice
der Kopf, ⸚e	the head	der Teil, -e	the part
das Ohr, -en	the ear	möglich	possible
der Mond, -e	the moon	richtig	right, correct
die Sonne, -n	the sun	stark	strong
der Stern, -e	the star	wichtig	important
der Sturm, ⸚e	the storm	brauchen	to need
der Wind, -e	the wind	regnen	to rain
die Antwort, -en	the answer	suchen	to look for, seek

aufhören	hört auf	aufgehört	to stop

denken	dachte	gedacht	to think
scheinen	schien	geschienen	to shine, to seem
verbringen	verbrachte	verbracht	to spend (*time*)

II. Oral Practice. Repeat the pattern sentence. Then substitute the items listed below in the appropriate places. Repeat the entire sentence with each substitute item, changing the verb where necessary.

a. Der Arm tut mir weh.
1. Der Fuß _____
2. Der Kopf _____
3. Das Ohr _____
4. _____ ihr_____
5. Der Kopf _____
6. Der Fuß _____
7. _____ ihm _____
8. Der Arm _____
9. Der Kopf_____
10. Der Fuß _____

b. Die Augen tun ihm weh.
1. Die Ohren _____
2. Die Arme _____
3. Die Füße _____
4. _____ ihr _____
5. Die Arme _____
6. Die Ohren _____
7. Die Augen _____
8. _____ meinem Vater _____

c. Es regnet jetzt.
1. _____ schon.
2. _____ hat _____ geregnet.
3. _____ gestern _____
4. _____ vorgestern _____

d. Scheint die Sonne jetzt?
1. _____ der Mond _____?
2. _____ schon?
3. _____ die Sterne_____?
4. _____ der Mond und die Sterne _____?

e. Es scheint richtig zu sein.
1. _____ möglich _____
2. _____ wichtig _____
3. Das _____
4. _____ möglich _____
5. _____ richtig _____
6. Dies _____
7. _____ möglich _____
8. _____ wichtig _____
9. Die Antwort _____
10. _____ richtig _____

f. Ich denke an ihn.
1. _____ Sie.
2. Er _____
3. _____ hat _____ gedacht.
4. Wir _____
5. _____ ihn _____
6. _____ unsere Freunde _____

g. Er hat aufgehört zu lesen.
1. schreiben
2. arbeiten
3. rauchen
4. singen
5. lachen
6. schwimmen

h. Sie verbringt acht Tage in Köln.
1. Ich _____
2. _____ habe _____ verbracht.

3. _____ Heidelberg _____   5. Der Arzt _____
4. Wir _____   6. _____ Berlin _____

i. Ich brauche Rat.

1. Er _____   5. _____ einen Kugelschreiber.
2. Die Jungen _____   6. Das Mädchen _____
3. Die Kinder _____   7. Der Schüler _____
4. Das Kind _____   8. _____ Kugelschreiber.

j. Sie sucht einen Kugelschreiber.

1. _____ ein Buch.   4. Mein Vetter _____
2. _____ Bleistifte.   5. Seine Freundin _____
3. _____ Rat.   6. Ihre Kusine _____

k. Wir lesen diesen Teil des Buches.

1. Die Jungen _____   4. _____ haben _____ gelesen.
2. Sie (*pl.*) _____   5. Mein Bruder _____
3. _____ der Geschichte.   6. Seine Tante _____

B. MODEL SENTENCES

I. Study each sentence until you can reproduce it correctly.

151. Er sagte, er besuche seinen Freund.
Er sagte, er besuchte seinen Freund.
152. Sie sagten, er gehe nach Hause.
Sie sagten, er ginge nach Hause.
153. Er glaubte, sie seien reich.
Er glaubte, sie wären reich.
154. Sie schrieb, sie habe Frau Meyer gesehen.
Sie schrieb, sie hätte Frau Meyer gesehen.
155. Sie glaubten, daß ihr kleiner Bruder nach Hause gegangen sei.
Sie glaubten, daß ihr kleiner Bruder nach Hause gegangen wäre.
156. Ich sagte, daß meine Verwandten fortgegangen sind.
157. Er wußte, daß sein Vetter in Deutschland war.
158. Er sagt, es hat geregnet.
159. Sie fragten, ob mein Bruder das Buch habe.
Sie fragten, ob mein Bruder das Buch hätte.
160. Der Lehrer sagte, der Schüler solle die Aufgabe lernen.
Der Lehrer sagte, der Schüler sollte die Aufgabe lernen.

151. He said he was visiting his friend.
152. They said he was going home.
153. He believed they were rich.
154. She wrote she had seen Mrs. Meyer.
155. They believed that their little brother had gone home.

156. I said (that) my relatives have gone away.
157. I knew that his cousin was in Germany.
158. He says it rained.
159. They asked whether my brother had the book.
160. The teacher said that the pupil should study the lesson.

II. Pattern Practice. Repeat the model sentence. Then substitute the items listed below in the equivalent part of the model sentence. Repeat the entire sentence with each substitute item.

a. Er sagte, er besuche seinen Freund.
   1. begrüße   3. suche
   2. brauche   4. höre

b. Sie sagten, er ginge nach Hause.
   1. der Junge   4. die Frau
   2. der Mann   5. das Mädchen
   3. der Arzt   6. das Kind

c. Er glaubte, sie wären reich.
   1. arm   3. jung
   2. alt   4. krank

d. Sie schrieb, sie hätte Frau Meyer gesehen.
   1. besucht   3. getroffen
   2. angerufen   4. geschrieben

e. Sie glaubten, ihr kleiner Bruder wäre nach Hause gegangen.
   1. gekommen   3. gefahren
   2. gelaufen   4. zurückgegangen

f. Ich sagte, daß meine Verwandten fortgegangen sind.
   1. abgefahren   3. angekommen
   2. aufgestanden   4. hereingekommen

g. Er wußte, daß sein Vetter in Deutschland war.
   1. wohnte   3. studierte
   2. arbeitete   4. blieb

h. Er sagt, es hat geregnet.
   1. Sein Freund   4. Das Kind
   2. Meine Freundin   5. Das Mädchen
   3. Sie (*sing.*)   6. Die Frau

i. Sie fragten, ob mein Bruder das Buch hätte.
   1. den Kugelschreiber   4. den Bleistift
   2. die Uhr   5. das Paket
   3. das Gepäck   6. das Papier

j. Der Lehrer sagte, der Schüler sollte die Aufgabe lernen.
   1. machen   3. schreiben
   2. lesen   4. bringen

C. STRUCTURE

1. Present subjunctive II forms of most weak verbs are identical with those of the past indicative. The present subjunctive II of **sagen** (*to say*):

ich **sagte**	wir **sagten**
du **sagtest**	ihr **sagtet**
er, sie, es **sagte**	sie **sagten**
	Sie **sagten**

2. The present subjunctive II of strong verbs is formed by adding the subjunctive endings to the stem of the past indicative, plus umlaut if the vowel can be umlauted:

INFINITIVE		PAST INDICATIVE	PRESENT SUBJUNCTIVE II
bleiben	*to stay*	ich **blieb**	ich **bliebe**
sehen	*to see*	ich **sah**	ich **sähe**
ziehen	*to pull*	ich **zog**	ich **zöge**
werden	*to become*	ich **wurde**	ich **würde**

The present subjunctive II of **sein** (*to be*) and **werden** (*to become*):

ich **wäre**	ich **würde**
du **wärest**	du **würdest**
er, sie, es **wäre**	er, sie, es **würde**
wir **wären**	wir **würden**
ihr **wäret**	ihr **würdet**
sie **wären**	sie **würden**
Sie **wären**	Sie **würden**

3. The subjunctive is used in indirect discourse (that is, when reporting someone's statement without quoting it). Indirect discourse is usually introduced by verbs of saying, thinking, or believing. Use the present subjunctive I or II in indirect discourse when the direct statement was or would be in the present tense.

Direct Discourse:

> Er sagte: „Ich besuche meinen Freund."
> *He said: "I'm visiting my friend."*

Indirect Discourse:

> Er sagte, er besuche seinen Freund.
> Er sagte, er besuchte seinen Freund.
> *He said he was visiting his friend.*

Direct Discourse:

> Sie sagten: „**Er geht nach Hause.**"
> *They said: "He's going home."*

Indirect Discourse:

> Sie sagten, **er gehe nach Hause.**
> Sie sagten, **er ginge nach Hause.**
> *They said he was going home.*

Direct Discourse:

> Er sagte: „**Sie sind reich.**"
> *He said: "They are rich."*

Indirect Discourse:

> Er glaubte, **sie seien reich.**
> Er glaubte, **sie wären reich.**
> *He believed they were rich.*

Note 1: Subjunctive I forms are generally preferred in formal and literary usage, subjunctive II forms in informal writing and in conversation, except when such forms are identical with the past indicative, in which case subjunctive I forms are favored. Forms of **sei** are also common in conversation.

Note 2: The conjunction **daß** (*that*) may be used with a corresponding change in word order. For example:

> Er sagte, **daß er seinen Freund besuche.**
> Sie sagten, **daß er nach Hause ginge.**
> Er glaubte, **daß sie reich wären.**

4. The past subjunctive I consists of the present subjunctive I of **haben** or **sein** plus past participle. The past subjunctive I of **sehen** (*to see*) and **kommen** (*to come*):

> ich **habe gesehen**
> du **habest gesehen**
> er, sie, es **habe gesehen**
> wir **haben gesehen**
> ihr **habet gesehen**
> sie **haben gesehen**
> Sie **haben gesehen**

ich **sei gekommen**
du **seist gekommen**
er, sie, es **sei gekommen**
wir **seien gekommen**
ihr **seiet gekommen**
sie **seien gekommen**
Sie **seien gekommen**

The past subjunctive II consists of the present subjunctive II of **haben** or **sein** plus past participle. The past subjunctive II of **sehen** (*to see*) and **kommen** (*to come*) follows:

ich **hätte gesehen**
du **hättest gesehen**
er, sie, es **hätte gesehen**
wir **hätten gesehen**
ihr **hättet gesehen**
sie **hätten gesehen**
Sie **hätten gesehen**

ich **wäre gekommen**
du **wärest gekommen**
er, sie, es **wäre gekommen**
wir **wären gekommen**
ihr **wäret gekommen**
sie **wären gekommen**
Sie **wären gekommen**

5. The past subjunctive I or II is used in indirect discourse when the direct statement was or would be in the past, compound past, or past perfect indicative:

Direct Discourse:

Sie schrieb: „**Ich sah meine Kusine.**"
Sie schrieb: „**Ich habe meine Kusine gesehen.**"
Sie schrieb: „**Ich hatte meine Kusine gesehen.**"

Indirect Discourse:

Sie schrieb, **sie habe ihre Kusine gesehen.**
Sie schrieb, **sie hätte ihre Kusine gesehen.**
She wrote she had seen her cousin.

Direct Discourse:

Sie schrieben: „**Unser Vater ging nach Hause.**"
Sie schrieben: „**Unser Vater ist nach Hause gegangen.**"
Sie schrieben: „**Unser Vater war nach Hause gegangen.**"

Indirect Discourse:

> Sie glaubten, **daß ihr Vater nach Hause gegangen sei.**
> Sie glaubten, **daß ihr Vater nach Hause gegangen wäre.**
> *They believed that their father had gone home.*

6. In indirect discourse, the verb is usually in the indicative (a) if the introductory verb is in the first person; (b) if the introductory verb expresses certainty; (c) if the indirect statement reports an obvious fact:

a. **Ich** sagte, daß meine Verwandten **fortgegangen sind.**
    I said that my relatives have gone away.
b. Er **wußte,** daß sein Vetter in Deutschland **war.**
    He knew that his cousin was in Germany
c. Er sagt, **es hat geregnet.**
    He says it rained.

7. The subjunctive may also be used in indirect questions introduced by **ob** (*whether, if*) and following an introductory verb in a past tense:

> Sie fragten, **ob mein Bruder das Buch habe.**
> Sie fragten, **ob mein Bruder das Buch hätte.**
> *They asked whether my brother had the book.*

8. The subjunctive of **sollen** (*to be supposed to*) is used in indirect commands:

> Der Lehrer sagte, **der Schüler solle die Aufgabe lernen.**
> Der Lehrer sagte, **der Schüler sollte die Aufgabe lernen.**
> *The teacher said the pupil should study the lesson.*

D. EXERCISES

Write the following sentences in German and be able to express them orally.

1. Our teacher (*f.*) believes that you have studied very little.
2. His grandmother said he should take a trip to Switzerland.
3. Her girl friends knew that she hadn't gone to town.
4. Your uncle said that he had not seen my father.
5. He said that his feet hurt.
6. We believe they live at the seashore.
7. My brother asked our father whether he might go to the movies.
8. Her cousin (*f.*) writes that she is spending a month in the country.
9. My friends wrote that I should visit them next week.
10. All her acquaintances said that she had departed yesterday morning.
11. We don't know where they work now.

12. His aunt thought that she had to go home.
13. The little girls say that their ears hurt.
14. The salesman asked whether we had seen his friend.
15. I believe you are wrong.
16. Do you know if the boys are at home?
17. They said that our aunt was looking for us.
18. The pupil (*f.*) thought that she could stay in town all afternoon.
19. She knows that her relatives have been living here for a month.
20. The travelers wrote that it had rained all summer in Austria.
21. They said that the sun was shining.
22. The students believed that the professor had gone away two weeks ago.
23. They asked whether it had stopped raining.
24. The boy's sister said that he shouldn't eat the cake.

E. COMPREHENDING AND SPEAKING

I. Repeat the following after your instructor (or the speaker) and study thoroughly.

DIE RHEINREISE

Kein anderer Fluß in Deutschland ist so berühmt wie der Rhein, und in keiner anderen Gegend[1] von Deutschland entstanden[2] so viele Sagen und Märchen[3] wie im romantischen Rheinland.

Unsere zwei Freunde fuhren von Frankfurt zuerst nach Koblenz
5 an den Rhein, weil sie gehört hatten, daß man in der Nähe[4] den Felsen[5] sehen könne, auf dem die Loreley, eine berühmte Gestalt[6] der deutschen Sage, ihre Lieder[7] gesungen habe. Auf einem Dampfer fuhren sie am Felsen vorbei,[8] den Rhein hinauf. Ein deutscher Herr, der auch auf dem Schiff fuhr, erzählte ihnen die Geschichte der
10 schönen Loreley, die die Schiffer ins Verderben gelockt habe.[9]

An beiden Ufern[10] des Rheins wachsen Reben.[11] ,,Aus dieser Gegend kommt unser bester Wein", sagte der Herr. ,,Sie haben sicher schon Johannisberger, Markobrunner oder Niersteiner getrunken!

[1]die Gegend, -en	region	[7]das Lied, -er	song
[2]entstehen	to originate	[8]am Felsen vorbei	past the rock
[3]Sagen und Märchen	legends and fairy tales	[9]die die Schiffer ins Verderben gelockt habe	who is said to have lured boatmen to disaster
[4]in der Nähe	in the vicinity, close by	[10]das Ufer, -	bank
[5]der Felsen, -	rock	[11]wachsen Reben	grape vines grow
[6]die Gestalt, -en	figure		

Am Loreley-Felsen

Der Rhein bei Bad Godesberg

An beiden Ufern des Rheins wachsen Reben.

Speyer: Im Dom sind die Gräber von acht deutschen Kaisern des Mittelalters.

German Information Center

Nicht? Dann müssen Sie unbedingt[12] ein Glas Rheinwein versuchen."
15 Damit lud er Peter und Walter in das Schiffsrestaurant ein,[13] wo sie eine Flasche Johannisberger tranken.

Am Morgen hatte es geregnet, aber jetzt schien die Sonne. Peter und Walter genossen[14] die Reise und stellten dem deutschen Herrn viele Fragen.

20 „Wie heißt die alte Stadt dort?" wollte Walter wissen.

„Das ist Speyer", entgegnete der Herr. „In dieser Stadt sind die Gräber[15] von acht deutschen Kaisern des Mittelalters."

In Speyer hörte die Rheinreise für die beiden Amerikaner auf. Sie dankten dem Herrn für seine interessanten Erklärungen[16] und
25 gingen dann in die Stadt, wo sie die Nacht verbrachten."

II. Beantworten Sie die folgenden Fragen auf deutsch!

1. Welches ist der berühmteste Fluß in Deutschland?
2. Warum fuhren die zwei Freunde nach Koblenz?
3. Wer war die Loreley?
4. Was erzählte der Herr den Studenten?
5. Nennen Sie drei deutsche Rheinweine!
6. Zu was lud der Herr Peter und Walter in das Schiffsrestaurant ein?
7. Hatte die Sonne den ganzen Tag geschienen?
8. Was kann man in Speyer sehen?
9. Wozu blieben die zwei Studenten in Speyer?

[12]**unbedingt**	absolutely	[15]**das Grab, ⸗er**	grave
[13]**ein-laden**	to invite	[16]**die Erklärung,**	explanation
[14]**genießen**	to enjoy	**-en**	

UNIT 23

A. UNITS OF SPEECH AND VOCABULARY

I. Study and Practice Aloud.

Sie biegen um die Ecke.	They are turning around the corner.
Dieser Weg führt zum Bahnhof.	This is the way to the railroad station.
Sie lernt ihre Nachbarin kennen.	She becomes acquainted with (meets) her neighbor (*f.*)
Er bleibt auf dieser Seite stehen.	He is stopping on this side.
Der Rhein fließt von Süden nach Norden.	The Rhine flows from south to north.
Der Hafen liegt in dieser Richtung.	The harbor is in this direction.
an der Ecke	on the corner, at the corner
um die Ecke	around the corner
nach rechts	to the right
nach links	to the left
von Osten	from (the) east
nach Westen	to (the) West
auf dieser Seite	on this side
auf der anderen Seite	on the other side
weit von hier	far from here

der Bahnhof, ⸚e	the railroad station	der Hafen, ⸚	the harbor
		der Platz, ⸚e	the square, place
die Ecke, -n	the corner	das Rathaus, ⸚er	the city hall

(*206*)

die Richtung, -en	the direction	**der Zahn, ⸚e**	the tooth
der Weg, -e	the way, road	**der Zahnarzt, ⸚e**	the dentist
der Norden	the north	**tausend**	a thousand, one
der Osten	the east		thousand
der Süden	the south	**links**	(on the) left
der Westen	the west	**rechts**	(on the) right
der Kellner, -	the waiter	**weit**	far
die Nachbarin,	the neighbor	**um**+*acc.*	around
-nen	(*f.*)	**bezahlen**	to pay
die Schuld, -en	the debt	**führen**	to lead
die Seite, -n	the side, page		

biegen	**bog**	**ist gebogen**	to turn
fließen	**floß**	**ist geflossen**	to flow
kennenlernen	**lernte kennen**	**kennengelernt**	to become acquainted with, meet (*for the first time*)
stehenbleiben	**blieb stehen**	**ist stehengeblieben**	to stop
sterben	**starb**	**ist gestorben**	to die
ziehen	**zog**	**gezogen**	to pull

II. Oral Practice. Repeat the pattern sentence. Then substitute the items listed below in the appropriate places. Repeat the entire sentence with each substitute item, changing the verb where necessary.

a. Sie biegen um die Ecke.

1. Wir _____
2. Er _____
3. _____ nach rechts.
4. Die Nachbarin _____

5. _____ ist _____ gebogen.
6. _____ nach links _____
7. Der Zahnarzt_____
8. Der Kellner _____

b. Dieser Weg führt zum Bahnhof.

1. Platz
2. Rathaus
3. Hafen

4. Postamt
5. Hotel
6. Garten

c. Sie lernt ihre Nachbarin kennen.

1. _____ meine _____
2. _____ hat _____ kennengelernt
3. Meine Schwester _____

4. Ich _____
5. _____ unsere _____
6. Wir _____

d. Er bleibt auf dieser Seite stehen.

1. Sie (*sing.*) _____
2. Ich _____
3. Wir _____
4. _____ auf der anderen
  Seite _____

5. _____ sind _____ stehengeblieben.
6. _____ an der Ecke _____
7. Das Auto _____
8. Die Straßenbahn _____

e. **Der Rhein fließt von Süden nach Norden.**

   1. Der Fluß _____
        4. _____ von Osten nach Westen.

   2. Die Flüsse _____
        5. Mehrere Flüsse _____

   3. Einige Flüsse _____
        6. Welche Flüsse _____?

f. **Der Hafen liegt in dieser Richtung.**

   1. Das Rathaus
        4. Die Universität

   2. Der Bahnhof
        5. Die Schule

   3. Der Platz
        6. Die Stadt

g. **Ist der Platz weit von hier?**

   1. das Rathaus
        4. der Bahnhof

   2. die Universität
        5. die Schule

   3. der Hafen
        6. die Kirche

h. **Sie bezahlen ihre Schulden.**

   1. _____ seine _____
        4. _____ den Kellner _____

   2. Er _____
        5. Ich _____

   3. _____ hat _____ bezahlt.
        6. Wir _____

i. **Der Zahnarzt zieht den Zahn.**

   1. _____ ihren _____
        4. _____ seinen _____

   2. _____ meinen _____
        5. _____ seine Zähne _____

   3. _____ hat _____ gezogen.
        6. _____ unsere Zähne _____

B. MODEL SENTENCES

I. Study each sentence until you can reproduce it correctly.

161. **Er sagte, daß er den Brief schreiben würde.**
162. **Wenn er jetzt käme, würde ich mit ihm reden.**
163. **Wenn sie in die Stadt gingen, könnten sie einige Sachen kaufen.**
164. **Wenn er sie nicht gesehen hätte, wäre er fortgegangen.**
165. **Dächte er öfter an seine Mutter, (so) würde er ihr schreiben.**
166. **Wäre er nur reich!**
167. **Wenn sie das gewußt hätten!**
168. **Ich möchte eine Tasse Kaffee haben.**
169. **Dürfte ich um ein Stück Kuchen bitten?**
170. **Könnten Sie mir dieses Buch zeigen?**
171. **Würden Sie heute mit mir ins Kino gehen?**

161. He said that he would write the letter.
162. If he came now, I'd talk with him.
163. If they went to town, they could buy a few things.
164. If he hadn't seen her, he would have gone away.
165. If he thought about his mother more often, he would write to her.
166. If he were only rich!

167. If they had known that!
168. I'd like to have a cup of coffee.
169. May I ask for a piece of cake?
170. Could you show me that book?
171. Would you go to the movies with me today?

II. Pattern Practice. Repeat the model sentence. Then substitute the items listed below in the equivalent part of the model sentence. Repeat the entire sentence with each substitute item.

a. **Er sagte, daß er den Brief schreiben würde.**

   1. lesen   4. suchen
   2. schicken   5. brauchen
   3. bringen   6. zerreißen

b. **Wenn er jetzt käme, würde ich mit ihm reden.**

   1. der Nachbar   4. sein Freund
   2. der Herr   5. ihr Verwandter
   3. der Junge   6. mein Bekannter

c. **Wenn sie in die Stadt gingen, könnten sie einige Sachen kaufen.**

   1. die Nachbarn   4. die Mädchen
   2. die Nachbarinnen 5. meine Schwestern
   3. die Frauen   6. unsere Eltern

d. **Wenn er sie nicht gesehen hätte, wäre er fortgegangen.**

   1. abgefahren   3. hinausgegangen
   2. hereingekommen   4. zurückgekommen

e. **Dächte er öfter an seine Mutter, so würde er ihr schreiben.**

   1. der Mann   4. der Schüler
   2. mein Vetter   5. der Junge
   3. unser Nachbar   6. der Student

f. **Wäre er nur reich!**

   1. mein Vater   3. ihr Onkel
   2. mein Großvater   4. sein Bruder

g. **Wenn sie das gewußt hätten!**

   1. Ihre Eltern   4. die Kinder
   2. die Nachbarn   5. die Jungen
   3. die Lehrer   6. die Mädchen

h. **Ich möchte eine Tasse Kaffee haben.**

   1. eine Tasse Tee   4. ein Glas Wasser
   2. eine Flasche Milch 5. ein Stück Kuchen
   3. ein Glas Milch   6. ein Stück Käse

i. **Dürfte ich um ein Stück Kuchen bitten?**

   1. ein Stück Käse   4. ein Glas Wasser
   2. eine Tasse Tee   5. ein Glas Milch
   3. eine Tasse Kaffee 6. eine Flasche Milch

j. Könnten Sie mir dieses Buch zeigen?
1. bringen   3. reichen
2. schicken   4. geben

k. Würden Sie heute mit mir ins Kino gehen?
1. ins Restaurant   3. in die Stadt
2. ins Postamt   4. in die Kirche

C. STRUCTURE

1. The future subjunctive consists of the present subjunctive I of **werden** and the infinitive of the main verb. The future subjunctive of **gehen** (*to go*):

ich **werde gehen**

du **werdest gehen**

er, sie, es **werde gehen**

wir **werden gehen**

ihr **werdet gehen**

sie **werden gehen**

Sie **werden gehen**

The conditional consists of the present subjunctive II of **werden** and the infinitive of the main verb. The conditional of **gehen** (*to go*):

ich **würde gehen**

du **würdest gehen**

er, sie, es **würde gehen**

wir **würden gehen**

ihr **würdet gehen**

sie **würden gehen**

Sie **würden gehen**

2. The future subjunctive and the conditional are used in indirect discourse to express future time:

> Er sagte, **daß er den Brief schreiben würde (werde).**
> *He said that he would write the letter.*

The future subjunctive is generally preferred in formal literary style, the conditional in conversation and informal writing.

3. Some irregular weak verbs umlaut the past-stem vowel in the present subjunctive II:

	INFINITIVE	PAST INDICATIVE	PRESENT SUBJUNCTIVE II
bringen	*to bring*	**brachte**	**brächte**
denken	*to think*	**dachte**	**dächte**
dürfen	*may, to be permitted to*	**durfte**	**dürfte**
haben	*to have*	**hatte**	**hätte**
können	*can, to be able to*	**konnte**	**könnte**
mögen	*to like, care to*	**mochte**	**möchte**
müssen	*must, to have to*	**mußte**	**müßte**
wissen	*to know*	**wußte**	**wüßte**

Irregular weak verbs with **a** as the stem vowel in the past indicative, have **e** in the present subjunctive II:

kennen	*to know*	**kannte**	**kennte**

4. There are two types of conditions, real and unreal (also called "contrary to fact"). Real conditions are expressed in the indicative:

> **Ich werde meinen Onkel sehen, wenn er uns besucht.**
> *I'll see my uncle if he visits us.*

Unreal conditions are expressed in the subjunctive. If the condition refers to the present or future, the present subjunctive II is used in the **wenn** clause and the conditional in the result clause:

> **Wenn er jetzt käme, würde ich mit ihm reden.**
> *If he came now, I'd talk with him.*

5. For **haben, sein,** and modal auxiliaries, the present subjunctive II is preferred to the conditional in the result clause:

   a. Wenn er mehr arbeitete, **hätte** er mehr Geld.
     If he worked more, he would have more money.
   b. Wenn ich länger schliefe, **wäre** ich nicht so müde.
     If I slept longer, I wouldn't be so tired.
   c. Wenn sie in die Stadt gingen, **könnten** sie einige Sachen kaufen.
     If they went to town, they could buy a few things.

6. The past subjunctive II is generally used in both clauses referring to the past:

> Wenn er sie nicht **gesehen hätte, wäre** er **fortgegangen.**
> *If he hadn't seen her, he would have gone away.*

7. The conjunction **wenn** (*if*) may be omitted in unreal conditional clauses; the finite verb then stands before the subject:

Dächte er öfter an seine Mutter, (so) **würde** er ihr schreiben.
If he thought of his mother more often, he would write her.

Note: With the omission of **wenn,** the main clause if often introduced by **so** or **dann.**

The examples cited in paragraphs 4, 5, and 6 may be expressed as follows with no change in meaning:

Käme er jetzt, (dann) **würde** ich mit ihm **reden.**
Gingen sie in die Stadt, (so) **könnten** sie einige Sachen **kaufen.**
Hätte er sie nicht **gesehen,** (so) **wäre** er **fortgegangen.**

8. The **wenn**-clause of an unreal condition may be used alone to express an unrealizable wish:

    a. **Wenn er nur reich wäre!**
      If he were only rich!
    b. **Wenn sie das gewußt hätten!**
      If they had known that!

Note that in these expressions, too, the conjunction **wenn** may be omitted; the finite verb is then placed before the subject:

    c. **Wäre er nur reich!**
      Were he only rich!
    d. **Hätten sie das gewußt!**
      Had they known that!

9. The present subjunctive II or the conditional is used in expressions of polite request:

    a. **Ich möchte** eine Tasse Kaffee **haben.**
      I'd like to have a cup of coffee.
    b. **Dürfte ich** um ein Stück Kuchen **bitten?**
      May I ask for a piece of cake?
    c. **Könnten Sie** mir dieses Buch **zeigen?**
      Could you show me that book?
    d. **Würden Sie** heute mit mir ins Kino **gehen?**
      Would you go to the movies with me today?

D. EXERCISES

Write the following sentences in German and be able to express them orally.

   1. We would have driven to the seashore, if the sun had been shining.

2. Would you like to have a glass of milk?
3. Were we only ten years younger!
4. If the children don't go to school, they won't learn much.
5. Could your uncle do something for us?
6. She wouldn't be so tired if she worked less.
7. Would your family go to the seashore with us next summer?
8. If the little girl ran faster, she'd be home at half past two.
9. If he only had a new car!
10. If her friends had come to the station, they would have seen her there.
11. If only he hadn't lost his money!
12. I am hungry and could eat a piece of cake.
13. My dentist would like to take a trip to England.
14. If you paid the bill, we could leave the restaurant.
15. Might we have more coffee?
16. If you knew my relatives, you would help them.
17. My grandmother would have died if my grandfather had not called the doctor.
18. Had the plane only left one hour later!
19. If the streetcar stops at the corner, we can get on.
20. We would read the books if he brought them to us.
21. My friends would like to buy a new house.
22. I'll see you in school on Monday if you are there.

E. COMPREHENDING AND SPEAKING

I. Repeat the following after your instructor (or the speaker) and study thoroughly.

„OH, ALTE BURSCHENHERRLICHKEIT[1] . . .“

„Wenn Herr Wagner hier wäre, würde er uns die ganze Stadt Heidelberg zeigen“, sagte Peter am anderen Tag bedauernd.[2] „Er war ja Student hier und kennt sicher jeden Winkel[3] in der Stadt.“

„Wie wäre es, wenn wir zuerst zur Universität gingen?“ meinte Walter. „Vielleicht werden wir einen Studenten finden, der uns umherführen[4] könnte.“

Sie hatten Glück.[5] Werner, ein netter[6] Student, hatte die beiden beobachtet und fragte sie, ob er ihnen die Stadt und die Universität

[1]**Oh, alte Burschen- herrlichkeit . . .**	O, old glory of student life	[3]**der Winkel, -**	corner
		[4]**umher-führen**	to show around
		[5]**Sie hatten Glück.**	They were in luck.
[2]**bedauernd**	regretfully	[6]**nett**	nice, friendly

Heidelberg

Leon Deller from Monkmeyer

Studenten in Heidelberg

10   zeigen solle. „Heidelberg ist die älteste Universität Deutschlands", so
      begann er, „sie wurde im 14. Jahrhundert gegründet."[7]

      „Wo ist der ‚campus'?" fragte Peter.

      „Deutsche Universitäten haben normalerweise[8] keinen ‚campus',
      da die Studenten gewöhnlich ein Zimmer bei einer Familie in der
      Stadt haben oder bei den Eltern wohnen. Auch sonst[9] sind die deut-
15   schen Universitäten in vielen Einrichtungen[10] anders als die ameri-
      kanischen, aber das kann ich nicht in wenigen Worten erklären."

      Walter fragte: „Warum tragen Sie eine blaue Mütze[11] auf dem
      Kopf?"

      „Ich gehöre zu einer Burschenschaft.[12] Viele Studenten gehören
20   dazu.[13] Man trifft sich einmal in der Woche,[14] trinkt Bier, singt Lieder
      und diskutiert."

      „Könnten Sie uns vielleicht das Schloß[15] Heidelberg zeigen?"
      fragte Peter.

      „Gerne", antwortete Werner und führte die zwei Freunde auf
25   einen Hügel,[16] von wo aus man die ganze Stadt sehen konnte. Im
      Schloß sahen sie das weltberühmte Faß,[17] in dem zweihunderttausend
      Flaschen Wein Platz haben. Vor dem Schloß sangen deutsche Studen-
      ten mit farbigen[18] Mützen ein altes Studentenlied:

                „Oh, alte Burschenherrlichkeit!
30   Wohin bist du entschwunden . . .?"[19]

II. Beantworten Sie die folgenden Fragen auf deutsch!

1. Was würde Herr Wagner tun, wenn er hier wäre?
2. Warum kennt Herr Wagner jeden Winkel der Stadt?
3. Wen hofft Walter bei der Universität zu finden?
4. Wer zeigt ihnen Heidelberg?
5. Wann wurde die Universität Heidelberg gegründet?
6. Wo wohnen die deutschen Studenten gewöhnlich?
7. Warum hat Werner eine blaue Mütze auf dem Kopf?
8. Was tut man in einer deutschen Burschenschaft?
9. Wie viele Flaschen Wein haben Platz im Heidelberger Faß?

[7]**sie wurde im 14. Jahrhundert gegründet**	it was founded in the 14th century	[13]**gehören zu**	to belong to
		[14]**Man trifft sich einmal in der Woche.**	They meet once a week.
[8]**normalerweise**	normally		
[9]**sonst**	otherwise	[15]**das Schloß, ⸗sser**	castle
[10]**in vielen Einrichtungen anders als**	in many respects different from	[16]**der Hügel, -**	hill
		[17]**das Faß, ⸗sser**	barrel
		[18]**farbig**	colored
[11]**die Mütze, -n**	cap	[19]**Wohin bist du entschwunden?**	Where have you disappeared to?
[12]**die Burschenschaft, -en**	fraternity		

UNIT 24

A. UNITS OF SPEECH AND VOCABULARY

I. Study and Practice Aloud.

er wäscht sich	he's washing himself
ich ziehe mich an	I'm dressing (myself)
Sie setzt sich an den Tisch.	She sits down at the table.
Sie sieht sich den Kölner Dom an.	She's looking at the Cathedral of Cologne.
Ich hole eine Medizin von der Apotheke.	I'm getting medicine from the drugstore.

der Anzug, ⸗e	the suit	die Medizin	the medicine
die Apotheke, -n	the pharmacy, drugstore	der Schaffner, -	the conductor
		der Schuh, -e	the shoe
der Berg, -e	the mountain	der Speise-	the dining car
die Dame, -n	the lady	wagen, -	
der Dom, -e	the cathedral	mich	myself
das Dorf, ⸗er	the village	dich	yourself
das Geschäft, -e	the shop, business	sich	himself, herself, itself, yourself, yourselves, themselves
der Geschäfts- mann, Geschäfts-	the businessman		
leute		uns	ourselves
		euch	yourselves
das Gesicht, -er	the face	Kölner	(of) Cologne

(*217*)

| **bestellen** | to order | **sich setzen** | to sit down |
| **holen** | to fetch, get | | |

sich ansehen (sieht sich an)	sah sich an	angesehen	to look at
anziehen	zog an	angezogen	to dress, put on
waschen (wäscht)	wusch	gewaschen	to wash

II. Oral Practice. Repeat the pattern sentence. Then substitute the items listed below in the appropriate places. Repeat the entire sentence with each substitute item, changing the verb where necessary.

a. Er wäscht sich.
1. Der Junge _____
2. Die Frau _____
3. Das Kind _____
4. _____ hat _____ gewaschen.
5. Die Kinder _____
6. Sie (*pl.*) _____

b. Ich ziehe mich an.
1. Wir _____ uns _____
2. _____ haben _____ angezogen.
3. Ich _____ mich _____
4. Er _____ sich _____
5. Das Kind _____
6. Der Junge _____

c. Sie setzt sich an den Tisch.
1. Die Dame _____
2. Der Geschäftsmann _____
3. Der Schaffner _____
4. _____ hat _____ gesetzt.
5. Die Dame _____
6. Die Damen _____
7. Die Geschäftsleute _____
8. Die Schaffner _____

d. Sie sieht sich den Kölner Dom an.
1. Die Dame _____
2. _____ hat _____ angesehen.
3. _____ das Dorf
4. Die Damen _____
5. _____ den Berg _____
6. Sie _____

e. Ich hole eine Medizin von der Apotheke.
1. Wir_____
2. Die Dame _____
3. Sie (*sing.*) _____
4. Der Schaffner _____
5. Der Geschäftsmann _____
6. Er _____

f. Sie bestellen Kaffee im Speisewagen.
1. Die Reisenden _____
2. Wir _____
3. _____ Tee _____
4. _____ Eis _____
5. Die Geschäftsleute _____
6. Die Damen _____

g. Er kauft einen blauen Anzug im Geschäft.
1. Mein Vetter _____
2. _____ zwei neue Anzüge _____
3. _____ schwarze Schuhe _____
4. _____ braune Schuhe _____

B. MODEL SENTENCES

I. Study each sentence until you can reproduce it correctly.

172. **Ich wasche mir das Gesicht.**
173. **Der Junge zieht sich die Schuhe an.**
174. **Unsere Freunde begrüßen sich.**
175. **Der Kellner fragte, ob ich Kaffee bestellt hätte.**
176. **Der Junge tat, als ob er krank wäre.**
177. **Sollte es morgen regnen, (so) bleiben wir hier.**

172. I am washing my face.
173. The boy is putting on his shoes.
174. Our friends are greeting one another.
175. The waiter asked whether I had ordered coffee.
176. The boy acted as if he were sick.
177. Should it rain tomorrow, we'll stay here.

II. Pattern Practice. Repeat the model sentence. Then substitute the following items below in the equivalent part of the model sentence. Repeat the entire sentence with each substitute item.

a. Ich wasche mir das Gesicht.

1. den Kopf	3. die Füße
2. die Hände	4. die Ohren

b. Der Junge zieht sich die Schuhe an.

1. Der Mann	4. Die Frau
2. Der Reisende	5. Das Mädchen
3. Er	6. Das Kind

c. Unsere Freunde begrüßen sich.

1. Meine Verwandten	4. Die Reisenden
2. Seine Bekannten	5. Die Damen
3. Die Geschäftsleute	6. Die Lehrerinnen

d. Der Kellner fragte, ob ich Kaffee bestellt hätte.

1. Tee	4. Bier
2. Kuchen	5. Käse
3. Wein	6. Fleisch

e. Der Junge tat, als ob er krank wäre.

1. Der Mann	4. Sein Onkel
2. Mein Bruder	5. Der Reisende
3. Ihr Vetter	6. Der Geschäftsmann

f. Sollte es morgen regnen, so bleiben wir hier.

1. dort	4. im Hotel
2. bei Ihnen	5. im Geschäft
3. zu Hause	6. in der Stadt

C. STRUCTURE

1. Verbs whose subject and object refer to the same person are called "reflexive":

   a. **Ich ziehe mich an.**
      I am dressing myself.
   b. **Wir waschen uns.**
      We are washing ourselves.
   c. **Er wäscht sich.**
      He is washing himself.

2. The complete present tense of **sich waschen:**

ich **wasche mich**	*I am washing myself, am getting washed*
du **wäscht dich**	*you are washing yourself, are getting washed*
er, sie, es **wäscht sich**	*he, she, it is washing himself, herself, itself, is getting washed*
wir **waschen uns**	*we are washing ourselves, are getting washed*
ihr **wascht euch**	*you are washing yourselves, are getting washed*
sie **waschen sich**	*they are washing themselves, are getting washed*
Sie **waschen sich**	*you are washing yourself (yourselves), are getting washed*

   Note that accusative reflexive pronouns are identical with accusative personal pronouns, except in the third person singular and plural and with the **Sie** form, which have a distinctive reflexive pronoun, **sich.**

3. If a reflexive verb has a direct noun object, the reflexive pronoun is in the dative case:

   a. Ich wasche **mir** das Gesicht.
      I am washing my face.
   b. Sie sieht **sich** den Kölner Dom an.
      She is looking at the Cologne Cathedral.
   c. Der Junge zieht **sich** die Schuhe an.
      The boy is putting on his shoes.

   Note that the reflexive pronoun **sich** is the same for both the dative and the accusative. Other dative reflexive pronouns are identical with dative object pronouns (**mir, dir, uns, euch**).

4. The reflexive pronoun may be used in a reciprocal sense:

   Unsere Freunde **begrüßen sich.**
   Our friends are greeting one another.

Note: **Einander** (*one another*) normally replaces **sich** in a reciprocal sense to avoid ambiguity:

> Die Kinder **waschen einander.**
> *The children are washing one another.*

Compare:

> Die Kinder **waschen sich.**
> *The children are washing themselves.*

5. Adjectives formed from names of cities end in **-er** and are not inflected. Such adjectives are always capitalized:

> Die Dame hat sich den **Kölner** Dom angesehen.
> *The lady looked at the Cologne Cathedral.*

6. Clauses introduced by **als ob** (*as if*) use the subjunctive:

> Der Junge tat, **als ob er krank wäre.**
> *The boy acted as if he were sick.*

Note: **Ob** may be omitted and its omission indicated by placing the inflected verb before the subject. The above sentence may be expressed as follows:

> Der Junge tat, **als wäre er krank.**

7. The present subjunctive II of **sollen** (in the sense of *should*) is used with a dependent infinitive in a **wenn**-clause. Note that **wenn** may be omitted, with the finite verb standing first:

  a. Wenn es morgen regnen sollte, bleiben wir hier.
    If it should rain tomorrow, we'll stay here.
  b. Sollte es morgen regnen, so bleiben wir hier.
    Should it rain tomorrow, we'll stay here.

D. EXERCISES

Write the following sentences in German and be able to express them orally.

1. His friends acted as if they didn't know him.
2. The students (*f.*) are telling each other stories.
3. Hans, put on your new suit.
4. Should you come to town at twelve o'clock, you can eat lunch with us.
5. The children ate as if they had not eaten the whole day.
6. Did your parents see the Heidelberg railroad station?
7. The boys have already dressed, haven't they?

Landschaft im Schwarzwald

8. Please sit down at the table, Mr. Schmidt.
9. Our relatives visited the Cologne Cathedral.
10. Her girl friend had sat down on a chair in the kitchen.
11. Children, wash your hands before you come into the dining room.
12. The conductor said that the train was leaving soon.
13. Will we see one another next Thursday?
14. The traveler wants to look at the Hamburg City Hall.
15. After the little girl had washed her hands, she went into the dining room.
16. The conductor thought that the traveler had lost his baggage.
17. Should your brother arrive tomorrow, bring him to our house.
18. Her niece said that the lady had gotten medicine in the drug store.
19. The teachers (*f.*) and the pupils (*f.*) greeted one another.
20. Richard, wash your face now.
21. His girl friend wrote that her cousins (*f.*) had taken a long trip.
22. My grandfather believed that I was going to the movies.
23. The salesgirl asked if we wanted to buy something.
24. As we were sitting down, some other guests were standing up.

E. COMPREHENDING AND SPEAKING

I. Repeat the following after your instructor (or the speaker) and study thoroughly.

BAHNFAHRT[1] NACH MÜNCHEN

Nachdem sich die beiden amerikanischen Studenten Heidelberg angesehen hatten, stiegen sie am nächsten Tag in einen Zug, der sie nach München bringen sollte.

5   Sie setzten sich im Speisewagen an einen freien Tisch und bestellten sich ein Frühstück. Während der Fahrt schauten sie zum Fenster hinaus und betrachteten die Landschaft.[2]

Der Zug fuhr durch eine waldige[3] Gegend. „Wir sind in der Nähe des Schwarzwalds",[4] sagte Peter, der eine Landkarte[5] auf den Knien[6] hatte, zu Walter. Aber dieser tat, als ob er schliefe.

10   „Wo wird der Zug das nächste Mal halten?"[7] fragte Peter den Schaffner, der sich eben näherte.

„In Ulm, mein Herr", sagte der Schaffner freundlich.

Ein Herr am nächsten Tisch hatte sich umgedreht.[8] „Da sind

[1]die Bahnfahrt, -en	train ride	[5]die Landkarte, -n	map
[2]die Landschaft	landscape	[6]das Knie, -	knee
[3]waldig	wooded	[7]halten	to stop
[4]der Schwarzwald	Black Forest	[8]sich um-drehen	to turn around

Ulm an der Donau

ja meine Amerikaner!" sagte er erfreut[9] zu der Dame, die neben ihm

15 saß. Peter erkannte[10] den deutschen Herrn, den sie auf ihrer Rheinreise getroffen hatten. Der Herr begrüßte die beiden und stellte sie
seiner Frau vor.[11] Er erzählte ihr, daß man sich auf einem Rhein-
dampfer getroffen und auf der Fahrt von Koblenz nach Speyer
kennengelernt habe.

20 „Fahren Sie auch nach München?" fragte die Dame. Peter und
Walter nickten.[12]

„Da müssen Sie uns aber besuchen!" sagte sie.

Die beiden Studenten bedankten sich für die Einladung[13] und
plauderten den ganzen Nachmittag mit dem sympathischen Ehepaar.[14]

II. Beantworten Sie die folgenden Fragen auf deutsch!

1. Wohin sollte der Zug die beiden Studenten bringen?
2. Was taten sie zuerst während der Fahrt?
3. Wo fährt der Zug durch?
4. Wer sagt Peter, wo der Zug das nächste Mal halten wird?
5. Wer sitzt am nächsten Tisch?
6. Woher kannten Peter und Walter den Herrn?
7. Was erzählte der Herr seiner Frau?
8. Warum nickten Peter und Walter?
9. Was taten die beiden Studenten den ganzen Nachmittag?

[9]**erfreut**	happily	[13]**bedankten sich**	thanked them for
[10]**erkennen**	to recognize	**für die**	the invitation
[11]**stellte sie seiner**	introduced them to	**Einladung**	
Frau vor	his wife	[14]**das sympathische**	the likeable couple
[12]**nicken**	to nod	**Ehepaar**	

UNIT 25

A. UNITS OF SPEECH AND VOCABULARY

I. Study and Practice Aloud.

Die Fahrt macht mir Freude.	The ride gives me pleasure.
Die Schüler nennen ihre Namen.	The pupils give their names.
Hat sie ein Paar Handschuhe?	Does she have a pair of gloves?
Er spricht ein paar Worte.	He is speaking a few words.
Diese Wörter haben dieselbe Bedeutung.	These words have the same meaning.
Ich sende es mit der Post.	I am sending it by mail.
Was bedeutet der Satz?	What does the sentence mean?
Er beeilt sich nie.	He never hurries.
Selbst sein Feind glaubt ihm.	Even his enemy believes him.
Haben Sie es je versucht?	Have you ever tried it?

die Bedeutung, -en	the meaning	der Satz, ∺e	the sentence
		der Wald, ∺er	the forest, woods
die Fahrt, -en	the ride	das Wort	the word
der Feind, -e	the enemy	die Worte	the words (*in a phrase*)
die Freude, -n	the joy, pleasure		
der Handschuh, -e	the glove	die Wörter	the words (*individually*)
der Name, -ns, -n	the name	ein paar	a few
das Paar, -e	the pair, couple	derselbe,	the same
die Post	the mail, post office	dieselbe, dasselbe	

(*226*)

selbst	even, self	**bedeuten**	to mean, signify
je	ever	**sich beeilen**	to hurry
nie	never	**versuchen**	to try

brennen	**brannte**	**gebrannt**	to burn
nennen	**nannte**	**genannt**	to name
rennen	**rannte**	ist **gerannt**	to run
senden	**sandte**	**gesandt**	to send

II. Oral Practice. Repeat the pattern sentence. Then substitute the items below in the appropriate places. Repeat the entire sentence with each substitute item, changing the verb where necessary.

a. Die Fahrt macht mir Freude.
1. uns
2. ihnen
3. den Leuten
4. ihr
5. ihm
6. meinem Freund

b. Die Schüler nennen ihre Namen.
1. Die Schülerinnen
2. Die Kinder
3. Die Mädchen
4. Die Jungen
5. Die Studenten
6. Die Studentinnen

c. Hat sie ein Paar Handschuhe?
1. _____ die Verkäuferin _____?
2. _____ das Mädchen _____?
3. _____ der Junge _____?
4. Trägt _____?
5. _____ Schuhe?
6. _____ das Kind _____?
7. _____ es _____?
8. _____ Sie _____?

d. Er spricht ein paar Worte.
1. Der Student
2. Der Professor
3. Der Junge
4. Der Schüler
5. Die Schülerin
6. Die Lehrerin

e. Diese Wörter haben dieselbe Bedeutung.
1. Einige
2. Mehrere
3. Beide
4. Manche

f. Ich sende es mit der Post.
1. Er _____
2. Sie (*sing.*) _____
3. _____ hat _____ geschickt.
4. Seine Tante _____
5. Der Zahnarzt _____
6. Meine Nachbarin _____

g. Was bedeutet der Satz?
1. _____ dieser Satz?
2. _____ der andere Satz?
3. _____ dieses Wort?
4. _____ das andere Wort?
5. _____ die Wörter?
6. _____ diese Wörter?

h. Er beeilt sich nie.

1. Der Arzt _____
2. Meine Kusine _____
3. _____ hat _____ beeilt.

4. Der Junge _____
5. Das Kind _____
6. Die Kinder _____

i. Selbst sein Feind glaubt ihm.

1. _____ ihr Feind _____ ihr.
2. _____ mein Feind _____ mir.
3. _____ meine Feinde _____

4. _____ haben _____ geglaubt.
5. _____ seine Feinde _____ ihm _____
6. _____ ihre Feinde _____ ihnen.

j. Haben Sie es je versucht?

1. _____ ihre Verwandten _____?
2. _____ das _____?
3. _____ Ihr Onkel _____?

4. _____ es _____?
5. _____ unser Vetter _____?
6. _____ das _____?

k. Das ist derselbe Handschuh.

1. derselbe Satz
2. derselbe Wald
3. dasselbe Paar
4. dasselbe Buch

5. dieselbe Post
6. dieselbe Medizin
7. derselbe Kugelschreiber
8. dieselbe Geschichte

l. Es brennt.

1. Das Postamt _____
2. Der Wald _____

3. _____ hat gebrannt.
4. Die Wälder _____

m. Er rennt in den Wald.

1. Der Junge
2. Die Schülerin
3. Sie (*sing.*)

4. _____ ist _____ gerannt.
5. Das Mädchen _____
6. Das Kind _____

B. MODEL SENTENCES

I. Study each sentence until you can reproduce it correctly.

178. **Die Wörter „Samstag" und „Sonnabend" haben dieselbe Bedeutung.**
179. **Das Buch hat mit diesen Worten geendet.**
180. **Wir sind mit einem jungen Paar gereist.**
181. **Er ist mit ein paar Freunden angekommen.**
182. **Mein Großvater hat es selbst getan.**
183. **Ich selbst habe sie gesehen.**
184. **Seine Geschichten waren nie kurz.**
185. **Hans war nie mein Feind.**
186. **Ihr Kind ist nie gerne in die Schule gegangen.**
187. **Sie ruft mich nie an.**

178. The words "Samstag" and "Sonnabend" have the same meaning.
179. The book ended with these words.
180. We traveled with a young couple.
181. He arrived with a couple of friends.
182. My grandfather did it himself.
183. I myself saw them.
184. His stories were never short.
185. Hans was never my enemy.
186. Her child never liked to go to school.
187. She never calls me up.

II. Pattern Practice. Repeat the model sentence. Then substitute the items below in the appropriate places. Repeat the entire sentence with each substitute item.

a. Die Wörter „Samstag" und „Sonnabend" haben dieselbe Bedeutung.
1. bevor und ehe
2. schicken und senden
3. rennen und laufen
4. eintreten und hereinkommen

b. Das Buch hat mit diesen Worten geendet.
1. Die Geschichte
2. Die Aufgabe
3. Der Satz
4. Der Lehrer

c. Wir sind mit einem jungen Paar gereist.
1. Meine Freunde
2. Unsere Verwandten
3. Seine Bekannten
4. Ihre Eltern
5. Seine Kinder
6. Meine Kusinen

d. Er ist mit ein paar Freunden angekommen.
1. Bekannten
2. Verwandten
3. Männern
4. Schülern
5. Kindern
6. Jungen

e. Mein Großvater hat es selbst getan.
1. Mein Neffe
2. Sein Sohn
3. Ihr Enkel
4. Meine Schwester
5. Das Mädchen
6. Das Kind

f. Ich selbst habe sie gesehen.
1. gehört
2. geschickt
3. genommen
4. gebracht
5. getragen
6. besucht

g. Seine Geschichten waren nie kurz.
1. _____ lang.
2. _____ interessant.
3. Ihre Geschichten _____
4. Ihre Bücher _____
5. _____ gut.
6. Seine Bücher _____

h. Hans war nie mein Feind.
1. unser Feind.
2. ihr Feind.
3. sein Feind.
4. sein Freund.
5. ihr Freund.
6. mein Freund.

i. Ihr Kind ist nie gerne in die Schule gegangen.

1. Sein Vetter _____   4. Seine Großmutter _____
2. Meine Schwester _____   5. Ihre Tante _____
3. _____ in die Stadt _____ 6. Die Alte _____

j. Sie ruft mich nie an.

1. Meine Freundin   4. Meine Schwester
2. Sein Onkel   5. Mein Vater
3. Ihr Verwandter   6. Mein Freund

C. STRUCTURE

1. **Der Name** (*the name*) adds **-ns** for the genitive singular, **-n** for all other forms:

	SINGULAR	PLURAL
NOMINATIVE	der Name	die Namen
GENITIVE	des Namens	der Namen
DATIVE	dem Namen	den Namen
ACCUSATIVE	den Namen	die Namen

Other nouns with endings like **der Name** are **der Gedanke** (*the thought*), **der Glaube** (*the belief*), **der Friede** (*peace*), and **der Wille** (*the will*).

2. The verbs **brennen** (*to burn*), **nennen** (*to name*), **rennen** (*to run*), and **senden** (*to send*) form their tenses like **kennen** (*to know*). The principal parts, plus the present subjunctive II, follow:

INFINITIVE	PAST INDICATIVE	PAST PARTICIPLE	PRESENT SUBJUNCTIVE II
brennen	brannte	gebrannt	brennte
nennen	nannte	genannt	nennte
rennen	rannte	ist gerannt	rennte
senden	sandte	gesandt	sendete

3. The adjective **derselbe, dieselbe, dasselbe** (*the same*) consists of the definite article plus **selb-** with weak adjective endings; the combination is always written as one word:

	MASCULINE	FEMININE	NEUTER	PLURAL
NOMINATIVE	derselbe	dieselbe	dasselbe	dieselben
GENITIVE	desselben	derselben	desselben	derselben
DATIVE	demselben	derselben	demselben	denselben
ACCUSATIVE	denselben	dieselbe	dasselbe	dieselben

4. **Das Wort** (*the word*) has two plural forms: **die Wörter** is used for isolated words (a); **die Worte,** for words in context (b):

a. Die Wörter „Samstag" und „Sonnabend" haben dieselbe Bedeutung.

The words "Samstag" and "Sonnabend" have the same meaning.

b. Das Buch hat mit diesen Worten geendet.

The book ended with these words.

5. **Ein Paar** (*a pair, a [married] couple*) is a noun; **ein** is inflected and **Paar** is capitalized:

> Wir sind mit **einem** jungen **Paar** gereist.
> *We traveled with a young couple.*
> Hat sie **ein Paar Handschuhe?**
> *Does she have a pair of gloves?*
> Er kauft sich **zwei Paar Schuhe.**
> *He is buying two pairs of shoes.*

Note that **Paar** used in a quantitative sense is invariable in the plural.

Ein paar (*a few*) is an adjective; **ein** is not inflected and **paar** is written with a small initial letter:

> Er ist mit **ein paar Freunden** angekommen.
> *He arrived with a few friends.*

6. The pronoun **selbst** (*self*) is used (a) after the verb and its objects or (b) immediately after the noun or pronoun it emphasizes:

a. Mein Großvater hat es **selbst** getan.

My grandfather did it himself.

b. Ich selbst habe es gesehen.

I myself saw it.

These two sentences may also be expressed as follows:

> **Der Großvater selbst** hat es getan.
> **Ich** habe es **selbst** gesehen.

Note that **selbst** may mean *myself, himself, herself, itself, themselves, yourself, yourselves, ourselves,* depending on the subject.

7. As an adverb, **selbst** precedes the element it emphasizes and means *even:*

> **Selbst sein Feind** glaubt ihm.
> *Even his enemy believes him.*

8. **Nie** (*never*), like **nicht** (*not*), usually follows the conjugated form of the verb and its objects in main clauses:

a. Er beeilt sich nie.

He never hurries.

Nie, like **nicht,** usually precedes (b) predicate adjectives or (c) predicate nouns, (d) adverbs, prepositional phrases of manner or place, and past participles, (e) infinitives, and (f) separable prefixes.

b. Seine Geschichten waren **nie kurz.**
  His stories were never short.

c. Hans war **nie mein Feind.**
  Hans was never my enemy.

d. Ihr Kind ist **nie gerne in die Schule gegangen.**
  Her child never liked to go to school.

e. Er wird es nie **verstehen.**
  He will never understand it.

f. Sie ruft mich **nie an.**
  She never calls me up.

D. EXERCISES

Write the following sentences in German and be able to express them orally.

1. You gave your name, didn't you?
2. The first words in his letter are very interesting.
3. My grandfather sent the package by mail.
4. His cousins called their daughter Marie.
5. The old man could not write his name.
6. The children are learning a few new words today.
7. The pupils believed that the school was burning.
8. His enemies will never find him.
9. Our uncle was never poor.
10. A few pencils are lying on the table.
11. Her cousin (*f.*) never became a teacher.
12. His grandmother always lived in the same house.
13. Your words gave me much pleasure.
14. My cousin never wears gloves.
15. His grandchildren have never eaten in a restaurant.
16. The boy and his best friend have the same teacher (*f.*).
17. The little girl had run into the house.
18. We never go into that building.
19. Even a child could do that.
20. Can you find her name in the book?
21. Do the pupils know what these two new words mean?
22. Our parents were never here.
23. Her girl friend is buying a pair of shoes.
24. Can you do it yourself?

E. COMPREHENDING AND SPEAKING

I. Repeat the following after your instructor (or the speaker) and study thoroughly.

IM THEATER

Peter und Walter blieben ein paar Tage in München. Der nette Herr, den sie mit seiner Frau im Zug getroffen hatten, lud sie zum Mittagessen ein. Nachher besuchten sie Herrn Hauser, der ihnen ein Hotelzimmer besorgt[1] hatte und sie am Abend ins Theater einlud.

5 Walter war etwas skeptisch darüber, ob sie das deutsche Theaterstück[2] verstehen würden, aber Peter meinte, man kenne nun schon so viele deutsche Wörter, daß man es ruhig wagen könne.[3]

Das Stück, das die zwei Studenten sehen sollten, hieß „Don Carlos". Es sei von Friedrich Schiller, einem der größten deutschen

10 Theaterdichter, sagte Herr Hauser und erklärte in ein paar Worten den Inhalt[4] des Stückes: Es handle von[5] einem spanischen Prinzen, der sich in seine Stiefmutter[6] verliebe.[7] Der Vater des Prinzen, Philipp der Zweite von Spanien, werde deswegen zum Feind seines Sohnes und bestrafe[8] ihn für seine Missetat.[9]

15 Als das Stück begann, hörten Walter und Peter aufmerksam zu.[10] Sie verstanden zwar[11] nicht jedes Wort; dennoch[12] ging es besser, als sie dachten. Selbst der skeptische Walter sagte am Schluß,[13] er habe die Bedeutung der meisten Sätze verstanden, und er klatschte kräftig in die Hände.[14]

II. Beantworten Sie die folgenden Fragen auf deutsch!

1. Wie lange blieben Peter und Walter in München?
2. Wohin lud sie Herr Wagner ein?
3. Worüber war Walter skeptisch?
4. Wie beruhigte[15] ihn Peter?

[1]besorgen	to obtain	[8]bestrafen	to punish
[2]das Theaterstück, -e	play	[9]die Missetat	misdeed
[3]daß man es ruhig wagen könne	that they could take a chance	[10]aufmerksam zuhören	to listen attentively
[4]der Inhalt	content	[11]zwar	to be sure
[5]es handle von	it concerns, deals with	[12]dennoch	nevertheless
[6]die Stiefmutter	stepmother	[13]am Schluß	at the end
[7]sich verlieben in	to fall in love with	[14]klatschte kräftig in die Hände	applauded furiously
		[15]beruhigen	to calm

5. Welches Theaterstück haben die Studenten gesehen?
6. Wer ist der Autor dieses Stückes?
7. Wovon handelt das Stück?
8. Wie haben Walter und Peter zugehört?
9. Haben sie jedes Wort verstanden?

REVIEW UNIT 5

A. *Supply the proper form of the word in parentheses in the space indicated.*

1. (haben) Der Schaffner glaubte, daß ich zuviel Gepäck _____.
2. (ich) Wohin soll ich _____ setzen?
3. (fahren) Hans wußte, daß sein Vater aufs Land _____.
4. (Hamburg) Das ist das _____ Rathaus.
5. (sollen) Die Eltern sagten, daß der Junge essen _____.
6. (Paar) Weißt du, daß sie sieben _____ Handschuhe hat?
7. (brennen) Er sah, daß sein neues Haus _____.
8. (sein) Er sagt, daß es jetzt zwei Uhr _____.
9. (derselbe) Der Junge spielt immer mit _____ Freund.
10. (Wort) Was bedeuten die _____ „Freund" und „Feind"?
11. (können) Das Kind fragte, ob ich ihm ein Glas Wasser geben _____.
12. (Name) Er sollte seinen _____ nicht nennen.
13. (senden) Wir haben ihm zwei Pakete _____.
14. (ein paar) Er hat von _____ _____ Schülern Abschied genommen.
15. (werden) Marie schrieb, daß sie uns morgen sehen _____.
16. (Wort) Seine ersten _____ waren interessant.
17. (haben) Ich glaube, das Kind _____ Durst.
18. (tun) Der Arzt fragte, ob mir die Ohren weh _____.

B. *Supply an appropriate word in the space indicated.*

1. Der Junge hat _____ angezogen.
2. Es _____ viele Wälder in Deutschland.
3. Ich möchte _____ das alte Rathaus ansehen.

4. Beeile _____, Hans!
5. Es _____ kein Wasser im Glas.
6. Setzen wir _____ an den Tisch!
7. Er _____ hoch, hoch, hoch!
8. Ich bin müde und die Augen tun mir _____.
9. Es _____ jetzt drei Studenten hier.
10. _____ er nur jetzt hier!
11. Mein Vetter sagte, daß er sein Buch verloren _____.
12. Es schien, als ob die Kinder krank _____.
13. _____ es warm werden, so werden wir an die See fahren.
14. Seine Freundin schrieb, sie _____ nach Deutschland gereist.
15. _____ ich nur mehr Geld!

C. *Select from the list one item to complete each sentence. Use each word only once.*

an	ein paar	es sind	sie
auf	ein Paar	in	uns
da ist	es gibt	man	zum
da sind	es ist	selbst	zur

1. Spricht _____ Deutsch in Italien?
2. _____ kein Tisch im Schlafzimmer.
3. Der Junge geht _____ Tante.
4. Das Mädchen trägt _____ weiße Handschuhe.
5. Wir haben es _____ gesehen.
6. _____ viel Schnee in Österreich.
7. Sie kommen wieder _____ Hotel zurück.
8. _____ nur drei Lehrer in dieser Schule.

D. *Repeat the following sentences, including* **nie** *in the proper place.*

1. Er bleibt an der Ecke stehen.
2. Das Haus war gelb.
3. Sie wird gerne zum Postamt gehen.
4. Mein Vetter war Arzt.
5. Das Kind hat am Tisch gesessen.

E. *Change the following sentences to unreal conditions.*

1. Wenn der Autobus stehenbleibt, können wir einsteigen.
2. Ich werde Sie in der Schule sehen, wenn Sie da sind.
3. Wenn er Durst hat, trinkt er ein Glas Milch.
4. Hans wird nicht viel lernen, wenn er seine Aufgaben nicht macht.
5. Wenn sie zu Hause waren, besuchten wir sie.

F. *Beantworten Sie die folgenden Fragen auf deutsch!*
1. Tragen Sie jetzt Handschuhe?
2. Womit schickt man Pakete?
3. Welches Wort hat dieselbe Bedeutung wie „rennen"?
4. Wohin setzt man sich, wenn man ißt?
5. Wo kann man Anzüge und Schuhe kaufen?
6. In welcher Richtung fließt der Rhein?
7. Wer zieht Zähne?
8. Regnet es jetzt?
9. Womit sieht man?
10. Wann scheinen die Sterne?
11. In welchen Ländern spricht man Deutsch?
12. Wohin bringt man Briefe?

G. *Recast the following sentences, starting each with* **Sie sagte, daß** ...
1. Jetzt kommt Hans in die Schule.
2. Sein Freund Günther begrüßt ihn und sie gehen zusammen ins Zimmer.
3. Manche Studenten sitzen schon an den Tischen und ihre Bücher liegen unter den Tischen.

H. *Rewrite the following sentences, replacing it with* **Der Mann schrieb, daß** ...
1. Um Viertel vor zwölf kamen sie in New York an.
2. Sie gingen in ein Restaurant.
3. Herr Braun bestellte, nachdem er die Speisekarte hatte.
4. Sie saßen eine Weile.
5. Dann bat Herr Braun um die Rechnung.

I. *Write a paragraph in German, stating where you would like to travel to and what places you would like to see, if you had a lot of money.*

UNIT 26

A. UNITS OF SPEECH AND VOCABULARY

I. Study and Practice Aloud.

Dieses Land besteht aus vielen Staaten.	This country consists of many states.
Er hat viel in seinem Leben erfahren.	He has experienced a lot in his life.
Jeder Mensch liebt die Freiheit und den Frieden.	Every human being loves freedom and peace.
Sie liebt die Natur.	She loves nature.
Ich besitze mein eigenes Haus.	I own my own house.
Sie war ein einziges Mal bei uns.	She was at our house only once.
Sie hat das Kleid einmal getragen.	She wore the dress once.
Jedesmal geht der Junge zu spät fort.	The boy leaves too late every time.
Manchmal kommt er zu früh an.	Sometimes he arrives too early.
Solche Menschen findet man selten.	You seldom find such people.
auf dem Bild	in the picture

das Bild, -er	the picture	**das Kleid, -er**	the dress
die Freiheit	(the) freedom	**die Kleider** *pl.*	the clothes
der Friede, -ns *(no pl.)*	(the) peace	**das Mal, -e**	the time, occasion
das Herz, -ens, -en	the heart	**der Mensch, -en, -en**	the human being

die Natur	(the) nature	bald	soon
der Ring, -e	the ring	selten	seldom
der Staat, -en	the state	einmal	once, one time
das Tier, -e	the animal	zweimal	twice, two times
eigen	own	dreimal	three times
einzig	only, single	jedesmal	every time
solcher,	such	manchmal	sometimes
solche,		lieben	to love, to like
solches			

besitzen	besaß	besessen	to own, possess
bestehen (+ aus + *dat.*)	bestand	bestanden	to consist (of)
erfahren (erfährt)	erfuhr	erfahren	to experience, find out
erkennen	erkannte	erkannt	to recognize

II. Oral Practice. Repeat the pattern sentence. Then substitute the items below in the appropriate places. Repeat the entire sentence with each substitute item, changing the verb where necessary.

a. Dieses Land besteht aus vielen Staaten.

1. _____ mehreren _____   3. _____ fünfzig _____
2. Unser Land _____   4. Amerika _____

b. Er hat viel in seinem Leben erlebt.

1. Der Reisende   4. Seine Tante
2. Mein Großvater   5. Die Lehrerin
3. Ihre Großmutter   6. Die Alte

c. Jeder Mensch liebt die Freiheit und den Frieden.

1. Jeder Amerikaner   3. Jede Engländerin
2. Jeder Engländer   4. Jede Amerikanerin

d. Sie liebt die Natur.

1. Meine Kusine   4. Er
2. Seine Schwester   5. Wir
3. Der Arzt   6. Die meisten Menschen

e. Ich besitze mein eigenes Haus.

1. Er _____ sein _____   4. Ihre Tante _____
2. Der Zahnarzt _____   5. Seine Verwandten _____
3. Die Verkäuferin _____   6. Ihre Eltern _____
   ihr _____

f. Sie war ein einziges Mal bei uns.

1. Seine Freundin   4. Unser Bekannter
2. Unsere Kusine   5. Der Beamte
3. Ihr Vetter   6. Der Schaffner

g. Sie hat das Kleid einmal getragen.

1. Meine Schwester _____   2. Seine Mutter _____

    3. Ihre Tante _____   5. Marie _____
    4. _____ diese Kleider _____   6. Sie (*sing.*) _____

h. Jedesmal geht der Junge zu spät fort.
    1. mein Bruder   4. das Mädchen
    2. sein Sohn   5. die Schülerin
    3. ihr Kind   6. der Schüler

i. Manchmal kommt er zu früh an.
    1. der Soldat   4. ihr Verwandter
    2. der Offizier   5. mein Vetter
    3. sein Bekannter   6. Ihr Enkel

j. Solche Menschen findet man selten.
    1. Kinder   4. Geschäftsleute
    2. Schüler   5. Freunde
    3. Lehrer   6. Verwandten

k. Man erkennt ihn auf dem Bild.
    1. _____ mich _____   4. _____ hat _____ erkannt.
    2. _____ den Mann _____   5. _____ bald _____
    3. _____ den Ring _____   6. Wir _____

B. MODEL SENTENCES

I. Study each sentence until you can reproduce it correctly.

188. **Das Leben ist kurz.**
189. **So eine Stadt haben wir nie gesehen.**
190. **Er lehrt die Schüler die Aufgabe.**
191. **Gestern hätten wir unsere Tante besuchen können.**
192. **Er hätte früher kommen sollen.**

188. Life is short.
189. We've never seen such a city.
190. He is teaching the pupils the lesson.
191. We could have visited our aunt yesterday.
192. He should have come sooner.

II. Pattern Practice. Repeat the model sentence. Then substitute the following items below in the equivalent part of the model sentence. Repeat the entire sentence with each substitute item.

a. Das Leben ist kurz.
    1. interessant   4. wichtig
    2. schwer   5. nicht leicht
    3. teuer   6. nicht lang

b. So eine Stadt haben wir nie gesehen.

1. einen Hut
2. einen Anzug
3. einen Dampfer
4. ein Auto
5. ein Flugzeug
6. ein Bild

c. Er lehrt die Schüler die Aufgabe.

1. die Schülerinnen
2. mich
3. den Schüler
4. ihn
5. die Schülerin
6. Sie

d. Gestern hätten wir unsere Tante besuchen können.

1. sehen
2. treffen
3. finden
4. hören
5. fragen
6. verlassen

e. Er hätte früher kommen sollen.

1. gehen
2. abfahren
3. ankommen
4. fortgehen

C. STRUCTURE

1. The noun **das Herz** (*the heart*) has the following forms:

	SINGULAR	PLURAL
NOMINATIVE	**das Herz**	**die Herzen**
GENITIVE	**des Herzens**	**der Herzen**
DATIVE	**dem Herzen**	**den Herzen**
ACCUSATIVE	**das Herz**	**die Herzen**

2. Das Mal may be used as a noun or combined with cardinal numbers or certain **der**-words to form adverbs:

ein einziges Mal   *only once, one single time*

einmal *once*	**jedesmal** *every time*
zweimal *twice*	**manchmal** *sometimes*
dreimal *three times*	

3. Abstract nouns are used with the definite article:

a. Sie liebt **die Natur.**
She loves nature.

b. Jeder Mensch liebt **die Freiheit** und **den Frieden.**
Every human being loves freedom and peace.

c. Das Leben ist kurz.
Life is short.

4. Singular forms of **solcher, solche, solches** (*such*) are preceded by the indefinite article:

> **Ein solcher Mensch** liebt die Natur.
> *Such a man loves nature.*
> **Solche Menschen** wird man selten finden.
> *You will seldom find such people.*

The uninflected form **solch** plus indefinite article (**solch ein[e]**) is normally replaced by the expression **so ein(e):**

> **So eine Stadt** haben wir nie gesehen.
> *We have never seen such a city.*

5. The verb **lehren** (*to teach*) may have two accusative objects:

> Er lehrt **die Schüler die Aufgabe.**
> *He is teaching the pupils the lesson.*

6. The past subjunctive II of **können** (*can, to be able to*) plus dependent infinitive is equivalent to English *could have* plus past participle:

> Gestern **hätten** wir unsere Tante **besuchen können.**
> *We could have visited our aunt yesterday.*

7. The past subjunctive II of **sollen** (*to be supposed to*) plus dependent infinitive is equivalent to English *should have* plus past participle:

> Er **hätte** früher **kommen sollen.**
> *He should have come sooner.*

D. EXERCISES

Write the following sentences in German and be able to express them orally.

1. We have never been in such a car.
2. Life in Switzerland is interesting.
3. He should have written his mother a letter a week ago.
4. This is the first time.
5. I should have stayed in town.
6. Next time they'll come to our house.
7. She helps her sister quite willingly.
8. You should have told the little girls a story.
9. His heart hurts when he sees that.
10. They say that Germany lies in the heart of Europe.
11. We called her up four times.
12. The children acted as if they were no longer tired.

13. Does your sister wear such expensive hats?
14. All human beings should love peace, shouldn't they?
15. Could your acquaintances have come Saturday evening?
16. I should have known that.
17. Nature is not always beautiful.
18. His girl friend likes to wear such shoes.
19. Did the new teacher teach the children the lesson?
20. His grandfather could have traveled to Spain in the summer.
21. Will he teach his relatives English?
22. I have seen his parents only once.
23. Your relatives visited us twice.
24. Our aunt has taught us German.

E. COMPREHENDING AND SPEAKING

I. Repeat the following after your instructor (or the speaker) and study thoroughly.

IM RESTAURANT

Am nächsten Tag betraten[1] Walter und Peter ein Restaurant, das Herr Hauser ihnen empfohlen[2] hatte. Die Tische waren mit weißen Tischtüchern bedeckt,[3] und auf jedem stand eine Vase mit frischen Blumen. „Du, das sieht teuer aus![4] Wir hätten nicht hierherkommen
5 sollen", sagte Walter kleinlaut.[5]

„Unsinn!"[6] entgegnete Peter, „in so einem typischen deutschen Restaurant haben wir noch nie gegessen. Wir können es uns schon leisten."[7] Damit ging er zu einem Tisch am Fenster.

Ein Kellner eilte herbei,[8] eine weiße Serviette[9] über dem Arm:
10 „Wünschen die Herren zu speisen?"[10]

Peter antwortete: „Jawohl![11] Bitte bringen Sie uns die Speisekarte!"

Als die beiden Freunde die Preise[12] auf der Speisekarte sahen,

[1]betreten	to enter	[7]**Wir können es uns schon leisten.**	We can afford it.
[2]empfehlen	to recommend		
[3]mit weißen Tischtüchern bedeckt	covered with white tablecloths	[8]**Ein Kellner eilte herbei.**	A waiter came hurrying up.
[4]das sieht teuer aus	that looks expensive	[9]die Serviette, -n	napkin
		[10]speisen	to dine
[5]kleinlaut	dejectedly	[11]jawohl	yes, indeed
[6]der Unsinn	nonsense	[12]der Preis, -e	price

Fritz Henle from Monkmeyer

Im Restaurant

wurden ihre Gesichter länger. Walter stieß Peter an: ,,Wollen wir nicht
15 lieber wieder gehen?‘‘

,,Wir hätten früher gehen sollen. Jetzt ist es zu spät.‘‘

Peter rechnete[13] ein paar Minuten, dann sagte er: ,,Es geht, wenn
wir heute abend nur belegte Brote[14] essen.‘‘ Walter war einverstanden.[15]

20 Das Essen bestand aus vier Gängen.[16] Zuerst brachte der Kellner
einen Fisch als Vorspeise.[17] Dann gab es Suppe, Braten,[18] verschie-
dene[19] Gemüse und Salate und zuletzt, als Nachtisch,[20] frische Erd-
beeren mit Schlagsahne.[21] Dazu hatte Peter eine Flasche Rheinwein
bestellt. ,,Man sagt, Rüdesheimer sei der beste‘‘, meinte er. Der Kellner
25 nickte lächelnd.

Ein älterer Herr hatte sich an den nächsten Tisch gesetzt. Walter
faßte Peter am Arm:[22] ,,Ist das nicht . . .?‘‘

Sie erkannten den Schauspieler,[23] der am Abend vorher den König
Philipp im Theater gespielt hatte. Jetzt aß er gerade ein großes Stück
30 Fleisch. ,,König sein macht hungrig‘‘, grinste[24] Peter.

Der Kellner brachte den schwarzen Kaffee und die Rechnung.
Peter gab ihm ein gutes Trinkgeld. ,,Das Essen war sehr gut‘‘, sagte
er zum Kellner. Dieser verbeugte sich[25] lächelnd, half den beiden in
den Mantel und öffnete ihnen die Tür.

II. Beantworten Sie die folgenden Fragen auf deutsch!

1. Wohin gingen Walter und Peter am nächsten Tag?
2. Womit waren die Tische bedeckt?
3. Was stand auf jedem Tisch?
4. Haben Peter und Walter schon früher einmal in einem typischen
   deutschen Restaurant gegessen?
5. Was fragte der Kellner?
6. Warum wurden die Gesichter der Freunde länger?
7. Woraus bestand das Essen?
8. Wer hatte sich an den nächsten Tisch gesetzt?
9. Kannten die beiden Studenten den Herrn?

[13]**rechnen**	to calculate	[21]**frische Erdbeeren**	fresh strawberries
[14]**belegte Brote**	sandwiches	**mit Schlagsahne**	with whipped
[15]**einverstanden**	in agreement		cream
[16]**der Gang, ⸚e**	course	[22]**faßte Peter am**	grabbed Peter's arm
[17]**die Vorspeise, -n**	appetizer	**Arm**	
[18]**der Braten, -**	roast	[23]**der Schauspieler, -**	actor
[19]**verschieden**	various, assorted	[24]**grinsen**	to grin
[20]**als Nachtisch**	for dessert	[25]**sich verbeugen**	to bow

UNIT 27

A. UNITS OF SPEECH AND VOCABULARY

I. Study and Practice Aloud.

Wie ist die Aussicht von der Brücke?	How is the view from the bridge?
Er hat Glück.	He is lucky.
Sie wohnt in der Nähe des Turms.	She lives near the tower.
Sie blicken auf das Schloß.	They glance at the castle.
Der Präsident dient dem Volk.	The President serves the people.
Er erinnert sich an die Stadt.	He remembers the city.
Sie erklärt alles auf französisch.	She explains everything in French.
Die Kunst interessiert mich.	Art interests me.
Mein Freund sammelt Gemälde.	My friend collects paintings.
Bayern ist wegen seiner Berge berühmt.	Bavaria is famous for its mountains.
Das Volk wählt den Präsidenten.	The people elect the President.

die Aussicht, -en	the view	das Glück	the (good) luck
Bayern	Bavaria	der König, -e	the king
die Brücke, -n	the bridge	die Kunst, ⸚e	(the) art
der Franzose, -n, -n	the Frenchman	der Maler, -	the painter
der Italiener, -	the Italian	die Nähe	the vicinity
der Spanier, -	the Spaniard	der Präsident, -en, -en	the president
das Gemälde, -	the painting		

(246)

das Schloß, des Schlosses, die Schlösser	the castle	**ändern**	to change
		blicken + **auf +** *acc.*	to glance (at)
der Turm, ⁓e	the tower	**dienen +** *dat.*	to serve
das Volk, ⁓er	the people, nation	**sich erinnern** **+ an +** *acc.*	to remember
berühmt	famous	**erklären**	to explain
französisch	French	**interessieren**	to interest
italienisch	Italian	**sammeln**	to collect
spanisch	Spanish	**wählen**	to elect
schließen	schloß	**geschlossen**	to close

II. Oral Practice. Repeat the pattern sentence. Then substitute the items below in the appropriate places. Repeat the entire sentence with each substitute item, changing the verbs where necessary.

a. **Wie ist die Aussicht von der Brücke?**
1. vom Turm
2. vom Schloß
3. von den Schlössern
4. von den Türmen
5. von den Brücken
6. von den Fenstern

b. **Er hat Glück.**
1. Der Maler
2. Der Präsident
3. Der König
4. Der Spanier
5. Der Franzose
6. Der Italiener

c. **Sie wohnt in der Nähe des Turmes.**
1. Der Maler _____
2. _____ des Schlosses.
3. Der Franzose _____
4. _____ der Universität.
5. Der Italiener _____
6. _____ des Kinos.
7. Der Spanier _____
8. _____ des Theaters.

d. **Sie blicken auf das Schloß.**
1. Er _____
2. _____ hat _____ geblickt.
3. _____ das Gemälde.
4. Wir _____
5. Die Reisenden _____
6. Sie (*pl.*) _____

e. **Der Präsident dient dem Volk.**
1. _____ hat _____ gedient.
2. _____ hatte _____
3. _____ wird _____ dienen.
4. Der König _____

f. **Er erinnert sich an die Stadt.**
1. _____ das Land.
2. _____ das Dorf.
3. _____ München.
4. Sie _____
5. _____ Berlin.
6. _____ Bayern.

g. **Sie erklärt alles auf französisch.**
1. Der Franzose _____
2. Der Maler _____
3. _____ italienisch.
4. _____ etwas _____

5. Er _____   7. Der Spanier _____

6. _____ spanisch.   8. Der Maler _____

h. Die Kunst interessiert mich.

1. _____ ihn.   4. München _____

2. Bayern _____   5. _____ den Präsidenten.

3. _____ uns.   6. Die Kunst _____

i. Mein Freund sammelt Gemälde.

1. Der König _____   4. Sein Onkel _____

2. Der Präsident _____   5. Der Franzose _____

3. _____ hat _____ gesammelt.   6. Er _____

j. Bayern ist wegen seiner Berge berühmt.

1. Deutschland _____   4. Bayern _____

2. Österreich _____   5. _____ seiner Kunst _____

3. _____ seiner Schlösser _____   6. _____ seines Biers _____

k. Das Volk wählt den Präsidenten.

1. _____ ihn.   3. _____ haben _____ gewählt.

2. Wir _____   4. _____ den Präsidenten _____

B. MODEL SENTENCES

I. Study each sentence until you can reproduce it correctly.

193. Die Geschichte wird von dem Jungen gelesen.

194. Die Tür wurde von der Frau geschlossen.

195. Die Aufgaben werden von den Schülern geschrieben werden.

196. Der Brief ist gestern geschrieben worden.

197. Sein Leben war durch den Krieg geändert worden.

198. Dem Mann wird von seinen Kindern geholfen.

199. Gestern abend wurde viel gesungen.

200. Die Tür war geschlossen.

193. The story is being read by the boy.

194. The door was (being) closed by the woman.

195. The lessons will be written by the pupils.

196. The letter was written yesterday.

197. His life had been changed by the war.

198. The man is being helped by his children.

199. There was a lot of singing yesterday evening.

200. The door was closed.

II. Pattern Practice. Repeat the model sentence. Then substitute the following items in the equivalent part of the model sentence. Repeat the entire sentence with each substitute item.

a. Die Geschichte wird von dem Jungen gelesen.

1. Studenten		4. Arzt
2. Präsidenten		5. Zahnarzt
3. Schüler		6. Verkäufer

b. Die Tür wurde von der Frau geschlossen.

1. Lehrerin	4. Schülerin
2. Verkäuferin	5. Dame
3. Studentin	6. Engländerin

c. Die Aufgaben werden von den Schülern geschrieben werden.

1. Schülerinnern	4. Jungen
2. Kindern	5. meinen Brüdern
3. Mädchen	6. seinen Töchtern

d. Der Brief ist gestern geschrieben worden.

1. Die Aufgabe	3. Der Satz
2. Die Geschichte	4. Das Wort

e. Sein Leben war durch den Krieg geändert worden.

1. Ihr Leben	4. Das Leben in England
2. Unser Leben	5. Das Leben in Deutschland
3. Das Leben in Europa	6. Das Leben in Italien

f. Dem Mann wird von seinen Kindern geholfen.

1. Dem Geschäftsmann	4. Meinem Onkel
2. Dem Verkäufer	5. Meinem Vetter
3. Dem Maler	6. Dem Soldaten

g. Gestern abend wurde viel gesungen.

1. gelacht	4. gespielt
2. geweint	5. geredet
3. gerufen	6. geplaudert

h. Die Tür war geschlossen.

1. Das Fenster	4. Das Geschäft
2. Das Haus	5. Das Restaurant
3. Das Gebäude	6. Der Laden

C. STRUCTURE

1. The passive voice consists of a form of the auxiliary verb **werden** and the past participle of the main verb:

Die Geschichte **wird** manchmal **gelesen.**
The story is occasionally read.
Die Tür **wurde geschlossen.**
The door was (being) closed.
Die Aufgaben **werden geschrieben werden.**
The lessons will be written.

Note the word order of a passive infinitive: **geschrieben werden.**

2. In a passive compound tense, the past participle of **werden** is shortened to **worden** (in place of **geworden**):

   a. Der Brief **ist** gestern **geschrieben worden.** (Note word order.)
   The letter was written yesterday.
   b. Sein Leben **war geändert worden.** (Note word order.)
   His life had been changed.

   Note that **Der Brief ist geschrieben worden** may be equivalent to both of the following:

   The letter was written.
   The letter has been written.

3. The agent (by whom something is done) is expressed as the dative object of the preposition **von** (*by*):

   a. Die Geschichte wird **von dem Jungen** gelesen.
   The story is being read by the boy.
   b. Die Tür wurde **von der Frau** geschlossen.
   The door was (being) closed by the woman.
   c. Die Aufgaben werden **von den Schülern** geschrieben werden.
   The lessons will be written by the pupils.

4. The instrument (by means of which something is done) is expressed as the accusative object of **durch** (*through, by*):

   Sein Leben war **durch den Krieg** geändert worden.
   His life had been changed by the war.

5. A verb requiring a dative object in the active voice also requires a dative object in the passive voice:

   Dem Mann wird von seinen Kindern **geholfen.**
   The man is being helped by his children.

6. Some verbs may be used in the passive voice without an expressed subject:

   Gestern abend **wurde** viel **gesungen.**
   There was a lot of singing yesterday evening.

Es may be used as the impersonal subject of such sentences. The above sentence could also be expressed:

    Es wurde gestern abend viel **gesungen.**

7. The verb **sein** (*to be*) is used with a past participle to express a state or a condition (the result of a passive action):

    a. Die Tür **war geschlossen.**
       The door was closed.

Compare:

    b. Die Tür **wurde geschlossen.**
       The door was (being) closed.

D. EXERCISES

Write the following sentences in German and be able to express them orally.

1. The red car has already been sold.
2. Why is this door closed?
3. Was their life changed by the war?
4. The bill will be paid by his grandfather.
5. The story was being explained by the teacher (*f.*) when the boy came into the room.
6. Their house was already sold.
7. When the airplane left, there was weeping and laughing.
8. The little girl will be dressed by her mother.
9. This bill must be paid tomorow morning.
10. These packages were sent on Saturday.
11. The windows are closed.
12. These pictures have been collected by my uncle.
13. There is a lot of talking in this room now.
14. Nothing was explained to us in English.
15. Will the meal be ordered by your mother or your father?
16. The sentence was changed by the pupil. (*f.*)
17. When will the new president be elected?
18. He was helped by his sons.
19. The yellow gloves were bought by my cousin (*f.*).
20. The notebook is torn to pieces.
21. Many books were collected by his aunt.
22. My package will be sent by mail.
23. The milk was drunk by the little child.
24. His lost book had been found.

Fritz Henle from Monkmeyer

München

E. COMPREHENDING AND SPEAKING

I. Repeat the following after your instructor (or the speaker) and study thoroughly.

EIN STUDENTENFEST[1]

München ist eine Kunststadt und hat viele berühmte Museen. Jedes Jahr wird in Schwabing, einem Stadtteil von München, ein Fest der Kunststudenten gefeiert.[2]

Die beiden Amerikaner, die unter[3] den Münchener Studenten
5 schon viele Freunde gefunden hatten, wurden zu einem solchen Studentenfest eingeladen.

Das Fest wurde in einem schönen alten Haus gefeiert. Walter und Peter hatten jeder eine deutsche Studentin eingeladen und saßen nun mit den Mädchen in einer großen Halle an einem Tisch. Ein
10 Orchester spielte Tanzmusik, und es wurde fröhlich[4] getanzt. Alle Studenten tranken entweder Bier oder Wein. Die meisten trugen farbige Studentenmützen, wie[5] sie die beiden Freunde in Heidelberg gesehen hatten.

Um Mitternacht gingen alle Gäste in den Garten. Ein prächtiges
15 Feuerwerk wurde Punkt zwölf Uhr abgebrannt.[6] Grüne, rote und blaue Raketen explodierten hoch über den Köpfen der Zuschauer.[7] Alle jauchzten[8] und lachten.

Ein Student hatte seine Gitarre mitgebracht. Die Studenten sammelten sich um ihn, und es wurden viele alte deutsche Studen-
20 tenlieder gesungen. Walter und Peter interessierten sich sehr für die Lieder, und die beiden Studentinnen, die mit ihnen gekommen waren, erklärten ihnen was sie bedeuteten.[9] Später tanzten sie.

Um drei Uhr wurden Tombolalose[10] verkauft. Walter gewann einen großen Blumenstock.[11] Alle blickten auf ihn und lachten. Walter
25 wurde rot und schenkte den Blumenstock seiner Tanzpartnerin. Peter hatte bei der Tombola kein Glück.

[1]**das Studentenfest, -e**	students' party	[7]**der Zuschauer, -**	spectator
[2]**feiern**	to celebrate	[8]**jauchzen**	to cheer
[3]**unter**	among	[9]**bedeuten**	to mean
[4]**fröhlich**	merrily	[10]**das Tombolalos, -e**	lottery ticket
[5]**wie**	such as	[11]**Blumenstock, ⸚e**	potted plant
[6]**ein prächtiges Feuerwerk wurde abgebrannt**	a splendid display of fireworks was set off		

Um fünf Uhr spielte das Orchester einen letzten Walzer, und dann zogen[12] alle Studenten singend durch die Straßen bis zu einem Restaurant, wo man frühstückte.

II. Beantworten Sie die folgenden Fragen auf deutsch!

1. Was für eine Stadt ist München?
2. Wo wird jedes Jahr ein Studentenfest gefeiert?
3. Wen hatten Peter und Walter eingeladen?
4. Was taten sie in der großen Halle?
5. Was geschah um Mitternacht?
6. Wer erklärte Peter und Walter die Bedeutung der Lieder?
7. Was wurde um drei Uhr verkauft?
8. Warum wurde Walter rot?
9. Wann spielte das Orchester den letzten Walzer?

[12]**ziehen**   to move

UNIT 28

A. UNITS OF SPEECH AND VOCABULARY

I. Study and Practice Aloud.

es freut mich	I'm glad
es gelingt mir	I succeed
es ist schade	it's a shame
Es klopft.	Someone is knocking (at the door).
Ich amüsiere mich glänzend.	I'm having a splendid time.
Sie sehen gut aus.	You look good.
Wo sind Sie geboren?	Where were you born?
Was für ein Haus haben sie?	What kind of house do they have?
Was für Krawatten kauft er?	What kind of ties is he buying?
Der Präsident läßt ein Museum bauen.	The President is having a museum built.
Er läßt sich ein Haus bauen.	He is having a house built.
mitten in der Stadt	in the middle of town
was für (ein)?	what kind of?

die Krawatte, -n	the necktie	**überall**	everywhere
das Museum, Museen	the museum	**sich amüsieren**	to have a good time
das Werk, -e	the work (of art)	**bauen**	to build
geboren	born	**freuen**	to give pleasure to
glänzend	splendid		
mitten + in + *dat.*	in the middle of	**klopfen**	to knock

(*255*)

aussehen (sieht aus)	sah aus	ausgesehen	to look, appear
gelingen	gelang	ist gelungen	to succeed
lassen (läßt)	ließ	gelassen	to let

II. Oral Practice. Repeat the pattern sentence. Then substitute the elements below in the appropriate places. Repeat the entire sentence with each substitute item, changing the verb where necessary.

a. **Es freut mich.**
  1. uns
  2. Sie
  3. ihn
  4. meinen Vater
  5. seine Mutter
  6. sie (*sing.*)

b. **Es gelingt mir.**
  1. _____ ihr.
  2. _____ uns.
  3. _____ ist _____ gelungen.
  4. _____ ihnen _____
  5. _____ ihm _____
  6. _____ unserem Freund _____

c. **Es ist schade, daß Sie seine Werke nicht gesehen haben.**
  1. _____ wir _____
  2. _____ Dürers _____
  3. _____ ich _____
  4. _____ Sie _____
  5. _____ Ihre Verwandten _____
  6. _____ seine Eltern _____

d. **Es klopft jetzt.**
  1. _____ hat _____ geklopft.
  2. _____ vor einer Stunde _____
  3. _____ vor fünf Minuten _____
  4. _____ um zehn Uhr _____

e. **Ich amüsiere mich glänzend.**
  1. Der Reisende _____
  2. Er _____
  3. _____ überall.
  4. Die Amerikanerin _____
  5. Unsere Bekannten _____
  6. Sie (*pl.*) _____

f. **Sie sehen gut aus.**
  1. Seine Eltern _____
  2. Die Kinder _____
  3. Ihre Freundin _____
  4. _____ hat _____ ausgesehen.
  5. Mein Großvater _____
  6. Seine Großmutter _____

g. **Wo sind Sie geboren?**
  1. _____ Ihre Eltern _____?
  2. _____ Ihre Geschwister _____?
  3. _____ seine Kinder _____?
  4. _____ das Mädchen _____?
  5. _____ das Kind _____?
  6. _____ der Junge _____?

h. **Was für ein Haus haben sie?**
  1. _____ Auto _____?
  2. _____ er?
  3. _____ Ihr Vetter?
  4. _____ Ihre Freunde?

i. **Was für Krawatten kauft er?**
  1. _____ Ihr Freund?
  2. _____ trägt _____
  3. _____ tragen Sie?
  4. _____ wollen _____?

j. Der Präsident läßt ein Museum bauen.

1. Er	3. Man
2. Der König	4. Die Stadt

k. Er läßt sich ein Haus bauen.

1. Mein Onkel	4. Der Professor
2. Seine Tante	5. Der Geschäftsmann
3. Der Zahnarzt	6. Der Arzt

l. Sie wohnt mitten in der Stadt.

1. _____ arbeitet _____	4. Der Mann _____
2. _____ im Zimmer.	5. _____ steht _____
3. Die Frau _____	6. _____ sitzt _____

B. MODEL SENTENCES

I. Study each sentence until you can reproduce it correctly.

201. **Es freut mich, daß Sie hier sind.**
202. **Es ist ihm gelungen, die Aufgabe zu lernen.**
203. **Ich bin in den Vereinigten Staaten geboren.**
204. **Goethe wurde in Frankfurt geboren.**
205. **Mein Onkel hat sich ein neues Haus bauen lassen.**
206. **Sie hatte ihn singen hören.**
207. **Die Mädchen haben ihre Freundinnen kommen sehen.**
208. **Mit was für einem Auto fährt er?**
209. **Unsere Verwandten haben uns im Jahre 1964 (neunzehnhundertvierundsechzig) besucht.**
210. **1963 (neunzehnhundertdreiundsechzig) sind sie nach Deutschland gefahren.**

201. I am glad (that) you are here.
202. He succeeded in learning the lesson.
203. I was born in the United States.
204. Goethe was born in Frankfurt.
205. My uncle had a new house built.
206. She had heard him sing.
207. The girls saw their girl friends coming.
208. In what kind of car is he going?
209. Our relatives visited us in (the year) 1964.
210. They went to Germany in 1963.

II. Pattern Practice. Repeat the model sentence. Then substitute the following items in the appropriate places. Repeat the entire sentence with each substitute item.

a. Es freut mich, daß Sie hier sind.
    1. _____, daß er gesund ist.
    2. _____, daß sie nicht mehr krank ist.
    3. _____, daß ich wieder zu Hause bin.
    4. _____, daß Ihre Freunde gekommen sind.

b. Es ist ihm gelungen, die Aufgabe zu lernen.

1. _____ ihr _____	4. _____ zu lesen.
2. _____ zu schreiben.	5. _____ das Buch _____
3. _____ den Brief _____	6. _____ uns _____

c. Ich bin in den Vereinigten Staaten geboren.

1. Er _____	4. Seine Großmutter _____
2. _____ in der Schweiz _____	5. _____ in Österreich _____
3. _____ in Deutschland _____	6. Mein Großvater _____

d. Goethe wurde in Frankfurt geboren.

1. _____ Deutschland _____	4. _____ Hamburg _____
2. Schiller _____	5. Er _____
3. Brahms _____	6. Beethoven _____ Bonn _____

e. Mein Onkel hat sich ein neues Haus bauen lassen.

1. Ihr Vater	4. Mein Onkel
2. Sein Bekannter	5. Ihr Vetter
3. Unser Freund	6. Sein Großvater

f. Sie hatte ihn singen hören.

1. sprechen	4. weinen
2. plaudern	5. rufen
3. laufen	6. spielen

g. Die Mädchen haben ihre Freundinnen kommen sehen.

1. gehen	4. hereinkommen
2. fahren	5. hinausgehen
3. rennen	6. abfahren

h. Mit was für einem Auto fährt er?

1. Dampfer	3. Schiff
2. Flugzeug	4. Zug

i. Unsere Verwandten haben uns im Jahre 1964 (neunzehnhundertvierundsechzig) besucht.

1. 1946	3. 1931
2. 1952	4. 1929

j. 1963 (Neunzehnhundertdreiundsechzig) sind sie nach Deutschland gefahren.

1. 1939	3. 1959
2. 1947	4. 1961

C. STRUCTURE

1. The neuter pronoun **es** (*it*) functions as the subject of impersonal verbs. To this group belong the following expressions:

es freut mich	*I am glad*
es klopft	*someone is knocking* (*at the door*)
es gelingt mir	*I succeed*
es regnet	*it is raining*
es schneit	*it is snowing*
es ist schade	*it's a shame*
es tut mir leid	*I'm sorry*

Note that some of these expressions require dative objects; for example, **es gelingt mir** and **es tut mir leid.**

2. Some of these expressions may be followed by **zu** + infinitive or by a clause introduced by **daß** (*that*):

   a. Es ist ihm gelungen, die Aufgabe zu lernen.
   He has succeeded in learning the lesson.
   b. Es freut mich, daß Sie hier sind.
   I'm glad (*that*) *you are here.*

3. The present tense of **sein** plus **geboren** (*born*) refers to living persons:

   Ich **bin** in den Vereinigten Staaten **geboren.**
   I was born in the United States.

   The past tense of **werden** plus **geboren** refers to persons who are no longer alive:

   Goethe **wurde** in Frankfurt **geboren.**
   Goethe was born in Frankfurt.

4. The verb **lassen** (*to let*) plus dependent infinitive expresses a causative action (having or letting someone do something):

   a. Der Präsident **läßt** ein Museum **bauen.**
   The President is having a museum built.
   b. Er **läßt** sich ein Haus **bauen.**
   He is having a house built.

5. In a compound tense of **lassen** plus dependent infinitive, the past participle is replaced by a form identical with the infinitive, thus forming a double infinitive:

   Mein Onkel **hat** sich ein neues Haus **bauen lassen** (instead of **gelassen**).
   My uncle had a new house built.

Note that in this double infinitive **lassen** functions like a modal auxiliary verb (page 121).

6. The verbs **hören** (*to hear*) and **sehen** (*to see*) also form a double infinitive in compound tenses plus dependent infinitive. Note that English uses either the infinitive or the present participle:

   a. Sie **hatte** ihn **singen hören** (instead of **gehört**).
     She had heard him sing.

   b. Die Mädchen **haben** ihre Freundinnen **kommen sehen** (instead of **gesehen**).
     The girls saw their girl friends coming.

7. In the interrogative expression **was für ein?** (*what kind of?*), the indefinite article **ein** is inflected and agrees with the noun it modifies, but **was** and **für** remain unchanged:

   a. **Was für ein Haus** haben sie?
     What kind of house do they have?

   b. **Mit was für einem Auto** fährt er?
     In what kind of car is he going?

   c. **Was für Krawatten** kauft er?
     What kind of ties is he buying?

8. Dates may be expressed by (a) **im Jahre** (*in the year*) plus the year, or by (b) the year alone:

   a. Unsere Verwandten haben uns **im Jahre 1964 (neunzehnhundertvierundsechzig)** besucht.
     Our relatives visited us in (the year) 1964.

   b. 1963 (**Neunzehnhundertdreiundsechzig**) sind sie nach Deutschland gefahren.
     They went to Germany in 1963.

D. EXERCISES

Write the following sentences in German and be able to express them orally.

1. Did you hear the children playing?
2. His cousins (*f.*) were born in 1947.
3. It looked as if it were raining.
4. Where was Bach born?
5. Have you succeeded in finding a doctor?
6. My uncle is having a blue suit made.
7. It was a shame that you came too late.

Fritz Henle from Monkmeyer

München: Hauptbahnhof

8. His aunt had a new table made.
9. When was Beethoven born?
10. I was sorry that I didn't see you this morning.
11. We saw the boys swimming.
12. In what kind of house do your relatives live?
13. Did this king have a castle built in 1700?
14. The war began in the year 1914.
15. Did you see the pupils writing?
16. What kind of ties do you like to wear?
17. The teacher (*f.*) is having the windows closed.
18. In what country was your grandfather born?
19. I am glad to read your letter.
20. My grandmother succeeded in selling her car yesterday.
21. Who was born in the year 1732?
22. Our neighbor is having flowers sent to his wife.
23. What kinds of books does your doctor like to read?

E. COMPREHENDING AND SPEAKING

I. Repeat the following after your instructor (or the speaker) and study thoroughly.

NACH HAMBURG

Eine Woche später fuhren Peter und Walter mit dem Zug nach Hamburg. Alle ihre Münchener Freunde waren zum Bahnhof gekommen, um von ihnen Abschied zu nehmen.

,,Es ist schade, daß ihr schon gehen müßt. Kommt bald wieder!"
5   so riefen sie. Peter und Walter mußten viele Hände schütteln, doch schließlich gelang es ihnen einzusteigen.

Punkt acht Uhr fuhr der Zug ab. Die beiden jungen Reisenden schauten zum Fenster hinaus und winkten:[1] ,,Auf Wiedersehen, es war sehr schön hier, es hat uns sehr gefallen!" riefen sie.

10   Die Reise nach Hamburg dauerte[2] sehr lange. Zuerst schauten sie zum Fenster hinaus, beobachteten die Landschaft oder lasen die Zeitung.[3] Gegen Mittag[4] ging ein Kellner durch den Wagen und läutete mit einer kleinen Glocke.[5] ,,Das Mittagessen wird soeben im

[1]**winken**	to wave	[4]**gegen Mittag**	around noon
[2]**dauern**	to last	[5]**läutete mit einer**	rang a bell
[3]**die Zeitung, -en**	newspaper	**Glocke**	

Fritz Henle from Monkmeyer

Mainz: Gutenbergdenkmal

15 Speisewagen serviert!"[6] rief er. Walter und Peter, die hungrig geworden
waren, gingen in den Speisewagen. Dort fanden sie glücklicherweise[7]
sofort[8] einen freien Tisch, und bald stand ein großer Teller mit Gemüse,
Kartoffeln[9] und Würsten[10] vor ihnen. Peter ließ auch zwei Glas Bier
kommen.

Am Nachmittag schlief Walter ein,[11] während Peter interessiert
20 in einem Reiseführer blätterte,[12] um noch mehr über Deutschland zu
erfahren.[13] Er las über die Stadt Mainz, wo Gutenberg, der Erfinder
der Buchdruckerkunst,[14] geboren wurde, über Ulm und sein berühmtes
Münster[15] und über die Universitätsstädte Tübingen, Göttingen und
Würzburg.

25 Der Zug fuhr jetzt durch eine öde, flache Gegend.[16] „Das muß
die Lüneburger Heide[17] sein", sagte sich Peter, der Herrn Hauser
davon hatte erzählen hören. Am Abend fuhr der Zug einen Fluß
entlang.[18]

„Wo sind wir, was für ein Fluß ist das?" fragte Walter, der soeben
30 erwachte.

„Das ist die Elbe", entgegnete Peter, „in ein paar Minuten werden
wir in Hamburg sein."

II. Beantworten Sie die folgenden Fragen auf deutsch!

1. Wer war zum Bahnhof gekommen?
2. Was riefen die Freunde von Peter und Walter?
3. Wann fuhr der Zug ab?
4. Wie lange dauerte die Reise nach Hamburg?
5. Was tat der Kellner mit der kleinen Glocke?
6. Wo wurde das Mittagessen serviert?
7. Was erfuhr Peter aus dem Reiseführer?
8. Wie sieht die Lüneburger Heide aus?
9. Welchen Fluß fuhr der Zug entlang?

[6]**wird soeben serviert**	is now being served	[13]**erfahren**	to learn
[7]**glücklicherweise**	fortunately	[14]**der Erfinder der Buchdruckerkunst**	the inventor of the art of printing
[8]**sofort**	immediately		
[9]**die Kartoffel, -n**	potato	[15]**das Münster, -**	cathedral
[10]**die Wurst, ⸚e**	sausage	[16]**eine öde, flache Gegend**	a desolate, flat region
[11]**ein-schlafen**	to fall asleep		
[12]**in einem Reiseführer blättern**	to leaf through a travel guide	[17]**die Heide, -n**	heath
		[18]**einen Fluß entlang**	along a river

UNIT 29

A. UNITS OF SPEECH AND VOCABULARY

I. Study and Practice Aloud.

Er macht das Licht an.	He's putting on the light.
Sie ärgert sich über das Kind.	She's annoyed at the child.
Sie kämmt sich die Haare.	She's combing her hair.
Das Konzert findet morgen statt.	The concert is taking place to-morrow.
Je mehr er sieht, desto mehr will er.	The more he sees, the more he wants.
Ich packe die Hosen in den Koffer.	I'm packing my trousers in the bag.
Die Stadt hat eine Million Einwohner.	The city has a million inhabitants.
im vorigen Jahrhundert	in the last century

der Dichter, -	the poet	das Licht, -er	the light
der Einwohner, -	the inhabitant	die Million, -en	the million
das Haar, -e	the hair	die Zeitung, -en	the newspaper
die Hose, -n	the (pair of) trousers	laut	loud
		jeder	everyone, everybody
die Jacke, -n	the jacket		
das Jahrhundert, -e	the century	jemand	someone, somebody
der Koffer, -	the bag, trunk	niemand	no one, nobody
das Konzert, -e	the concert		

je (+ *comp.*)	the (+ *comp.*)	**kämmen**	to comb
. . . desto (+ *comp.*)	. . . the (+ *comp.*)	**leben**	to live, to be alive
sich ärgern + über + *acc.*	to be annoyed at	**packen**	to pack

anmachen	**machte an**	**angemacht**	to put on (a light)
stattfinden	**fand statt**	**stattgefunden**	to take place

II. Oral Prcctice. Repeat the pattern sentence. Then substitute the items listed below in the appropriate places. Repeat the entire sentence with each substitute item, changing the verb where necessary.

a. Er macht das Licht an.
1. Jemand _____
2. Niemand _____
3. _____ hat _____ angemacht.
4. Jemand _____
5. _____ wird _____ anmachen.
6. Niemand _____

b. Sie ärgert sich über das Kind.
1. Jeder _____
2. _____ den Jungen.
3. _____ hat _____ geärgert.
4. Niemand _____
5. _____ wird _____ ärgern.
6. Jeder _____

c. Sie kämmt sich die Haare.
1. Er
2. Jeder
3. Jemand
4. Niemand
5. Das Kind
6. Der Junge

d. Das Konzert findet morgen statt.
1. _____ nächste Woche _____
2. _____ heute _____
3. _____ hat _____ stattgefunden.
4. _____ gestern _____
5. _____ vorgestern _____
6. _____ am Freitag _____

e. Je mehr er sieht, desto mehr will er.
1. der Junge
2. der Schüler
3. dieser Mann
4. mein Bruder
5. Sein Vetter
6. ihr Sohn

f. Ich packe die Hosen in den Koffer.
1. Der Reisende _____
2. Der Schaffner _____
3. _____ hat _____ gepackt.
4. _____ die Jacke _____
5. Der Geschäftsmann _____
6. Er _____

g. Die Stadt hat eine Million Einwohner.
1. Dieser Staat _____
2. München _____
3. Es _____
4. _____ tausend _____
5. Das Dorf _____
6. Mein Dorf _____

h. Der Dichter hat im vorigen Jahrhundert gelebt.

1. Der König _____
2. Er _____
3. _____ ist _____ gestorben.
4. Der König _____
5. Der Dichter _____
6. Die Dichter _____

i. Lesen Sie jetzt die Zeitung?

1. Ihre Eltern
2. Ihr Vater
3. er
4. Ihre Mutter
5. sie (*sing.*)
6. der Arzt

j. Die Kinder sind sehr laut.

1. _____ singen _____
2. _____ zu laut.
3. _____ sprechen _____
4. _____ lauter.

B. MODEL SENTENCES

I. Study each sentence until you can reproduce it correctly.

211. Hunderte von Kindern gehen in die Schule.
212. Tausende von Menschen waren auf der Straße.
213. Berlin hat drei Millionen Einwohner.
214. Je langsamer das Kind spricht, desto besser verstehe ich es.
215. Es versteht sich.
216. Diese Rechnung ist noch zu bezahlen.
217. Das Lernen ist schwer.
218. Beim Essen liest er immer die Zeitung.
219. Er wartet darauf, daß seine Freunde kommen.
220. Bitte seien Sie nicht so laut!

211. Hundreds of children go to school.
212. Thousands of people were on the street.
213. Berlin has three million inhabitants.
214. The slower the child speaks, the better I understand him.
215. It's understood.
216. This bill is yet to be paid.
217. Learning is difficult.
218. He always reads the newspaper while eating.
219. He's waiting for his friends to come.
220. Please don't be so loud.

II. Pattern Practice. Repeat the model sentence. Then substitute the items listed below in the appropriate places. Repeat the entire sentence with each substitute item, changing the pronouns where necessary.

a. Hunderte von Kindern gehen in die Schule.

1. Schülern
2. Schülerinnen
3. Jungen
4. Mädchen

b. Tausende von Menschen waren auf der Straße.

1. Männern   4. Herren
2. Frauen   5. Mädchen
3. Damen   6. Jungen

c. Berlin hat drei Millionen Einwohner.

1. Die Stadt _____   4. Wien _____
2. _____ zwei _____   5. Dieser Staat _____
3. Hamburg _____   6. _____ zehn _____

d. Je langsamer das Kind spricht, desto besser verstehe ich es.

1. das Mädchen   4. die Jungen
2. der Junge   5. die Mädchen
3. der Schüler   6. die Kinder

e. Er versteht sich, daß er hier bleibt.

1. _____, daß wir morgen kommen.
2. _____, daß sie nach Hause geht.
3. _____, daß Sie mir helfen.
4. _____, daß ich in die Schule gehe.

f. Diese Rechnung ist noch zu bezahlen.

1. jetzt   3. morgen
2. heute   4. übermorgen

g. Das Lernen ist schwer.

1. _____ wichtig.   4. Das Schwimmen _____
2. _____ interessant.   5. Das Singen _____

h. Beim Essen liest er immer die Zeitung.

1. mein Onkel   3. sie (*sing.*)
2. meine Tante   4. ich

i. Er wartet darauf, daß seine Freunde kommen.

1. _____, daß seine Verwandten abfahren.
2. _____, daß seine Freundin ihn besucht.
3. _____, daß sein Onkel zurückkommt.
4. _____, daß das Konzert beginnt.
5. _____, daß sein Bruder den Koffer packt.

j. Bitte, seien Sie nicht so laut, Herr Schmidt!

1. Frau Meyer   3. Mein Herr
2. Fräulein Braun   2. Meine Herren

C. STRUCTURE

1. **Hundert** (*hundred*) and **Tausend** (*thousand*), when used as nouns, are capitalized, form their plural by adding **-e,** and are followed by **von** (*of*) plus dative:

a. Hunderte von Kindern gehen in die Schule.
Hundreds of children go to school.

b. Tausende von Menschen waren auf der Straße.
Thousands of people were on the street.

2. **Million** (*million*) is always a noun and therefore always capitalized. It is followed directly by a noun:

a. Die Stadt hat **eine Million Einwohner.**
The city has a million inhabitants.

b. Berlin hat **drei Millionen Einwohner.**
Berlin has three million inhabitants.

3. Passive constructions are not as frequent in German as in English. Among common substitutes are reflexive constructions:

a. Es versteht sich.   **b. Das lernt sich leicht.**
It's understood.   *That's easily learned.*

4. The verb **sein** (*to be*) plus **zu** plus infinitive may also be substituted for the passive:

Diese Rechnung **ist** noch **zu bezahlen.**
This bill is yet to be paid.

5. An active construction with **man** is another substitute for the passive:

a. Man tut so etwas nicht.
Such things are not done.

b. Man spricht Deutsch in Österreich.
German is spoken in Austria.

6. An infinitive may be used as a neuter noun:

a. Das Lernen ist schwer.
Learning is difficult.

b. Beim Essen liest er immer die Zeitung.
He always reads the newspaper while eating.

7. A **da(r)**-compound is used to anticipate a clause that is dependent on a verb followed by a preposition, such as **warten auf** (*to wait for*):

Er wartet **darauf, daß seine Freunde kommen.**
He is waiting for his friends to come.

8. The command forms of **sein** (*to be*) are:

sei!	*be*	(for persons addressed as **du**)
seid!	*be*	(for persons addressed as **ihr**)
seien Sie!	*be*	(for persons addressed as **Sie**)

D. EXERCISES

Write the following sentences in German and be able to express them orally.

1. My younger brother listens to the radio while dressing.
2. Klara, be here at twelve o'clock sharp.
3. Don't wait for me to open the door.
4. His grandfather has hundreds of books.
5. Children, be here when your parents come back.
6. The businessman was smoking a cigarette while eating.
7. No one was to be seen in town.
8. Which bills are yet to be paid?
9. This letter is to be written in German.
10. The more the children read, the more they learn.
11. Your pen will soon be found.
12. The longer my cousin works, the more tired he looks.
13. How many million inhabitants does this city have?
14. The little girl was talking while writing.
15. Are these lessons easily done?
16. He was annoyed that the children were talking so loudly.
17. They built thousands of houses last year.
18. Ten million Germans have read the works of this poet.
19. His cousin (*f.*) remembered that he had traveled by airplane.
20. We saw hundreds of museums in Europe.
21. These tables are not to be sold.
22. Does Munich now have a million inhabitants?
23. The louder the little boy talks, the less I understand him.
24. Thousands of pupils have visited this museum.

E. COMPREHENDING AND SPEAKING

I. Repeat the following after your instructor (or the speaker) and study thoroughly.

IM HAMBURGER HAFEN

Hamburg ist die größte Stadt der Bundesrepublik Deutschland und hat den größten Hafen an der Nordseeküste.[1] Ungefähr zwei Millionen Menschen wohnen in Hamburg, und Tausende arbeiten im Hafen.

[1]**die Nordseeküste,**
   -n   North Sea coast

Im Hafen von Hamburg

5   Hamburg war die letzte deutsche Stadt, die Peter und Walter
     besuchten, bevor sie wieder nach den Vereinigten Staaten zurückreisten.
     Sie hatten schon viel vom Hamburger Hafen gehört und wollten ihn
     nun besichtigen.[2]

     Früh am Morgen fuhren sie zum Kai,[3] wo die großen Ozean-
10   dampfer aus aller Welt lagen und von den Arbeitern beladen oder
     entladen wurden.[4]

     Kleine Schleppdampfer[5] zogen eben ein großes Schiff, einen
     Passagierdampfer, an den Kai. Hunderte von Reisenden waren oben
     auf dem Deck zu sehen. Die meisten winkten mit den Taschentüchern.[6]

15   Es versteht sich, daß Peter und Walter zuschauten, wie das Schiff
     landete und wie die Passagiere ausstiegen. Je länger sie im Hafen
     waren, desto faszinierender[7] fanden sie die vielen Dinge,[8] die es hier
     zu sehen gab. Mit der Zeit aber wurden sie vom Zuschauen müde und
     dachten daran, ins Hotel zurückzugehen.

20   Da hatte Walter eine glänzende Idee.[9] ,,Weißt du was?" sagte er.
     ,,Wir fahren zur Insel Helgoland.[10] Das läßt sich leicht machen. Ein
     kleiner Dampfer fährt in einer halben Stunde hinüber."

     Peter ärgerte sich zuerst über Walters Idee, denn er war müde
     und hungrig, aber schließlich ließ er sich überreden.[11] Er mußte es
25   nicht bereuen.[12] Auf Helgoland, dem roten Felsen, der vor dem Hafen
     von Hamburg liegt, verbrachten Walter und Peter einen der schönsten
     Tage, die sie in Deutschland erlebt hatten.

II. Beantworten Sie die folgenden Fragen auf deutsch!
1. Welches ist die größte Stadt der Bundesrepublik Deutschland?
2. Wie viele Einwohner hat diese Stadt?
3. Was wollten die beiden Studenten besichtigen?
4. Was sehen sie am Kai?
5. Wovon wurden sie müde?
6. Was für eine glänzende Idee hatte Walter?
7. War Peter davon begeistert?
8. Wie fühlte sich Peter?
9. Warum mußte er nicht bereuen, daß er sich überreden ließ?

[2]**besichtigen**	to view	[7]**faszinierend**	fascinating
[3]**der Kai, -s**	wharf	[8]**das Ding, -e**	thing
[4]**von den Arbeitern**	were loaded or un-	[9]**eine glänzende**	a brilliant idea
beladen oder	loaded by the	**Idee**	
entladen wurden	workers	[10]**zur Insel**	to the island of
[5]**der**	tugboat	**Helgoland**	Helgoland
Schleppdampfer, -		[11]**überreden**	to persuade, con-
[6]**winkten mit den**	waved their hand-		vince
Taschentüchern	kerchiefs	[12]**bereuen**	to regret

UNIT 30

A. UNITS OF SPEECH AND VOCABULARY

I. Study and Practice Aloud.

Sie kosten vier Mark das Dutzend.	They cost four marks a dozen.
Es kostet eine Mark das Kilo.	It costs one mark a kilogram.
Das Kalbfleisch schmeckt mir.	I like the veal.
Wir machen einen Spaziergang.	We are taking a walk.
Ich setze mir den Hut auf.	I'm putting on my hat.
Ich freue mich auf meinen Geburtstag.	I'm looking forward to my birthday.
Sie freut sich über das Geschenk.	She's pleased with the gift.
Die Schreibmaschine gehört ihm.	The typewriter belongs to him.
Ich interessiere mich für alte Briefmarken.	I'm interested in old stamps.
Sie wohnen in der Goethestraße.	They live on Goethe Street.
einen Spaziergang machen	to take a walk
in der Goethestraße	on Goethe Street

die Birne, -n	the pear	das Geschenk, -e	the gift
die Briefmarke, -n	the (postage) stamp	das Kalbfleisch	the veal
		das Kilo, -s	the kilogram
das Dutzend, -e	the dozen	die Mark, -	the mark
der Fisch, -e	the fish	die Münze, -n	the coin
der Geburtstag, -e	the birthday	der Nachtisch, -e	the dessert
		der Park, -s	the park

(*273*)

der Pfirsich, -e	the peach	sich freuen +	to be pleased
das Rindfleisch	the beef	über + *acc.*	with
der Schinken, -	the ham	gehören +	to belong (to)
die Schreib-	the typewriter	*dat.*	
maschine,		schmecken	to taste (good
-n		+ *dat.*	to)
der Spaziergang,	the walk	sich interessieren	to be interested
⸚e		+ für +	(in)
sich freuen +	to look forward	*acc.*	
auf + *acc.*	(with plea-		
	sure) to		

sich aufsetzen	setzte sich auf	aufgesetzt	to put on (oneself)

II. Oral Practice. Repeat the pattern sentence. Then substitute the items listed below in the appropriate places. Repeat the entire sentence with each substitute item, changing the verb or pronoun where necessary.

a. Sie kosten vier Mark das Dutzend.
1. fünf
2. sechs
3. drei
4. sieben

b. Es kostet eine Mark das Kilo.
1. Die Birnen
2. Diese Birnen
3. Die großen Birnen
4. Die großen Pfirsiche
5. Diese Pfirsiche
6. Die Pfirsiche

c. Das Kalbfleisch schmeckt mir.
1. Das Rindfleisch _____
2. Der Schinken _____
3. Der Fisch _____
4. Der Nachtisch _____
5. _____ ihm.
6. Der Fisch _____
7. Der Schinken _____
8. Das Rindfleisch _____
9. Das Kalbfleisch _____
10. _____ ihr.
11. Das Rindfleisch _____
12. Der Schinken _____
13. Der Fisch _____
14. Der Nachtisch _____

d. Wir machen einen Spaziergang im Park.
1. Ich
2. Der Dichter
3. Er
4. Die alte Dame
5. Das Mädchen
6. Das Kind

e. Ich setze mir den Hut auf.
1. Der Arzt
2. Der Schaffner
3. Er
4. Die Verkäuferin
5. Die Lehrerin
6. Die Studentin

f. Ich freue mich auf meinen Geburtstag.
1. Der Junge
2. Das Kind
3. Das Mädchen
4. Der Schüler
5. Mein Bruder
6. Unser Vetter

g. Sie freut sich über das Geschenk.
1. Die Lehrerin
2. Die Studentin
3. Der Junge
4. Er
5. Ich
6. Wir

h. Die Schreibmaschine gehört ihm.
1. ihr
2. mir
3. uns
4. ihnen

i. Ich interessiere mich für alte Briefmarken.
1. Wir _____
2. Er _____
3. _____ alte Münzen.
4. Ihr Großvater
5. Seine Großmutter
6. Meine Tante

j. Sie wohnen in der Goethestraße.
1. Schillerstraße
2. Friedrichstraße
3. Königstraße
4. Kaiserstraße

B. MODEL SENTENCES

I. Study each sentence until you can reproduce it correctly.

221. **Hamburg ist eine in der ganzen Welt bekannte Stadt.**
222. **Der eben angekommene Brief ist von meiner Schwester.**
223. **Ohne zu antworten, hat er das Haus verlassen.**
224. **Anstatt mit uns zu kommen, ist er nach Hause gegangen.**
225. **Die Schuhe kosten dreißig Mark das Paar.**
226. **Wollen Sie diesen Hut oder d e n Hut?**
227. **Wer das kaufen kann, (der) muß reich sein.**
228. **Wer dieses Buch liest, dem wird es bestimmt gefallen.**
229. **Was sie kauft, ist meistens teuer.**

221. Hamburg is a city well know throughout the whole world.
222. The letter that just arrived is from my sister.
223. He left the house without answering.
224. He went home instead of coming with us.
225. The shoes cost thirty marks a pair.
226. Do you want this hat or that hat?
227. Whoever can buy that must be rich.
228. Whoever reads this book will definitely like it.
229. What ever she buys is usually expensive.

II. Pattern Practice. Repeat the model sentence. Then substitute the items listed below in the appropriate places. Repeat the entire sentence with each substitute item.

a. Hamburg ist eine in der ganzen Welt bekannte Stadt.
1. Berlin
2. München
3. Wien
4. Bonn

b. Der eben angekommene Brief ist von meiner Schwester.

1. meiner Mutter.   3. unserem Onkel.
2. Ihrer Schwester.   4. meinem Vater.

c. Ohne zu antworten, hat er das Haus verlassen.

1. sprechen   4. essen
2. packen   5. trinken
3. warten   6. schlafen

d. Anstatt mit uns zu kommen, ist er nach Hause gegangen.

1. gehen   4. sprechen
2. fahren   5. warten
3. essen   6. bleiben

e. Die Schuhe kosten dreißig Mark das Paar.

1. Seine Schuhe   4. Diese Handschuhe
2. Ihre Schuhe   5. Meine Handschuhe
3. Die Handschuhe   6. Die weißen Handschuhe

f. Wollen Sie diesen Hut oder d e n Hut?

1. Anzug   4. Koffer
2. Nachtisch   5. Ring
3. Bleistift   6. Apfel

g. Wer das kaufen kann, (der) muß reich sein.

1. schicken   3. besitzen
2. haben   4. tragen

h. Wer dieses Buch liest, dem wird es bestimmt gefallen.

1. kauft   3. besitzt
2. bekommt   4. hat

i. Was sie kauft, ist meistens teuer.

1. verkauft   4. bringt
2. sucht   5. trägt
3. braucht   6. bestellt

C. STRUCTURE

1. A participle or a descriptive adjective modifying a noun may itself be preceded by modifying elements. The participle or adjective has strong or weak endings like any descriptive adjective preceding a noun:

   a. Hamburg ist eine **in der ganzen Welt bekannte** Stadt.
   Hamburg is a city well known throughout the world.

   b. Der **eben angekommene** Brief ist von meiner Schwester.
   The letter which just arrived is from my sister.

These modified-adjective constructions are rare in conversation but common in literature and especially in scientific writing. In conversation, such constructions are normally replaced by relative clauses:

a. Hamburg ist eine Stadt, **die in der ganzen Welt bekannt ist.**
b. Der Brief, **der eben angekommen ist,** ist von meiner Schwester.

2. The prepositions **anstatt** (*instead of*), **ohne** (*without*), and **um** (*in order*) may be used with **zu** plus infinitive:

a. **Ohne zu antworten,** hat er das Haus verlassen.
He left the house without answering.
b. **Anstatt** mit uns **zu kommen,** ist er nach Hause gegangen.
He went home instead of coming with us.
c. Er ist früh fortgegangen, **um** vor zwei Uhr **zurückzukommen.**
He went away early in order to come back before two o'clock.

3. Nouns denoting units of measure require the definite article when used distributively:

a. Es kostet eine Mark **das Kilo.**
It costs one mark a kilogram.
b. Sie kosten vier Mark **das Dutzend.**
They cost four marks a dozen.
c. Die Schuhe kosten dreißig Mark **das Paar.**
The shoes cost thirty marks a pair.

Note that **Mark** is unchanged in the plural.

4. The definite article may be used with stress as a demonstrative:

Wollen Sie diesen Hut oder **den** Hut?
Do you want this hat or that hat?

5. **Wer** (*who, whoever*) is used as a relative pronoun without antecedents (referring to no specific person). The main clause begins with demonstrative **der** (*he, that one*), which is usually omitted in the nominative, but may not be omitted in other cases:

a. **Wer** das kaufen kann, **(der)** muß reich sein.
Whoever can buy that must be rich.
b. **Wer** dieses Buch liest, **dem** wird es bestimmt gefallen.
Whoever reads this book will definitely like it.

6. **Was** (*what, whatever, that which*) is used as a relative pronoun without antecedent (referring to no specific thing or idea):

Was sie kauft, ist meistens teuer.
Whatever she buys is usually expensive.

D. EXERCISES

Write the following sentences in German and be able to express them orally.

1. The little boy wants whatever he sees.
2. This pen belongs to me and that pen belongs to her.
3. That is a book famous throughout the entire world.
4. Their gloves will cost twenty marks a pair.
5. The dentist paid for the clothes ordered by his children.
6. Whoever was here this morning will come back again this evening.
7. Do you like this car or that one.
8. The little girl played with her friends instead of studying her lessons.
9. The ham costs eight marks a kilogram.
10. These shoes cost forty marks a pair.
11. She gave me the letter without opening it.
12. That house is newer than this house.
13. Whoever was in the kitchen drank the whole bottle of milk.
14. The doctor went back to the office without eating lunch.
15. You can have either this chair or that chair.
16. Whoever lives in this village knows my grandfather.
17. The woman waiting on the corner got on the streetcar.
18. Whatever this poet writes is interesting.
19. My sister went out of the house without closing the windows.
20. Whoever eats this beef likes it.
21. The child ran quickly in order to be in school before nine o'clock.
22. Did you see the people standing in front of the house?
23. Her brother wants to earn more money in order to take a trip to Austria.
24. Wear whatever you will.

E. COMPREHENDING AND SPEAKING

I. *Repeat the following after your instructor (or the speaker) and study thoroughly.*

EIN BRIEF

Am Tage der Abreise[1] fand Walter in der Nähe des Hafens einen Kuriositätenladen, der ihm sehr gefiel. Merkwürdige[2] Dinge, die von Seeleuten[3] aus aller Welt zusammengetragen worden waren, gab es hier zu sehen: farbige Muscheln[4] in allen Größen,[5] das Stück zu fünfzig

[1]**die Abreise, -n**	departure	[4]**die Muschel, -n**	shell
[2]**merkwürdig**	remarkable	[5]**die Größe, -n**	size
[3]**der Seemann, Seeleute**	seaman, sailor		

5   Pfennig,[6] Haifischzähne[7] und Korallen.[8] Ein vor dem Laden sitzender Mann zeigte Walter ein kleines Segelschiff,[9] das in einer Flasche eingeschlossen[10] war. „Wer das besitzt, vergißt Hamburg nie!" sagte er.

10   Walter kaufte sich das Schiff als Souvenir und ging dann zum Hotel zurück. Später ging er mit Peter in ein Café am Hafen. Dort schrieb Peter einen Brief:

Hamburg, den 20. Juli 1967

Liebe[11] Käthe,

   Unsere Reise geht zu Ende, und dies wird der letzte Brief sein,
15   den Du von mir aus Deutschland empfangen[12] wirst.

   Wir sitzen jetzt gerade in einem Café im Hamburger Hafen und essen unser letztes deutsches Frühstück, das uns gut schmeckt. Am Kai, uns unmittelbar gegenüber,[13] liegt die ‚Aurora', der große Ozeandampfer, der uns nach Amerika zurückbringen wird. In einer halben
20   Stunde werden wir an Bord gehen.

   Walter und ich sind etwas traurig,[14] daß die schöne Zeit in Deutschland so schnell vorbeigegangen ist. Ohne zu übertreiben,[15] können wir sagen, daß wir noch nie zuvor[16] so herrliche Ferien erlebt haben. Was haben wir nicht alles gesehen! Alte Städte, romantische
25   Landschaften, Museen und Universitäten! Wir haben uns für alles interessiert und viel gelernt.

   Kreuz und quer[17] im Lande umherreisend, haben wir viele nette Leute getroffen, die uns immer wieder geholfen haben. Viele sind unsere Freunde geworden. Was sie für uns getan haben, werden wir
30   nicht vergessen. Ich bin sicher, daß wir eines Tages zurückkehren[18] werden, und ich hoffe, daß Du dann mitkommen kannst.

   Die Schiffsirene heult.[19] Wir müssen gehen. In acht Tagen werden **wir** in New York sein. Ich freue mich auf das Wiedersehen!

   Bis dahin sei herzlich gegrüßt von[20]

Deinem Peter.

35
   P.S. Auch Walter läßt Dich natürlich grüßen.

[6]das Stück zu fünfzig Pfennig	fifty pfennigs a piece	[14]traurig	sad
[7]die Haifischzähne	shark's teeth	[15]übertreiben	to exaggerate
[8]die Koralle, -n	coral	[16]zuvor	before
[9]das Segelschiff, -e	sailboat	[17]kreuz und quer	in all directions
[10]ein-schließen	to enclose, lock up	[18]zurück-kehren	to come back, return
[11]lieb	dear	[19]die Schiffsirene heult	the ship's siren is howling
[12]empfangen	to receive	[20]sei herzlich gegrüßt von	cordial greetings from
[13]uns unmittelbar gegenüber	directly opposite us		

II. *Beantworten Sie die folgenden Fragen auf deutsch!*

1. Was fand Walter am Tage der Abreise?
2. Welche Kuriositäten gab es zu sehen?
3. Wer zeigte Walter ein Schiff in einer Flasche?
4. Wohin gingen Walter und Peter später?
5. Wem schrieb Peter einen Brief?
6. Wie hieß das Schiff, das die beiden Studenten nach Amerika zurückbringen sollte?
7. Wann mußten sie an Bord gehen?
8. Warum waren sie traurig?
9. Was hoffte Peter?

REVIEW UNIT 6

A. *Supply the proper form of the word in parentheses in the place indicated.*

1. (Herz) Welches Land liegt im _____ Europas?
2. (sein) _____ zu Hause, wenn ich zurückkomme, Walter!
3. (hören) Der Lehrer hat die Schüler plaudern _____.
4. (werden) Der rote Hut ist von meiner Schwester gekauft _____.
5. (alt) Je _____ mein Großvater wird, desto mehr arbeitet er.
6. (ein) In so _____ Haus haben wir nie gewohnt.
7. (singen) Es wurde am Sonnabend wenig _____.
8. (hundert) Der Dichter hat _____ von Geschichten geschrieben.
9. (können) Wenn ich in die Stadt gefahren wäre, hätte ich sie sehen _____.
10. (liegen) Der auf dem Sofa _____ Junge hört Radio.
11. (sehen) Wir haben das Flugzeug ankommen _____.
12. (Million) Wie viele _____ Einwohner hat Berlin?
13. (sein) _____ nicht so laut, meine Kinder!
14. (bestellen) Der von den Kindern _____ Nachtisch war teuer.
15. (solch) _____ Autos fahren gut.
16. (sollen) Ich hätte meiner Mutter schreiben _____.
17. (lassen) Ich habe mir einen neuen Anzug machen _____.

B. *Supply an appropriate word in the place indicated. If the sentence is complete as is, supply nothing.*

1. Es freut mich, _____ Sie mich besuchen werden.
2. Wer diesen Wein trinkt, _____ schmeckt er.

3. Wo _____ Washington geboren?
4. Keine Handschuhe sind in diesem Geschäft _____ kaufen.
5. _____ dieses Auto besitzt, fährt sehr schnell.
6. Was für _____ Kugelschreiber haben Sie da?
7. Das Paket wurde _____ meiner Mutter geschickt.
8. Kosten die Äpfel eine Mark _____ Kilo?
9. Interessieren Sie sich für _____ Kunst?
10. Meine jüngere Schwester _____ in New York geboren.
11. Goethe _____ in Frankfurt geboren.
12. Es ist _____, daß Ihre Großmutter wieder krank ist.
13. Ist es _____ Kind gelungen, den Brief zu schreiben?
14. Macht sie das Kleid selbst oder _____ sie es sich machen.
15. _____ Singen lächelt er nie.
16. Er wird weder _____ Auto noch dieses Auto kaufen.
17. Er sah aus, _____ hätte er alle seine Freunde verloren.
18. Das Fenster wurde vor einer Stunde geschlossen und es _____ noch geschlossen.
19. Regnet _____ schon?
20. Dieses Geschäft verkauft Tausende _____ Schreibmaschinen.
21. _____ 1945 hat der Krieg geendet.
22. Dieses Land hat fünf Millionen _____ Einwohner.
23. Es _____ uns, Sie bei uns zu sehen.
24. Wenn ich um acht Uhr in die Schule kam, _____ die Tür immer geschlossen.
25. Wollen Sie mehr Geld verdienen? — Das versteht _____.
26. Anstatt nach Hause _____ gehen, ist er in der Stadt geblieben.
27. Sie lehrt _____ Schülerinnen Englisch.
28. Mit was _____ einem Schiff reist er?
29. Je mehr er verdient, _____ weniger hat er.
30. Ich erinnere _____ daran.

C. *Change the following sentences to the passive.*

1. Das junge Mädchen lehrt das kleine Kind.
2. Die alte Dame hat den neuen Hut gekauft.
3. Der Student wird die Aufgabe schreiben.
4. Diese Rechnung ist noch zu bezahlen.
5. Man spricht Deutsch in Österreich.

D. *Beantworten Sie die folgenden Fragen auf deutsch!*

1. Aus wie vielen Staaten bestehen die Vereinigten Staaten?
2. Wohnen Sie in der Nähe der Universität?
3. Wie heißt der Präsident der Vereinigten Staaten?

4. Welches Land ist wegen seiner Berge berühmt?
5. Wann sind Sie geboren?
6. Ist Ihre Universität (oder Ihre Schule) mitten in der Stadt?
7. Was macht man an, wenn es dunkel wird?
8. Wann kämmen Sie sich die Haare?
9. Wie viele Einwohner hat Berlin?
10. In welchem Jahrhundert leben wir?
11. Was muß man bezahlen, wenn man in einem Restaurant ißt?
12. Haben Sie eine Schreibmaschine?
13. Sammeln Sie alte Briefmarken oder alte Münzen?
14. In welcher Straße wohnen Sie?
15. Essen Sie lieber Eis oder Kuchen zum Nachtisch?

E. *Write a brief autobiography in German, telling when and where you were born, the population of your native town; describe your family, where you live and have lived, when you began to attend school, how long you have been attending school, when you began to study German, how long you have been studying German, and so on.*

APPENDIX A

PRONUNCIATION GUIDE

The best way to learn to pronounce any language properly is to imitate the pronunciation of a good speaker. The following guide is provided for reference. The student must realize that English equivalents are only approximate.

1. Vowels.

All German vowels are usually short before double consonants and long otherwise. Double vowels and vowels followed by **h** are long.

SHORT VOWELS

GERMAN SPELLING	APPROXIMATE ENGLISH EQUIVALENT	ILLUSTRATION
a	*a*rt	Mann
ä	b*e*d	hätte
e	b*e*t	Bett
i	p*i*n	bin
o	*o*ral	kommen
ö	No equivalent. Round lips for *o* as in c*o*me, and pronounce *e* as in b*e*d.	könnte
u	p*u*ll	Fluß
ü	No equivalent. Round lips for *u* as in p*u*ll, and pronounce *i* as in p*i*n.	Flüsse

GERMAN SPELLING	APPROXIMATE ENGLISH EQUIVALENT	ILLUSTRATION
	LONG VOWELS	
a	f*a*ther	Vater
ä	f*ai*r	Väter
e	th*e*y	Weg Tee geht
i	mach*i*ne	gib ihr
ie[1]	bel*ie*ve	sie
o	Like *o* in r*o*pe, but without glide into *u*.	so Boot Ohr
ö	No equivalent. Round lips for *o* as in r*o*pe, and pronounce *e* as in th*e*y.	Söhne
u	p*oo*l	Fuß
ü	No equivalent. Round lips for *oo* as in p*oo*l, and pronounce *i* as in mach*i*ne.	Füße

2. *Diphthongs.*

au	b*ou*gh	Baum
ai	r*i*de	Mai
ei	r*i*de	mein
äu	b*oy*	Bäume
eu	b*oy*	Leute

[1] Although written with two symbols, this is only a single sound. The pronunciation of **ie** in **sie** is exactly the same as that of **i** in **gib** or **ihr.**

3. *Consonants.*

GERMAN SPELLING	APPROXIMATE ENGLISH EQUIVALENT	ILLUSTRATION
b beginning a syllable	*b*ad	Bett geben
b ending a syllable	li*p*	gab
d beginning a syllable	*d*o	da jeder
d ending a syllable	bel*t*	Geld
f	*f*ive	fünf
g beginning a syllable	*g*ive	geben Tage
g ending a syllable	mil*k*	Tag Weg
h at beginning of word	*h*ave	haben
h other than above	*h*onor, a*h*	sehen sah
j	*y*es	ja
k	*k*ing	Katze
l	*l*augh, *never* like *l* in ba*ll*	lachen soll
m	*m*an	Mann
n	*n*ame	Name
p	*p*ost	Post
r	No equivalent. Made by vibrating back of tongue against soft palate. At end of syllable, similar to final *r* in American English.	reden durch hier
s at beginning of syllable	zebra	so Gläser
s at end of syllable	thi*s*	Glas
t	*t*o	tat

GERMAN SPELLING	APPROXIMATE ENGLISH EQUIVALENT	ILLUSTRATION
v	*f*or	vor
v in words of Latin or French origin	No*v*ember	November
w	*v*ine	Wein
z	ca*ts*	zehn schwarz

4. Consonant Combinations.

ch after a, o, u, au	No equivalent. Like *h* in a*h*em when clearing one's throat.	lachen noch Buch
ch other than above	No equivalent. Like *h* in *h*ue.	lächeln ich möchte solch durch
ck	sti*ck*er	stecken
ng	si*ng*	singen
pf	cu*pf*ul	Apfel
sch	*sh*ave	schreiben
ß	*s*o	Fluß
th	*Th*omas	Theater
tz	ca*ts*	sitzen

Several letters occurring only in words of non-German origin:

c before a, o, u, au	*k*ing	Café
c before ä, e, i	ca*ts*	Cäsar
qu	Like *kv*	Quelle
x	fo*x*	Max
y	Like German **ü.**	Physiker

5. Syllabication.

When it becomes necessary to break a word at the end of a line, single consonants usually go with the following syllable, for example: **a-ber, De-zem-ber.** Consonant combinations representing a single consonant sound stay together: **Ti-sche.** Exceptions are **ng** and **ck,** which are broken up into **n-g** and **k-k** respectively: **sin-gen, stek-ken.** Compound words are broken so as to keep their component parts intact: **ein-ander.**

6. Punctuation.

All subordinate clauses, including relative clauses, and infinitive phrases consisting of one or more words in addition to **zu** and the infinitive, are set off by commas:

a. Ich werde meinen Onkel sehen, **wenn er uns besucht.**
b. Die Mädchen, **die hier waren,** sind jetzt fortgegangen.
c. Der Schüler lief schnell, **um vor ein Uhr zu Hause zu sein.**
d. Er geht zur Schule, **um Deutsch zu lernen.**

APPENDIX B

DECLENSIONS

1. Declension of Nouns.

	SINGULAR	PLURAL
NOM.	der Lehrer	die Lehrer
GEN.	des Lehrers	der Lehrer
DAT.	dem Lehrer	den Lehrern
ACC.	den Lehrer	die Lehrer
NOM.	die Hand	die Hände
GEN.	der Hand	der Hände
DAT.	der Hand	den Händen
ACC.	die Hand	die Hände
NOM.	das Haus	die Häuser
GEN.	des Hauses	der Häuser
DAT.	dem Hause	den Häusern
ACC.	das Haus	die Häuser
NOM.	die Aufgabe	die Aufgaben
GEN.	der Aufgabe	der Aufgaben
DAT.	der Aufgabe	den Aufgaben
ACC.	die Aufgabe	die Aufgaben

	SINGULAR	PLURAL
NOM.	der Professor	die Professoren
GEN.	des Professors	der Professoren
DAT.	dem Professor	den Professoren
ACC.	den Professor	die Professoren
NOM.	der Student	die Studenten
GEN.	des Studenten	der Studenten
DAT.	dem Studenten	den Studenten
ACC.	den Studenten	die Studenten
NOM.	das Hotel	die Hotels
GEN.	des Hotels	der Hotels
DAT.	dem Hotel	den Hotels
ACC.	das Hotel	die Hotels

2. Strong Declension of Adjective.

	SINGULAR	PLURAL
NOM.	gut**er** Freund	gut**e** Freunde
GEN.	gut**en**[1] Freundes	gut**er** Freunde
DAT.	gut**em** Freund(e)	gut**en** Freunden
ACC.	gut**en** Freund	gut**e** Freunde
NOM.	gut**e** Freundin	gut**e** Freundinnen
GEN.	gut**er** Freundin	gut**er** Freundinnen
DAT.	gut**er** Freundin	gut**en** Freundinnen
ACC.	gut**e** Freundin	gut**e** Freundinnen
NOM.	gut**es** Kind	gut**e** Kinder
GEN.	gut**en**[1] Kindes	gut**er** Kinder
DAT.	gut**em** Kind(e)	gut**en** Kindern
ACC.	gut**es** Kind	gut**e** Kinder

3. Weak Declension of Adjectives.

	SINGULAR	PLURAL
NOM.	der alt**e** Mann	die alt**en** Männer
GEN.	des alt**en** Mannes	der alt**en** Männer
DAT.	dem alt**en** Mann(e)	den alt**en** Männern
ACC.	den alt**en** Mann	die alt**en** Männer

[1] The **en** ending of the masculine genitive singular and of the neuter genitive singular occurs rarely in conversational German.

	SINGULAR	PLURAL
NOM.	welche jung**e** Frau	welche jung**en** Frauen
GEN.	welcher jung**en** Frau	welcher jung**en** Frauen
DAT.	welcher jung**en** Frau	welchen jung**en** Frauen
ACC.	welche jung**e** Frau	welche jung**en** Frauen

NOM.	dieses neu**e** Buch	diese neu**en** Bücher
GEN.	dieses neu**en** Buches	dieser neu**en** Bücher
DAT.	diesem neu**en** Buch(e)	diesen neu**en** Büchern
ACC.	dieses neu**e** Buch	diese neu**en** Bücher

4. Declension of Adjectives after Ein-Words.

	SINGULAR	PLURAL
NOM.	kein gut**er** Mann	keine gut**en** Männer
GEN.	keines gut**en** Mannes	keiner gut**en** Männer
DAT.	keinem gut**en** Mann(e)	keinen gut**en** Männern
ACC.	keinen gut**en** Mann	keine gut**en** Männer

NOM.	ihre jung**e** Tochter	ihre jung**en** Töchter
GEN.	ihrer jung**en** Tochter	ihrer jung**en** Töchter
DAT.	ihrer jung**en** Tochter	ihren jung**en** Töchtern
ACC.	ihre jung**e** Tochter	ihre jung**en** Töchter

NOM.	unser neu**es** Buch	unsere neu**en** Bücher
GEN.	unseres neu**en** Buches	unserer neu**en** Bücher
DAT.	unserem neu**en** Buch(e)	unseren neu**en** Büchern
ACC.	unser neu**es** Buch	unsere neu**en** Bücher

5. Declension of Personal Pronouns.

		SINGULAR		
NOM.	ich	du	er	es	sie
GEN.	meiner[1]	deiner[1]	seiner[1]	seiner[1]	ihrer[1]
DAT.	mir	dir	ihm	ihm	ihr
ACC.	mich	dich	ihn	es	sie

		PLURAL	
NOM.	wir	ihr	sie	Sie
GEN.	unser[1]	euer[1]	ihrer[1]	Ihrer[1]
DAT.	uns	euch	ihnen	Ihnen
ACC.	uns	euch	sie	Sie

[1] The genitive forms of the personal pronouns are rarely used in modern German.

APPENDIX C

VERBS

1. Auxiliary Verbs.

haben *to have*	**sein** *to be*	**werden** *to become*

PAST PARTICIPLE

gehabt	gewesen	geworden

PRESENT INDICATIVE

ich habe	ich bin	ich werde
du hast	du bist	du wirst
er hat	er ist	er wird
wir haben	wir sind	wir werden
ihr habt	ihr seid	ihr werdet
sie haben	sie sind	sie werden
Sie haben	Sie sind	Sie werden

PAST INDICATIVE

ich hatte	ich war	ich wurde
du hattest	du warst	du wurdest
er hatte	er war	er wurde

wir hatten	wir waren	wir wurden
ihr hattet	ihr wart	ihr wurdet
sie hatten	sie waren	sie wurden
Sie hatten	Sie waren	Sie wurden

FUTURE INDICATIVE

ich werde haben	ich werde sein	ich werde werden
du wirst haben	du wirst sein	du wirst werden
er wird haben	er wird sein	er wird werden
wir werden haben	wir werden sein	wir werden werden
ihr werdet haben	ihr werdet sein	ihr werdet werden
sie werden haben	sie werden sein	sie werden werden
Sie werden haben	Sie werden sein	Sie werden werden

PRESENT PERFECT

ich habe gehabt	ich bin gewesen	ich bin geworden
du hast gehabt	du bist gewesen	du bist geworden
er hat gehabt	er ist gewesen	er ist geworden
wir haben gehabt	wir sind gewesen	wir sind geworden
ihr habt gehabt	ihr seid gewesen	ihr seid geworden
sie haben gehabt	sie sind gewesen	sie sind geworden
Sie haben gehabt	Sie sind gewesen	Sie sind geworden

PAST PERFECT

ich hatte gehabt	ich war gewesen	ich war geworden
du hattest gehabt	du warst gewesen	du warst geworden
er hatte gehabt	er war gewesen	er war geworden
wir hatten gehabt	wir waren gewesen	wir waren geworden
ihr hattet gehabt	ihr wart gewesen	ihr wart geworden
sie hatten gehabt	sie waren gewesen	sie waren geworden
Sie hatten gehabt	Sie waren gewesen	Sie waren geworden

FUTURE PERFECT

ich werde gehabt haben	ich werde gewesen sein
du wirst gehabt haben	du wirst gewesen sein
er wird gehabt haben	er wird gewesen sein
wir werden gehabt haben	wir werden gewesen sein
ihr werdet gehabt haben	ihr werdet gewesen sein
sie werden gehabt haben	sie werden gewesen sein
Sie werden gehabt haben	Sie werden gewesen sein

FUTURE PERFECT

ich werde geworden sein
du wirst geworden sein
er wird geworden sein
wir werden geworden sein
ihr werdet geworden sein
sie werden geworden sein
Sie werden geworden sein

PRESENT SUBJUNCTIVE I

ich habe	ich sei	ich werde
du habest	du seist	du werdest
er habe	er sei	er werde
wir haben	wir seien	wir werden
ihr habet	ihr seiet	ihr werdet
sie haben	sie seien	sie werden
Sie haben	Sie seien	Sie werden

PRESENT SUBJUNCTIVE II

ich hätte	ich wäre	ich würde
du hättest	du wärest	du würdest
er hätte	er wäre	er würde
wir hätten	wir wären	wir würden
ihr hättet	ihr wäret	ihr würdet
sie hätten	sie wären	sie würden
Sie hätten	Sie wären	Sie würden

PAST SUBJUNCTIVE I

ich habe gehabt	ich sei gewesen	ich sei geworden
du habest gehabt	du seist gewesen	du seist geworden
er habe gehabt	er sei gewesen	er sei geworden
wir haben gehabt	wir seien gewesen	wir seien geworden
ihr habet gehabt	ihr seiet gewesen	ihr seiet geworden
sie haben gehabt	sie seien gewesen	sie seien geworden
Sie haben gehabt	Sie seien gewesen	Sie seien geworden

PAST SUBJUNCTIVE II

ich hätte gehabt	ich wäre gewesen	ich wäre geworden
du hättest gehabt	du wärest gewesen	du wärest geworden
er hätte gehabt	er wäre gewesen	er wäre geworden

wir hätten gehabt	wir wären gewesen	wir wären geworden
ihr hättet gehabt	ihr wäret gewesen	ihr wäret geworden
sie hätten gehabt	sie wären gewesen	sie wären geworden
Sie hätten gehabt	Sie wären gewesen	Sie wären geworden

FUTURE SUBJUNCTIVE

ich werde haben	ich werde sein	ich werde werden
du werdest haben	du werdest sein	du werdest werden
er werde haben	er werde sein	er werde werden
wir werden haben	wir werden sein	wir werden werden
ihr werdet haben	ihr werdet sein	ihr werdet werden
sie werden haben	sie werden sein	sie werden werden
Sie werden haben	Sie werden sein	Sie werden werden

CONDITIONAL

ich würde haben	ich würde sein	ich würde werden
du würdest haben	du würdest sein	du würdest werden
er würde haben	er würde sein	er würde werden
wir würden haben	wir würden sein	wir würden werden
ihr würdet haben	ihr würdet sein	ihr würdet werden
sie würden haben	sie würden sein	sie würden werden
Sie würden haben	Sie würden sein	Sie würden werden

FUTURE PERFECT SUBJUNCTIVE

ich werde gehabt haben   ich werde gewesen sein
          etc.   etc.

ich werde geworden sein
          etc.

CONDITIONAL PERFECT

ich würde gehabt haben   ich würde gewesen sein
          etc.   etc.

ich würde geworden sein
          etc.

IMPERATIVE

habe!	sei!	werde!
habt!	seid!	werdet!
haben Sie!	seien Sie!	werden Sie!

2. *Modal Auxiliaries.*

PRESENT INDICATIVE

dürfen	**können**	**mögen**
(may, to be permitted to)	(can, to be able to)	(to like to, to care to)
ich darf	ich kann	ich mag
du darfst	du kannst	du magst
er darf	er kann	er mag
wir dürfen	wir können	wir mögen
ihr dürft	ihr könnt	ihr mögt
sie dürfen	sie können	sie mögen
Sie dürfen	Sie können	Sie mögen

müssen	**sollen**	**wollen**
(must, to have to)	(to be to, to be supposed to)	(to want to)
ich muß	ich soll	ich will
du mußt	du sollst	du willst
er muß	er soll	er will
wir müssen	wir sollen	wir wollen
ihr müßt	ihr sollt	ihr wollt
sie müssen	sie sollen	sie wollen
Sie müssen	Sie sollen	Sie wollen

PAST INDICATIVE

ich durfte	ich konnte	ich mochte
du durftest	du konntest	du mochtest
er durfte	er konnte	er mochte
wir durften	wir konnten	wir mochten
ihr durftet	ihr konntet	ihr mochtet
sie durften	sie konnten	sie mochten
Sie durften	Sie konnten	Sie mochten

ich mußte	ich sollte	ich wollte
du mußtest	du solltest	du wolltest
er mußte	er sollte	er wollte
wir mußten	wir sollten	wir wollten
ihr mußtet	ihr solltet	ihr wolltet
sie mußten	sie sollten	sie wollten
Sie mußten	Sie sollten	Sie wollten

FUTURE INDICATIVE

ich werde dürfen (können, mögen, müssen, sollen, wollen) etc.

PRESENT PERFECT

ich habe gedurft (gekonnt, gemocht, gemußt, gesollt, gewollt) etc.

PAST PERFECT

ich hatte gedurft (gekonnt, gemocht, gemußt, gesollt, gewollt) etc.

FUTURE PERFECT

ich werde gedurft (gekonnt, gemocht, gemußt, gesollt, gewollt) haben etc.

PRESENT SUBJUNCTIVE I

ich dürfe	ich könne	ich möge
du dürfest	du könnest	du mögest
er dürfe	er könne	er möge
wir dürfen	wir können	wir mögen
ihr dürfet	ihr könnet	ihr möget
sie dürfen	sie können	sie mögen
Sie dürfen	Sie können	Sie mögen
ich müsse	ich solle	ich wolle
du müssest	du sollest	du wollest
er müsse	er solle	er wolle
wir müssen	wir sollen	wir wollen
ihr müsset	ihr sollet	ihr wollet
sie müssen	sie sollen	sie wollen
Sie müssen	Sie sollen	Sie wollen

PRESENT SUBJUNCTIVE II

ich dürfte, ich könnte, ich möchte, ich müßte, ich sollte, ich wollte etc.

PAST SUBJUNCTIVE I

ich habe gedurft (gekonnt, gemocht, gemußt, gesollt, gewollt)
du habest gedurft (gekonnt, gemocht, gemußt, gesollt, gewollt) etc.

PAST SUBJUNCTIVE II

ich hätte gedurft (gekonnt, gemocht, gemußt, gesollt, gewollt) etc.

FUTURE SUBJUNCTIVE

ich werde dürfen (können, mögen, müssen, sollen, wollen)
du werdest dürfen (können, mögen, müssen, sollen, wollen) etc.

CONDITIONAL

ich würde dürfen (können, mögen, müssen, sollen, wollen) etc.

FUTURE PERFECT SUBJUNCTIVE

ich werde gedurft (gekonnt, gemocht, gemußt, gesollt, gewollt) haben
du werdest gedurft (gekonnt, gemocht, gemußt, gesollt, gewollt) haben etc.

CONDITIONAL PERFECT

ich würde gedurft (gekonnt, gemocht, gemußt, gesollt, gewollt) haben etc.

3. Inflection of a Weak and a Strong Verb.

Active

INFINITIVE

sagen   to say   **laufen**   to run

PRESENT PARTICIPLE

sagend   laufend

PAST PARTICIPLE

gesagt   gelaufen

PRESENT INDICATIVE

ich sage	ich laufe
du sagst	du läufst
er sagt	er läuft
wir sagen	wir laufen
ihr sagt	ihr lauft
sie sagen	sie laufen
Sie sagen	Sie laufen

PAST INDICATIVE

ich sagte	ich lief
du sagtest	du liefst
er sagte	er lief

wir sag**ten**	wir liefen
ihr sag**tet**	ihr lieft
sie sag**ten**	sie liefen
Sie sag**ten**	Sie liefen

FUTURE INDICATIVE

ich werde sagen	ich werde laufen
du wirst sagen	du wirst laufen
er wird sagen	er wird laufen
wir werden sagen	wir werden laufen
ihr werdet sagen	ihr werdet laufen
sie werden sagen	sie werden laufen
Sie werden sagen	Sie werden laufen

PRESENT PERFECT

ich habe gesagt	ich bin gelaufen
du hast gesagt	du bist gelaufen
er hat gesagt	er ist gelaufen
wir haben gesagt	wir sind gelaufen
ihr habt gesagt	ihr seid gelaufen
sie haben gesagt	sie sind gelaufen
Sie haben gesagt	Sie sind gelaufen

PAST PERFECT

ich hatte gesagt	ich war gelaufen
du hattest gesagt	du warst gelaufen
er hatte gesagt	er war gelaufen
wir hatten gesagt	wir waren gelaufen
ihr hattet gesagt	ihr wart gelaufen
sie hatten gesagt	sie waren gelaufen
Sie hatten gesagt	Sie waren gelaufen

FUTURE PERFECT

ich werde gesagt haben	ich werde gelaufen sein
du wirst gesagt haben	du wirst gelaufen sein
er wird gesagt haben	er wird gelaufen sein
wir werden gesagt haben	wir werden gelaufen sein
ihr werdet gesagt haben	ihr werdet gelaufen sein
sie werden gesagt haben	sie werden gelaufen sein
Sie werden gesagt haben	Sie werden gelaufen sein

IMPERATIVE

sage!	laufe!
sagt!	lauft!
sagen Sie!	laufen Sie!

PRESENT SUBJUNCTIVE I

ich sage	ich laufe
du sagest	du laufest
er sage	er laufe
wir sagen	wir laufen
ihr saget	ihr laufet
sie sagen	sie laufen
Sie sagen	Sie laufen

PRESENT SUBJUNCTIVE II

ich sagte	ich liefe
du sagtest	du liefest
er sagte	er liefe
wir sagten	wir liefen
ihr sagtet	ihr liefet
sie sagten	sie liefen
Sie sagten	Sie liefen

PAST SUBJUNCTIVE I

ich habe gesagt	ich sei gelaufen
du habest gesagt	du seiest gelaufen
er habe gesagt	er sei gelaufen
wir haben gesagt	wir seien gelaufen
ihr habet gesagt	ihr seiet gelaufen
sie haben gesagt	sie seien gelaufen
Sie haben gesagt	Sie seien gelaufen

PAST SUBJUNCTIVE II

ich hätte gesagt	ich wäre gelaufen
du hättest gesagt	du wärest gelaufen
er hätte gesagt	er wäre gelaufen
wir hätten gesagt	wir wären gelaufen
ihr hättet gesagt	ihr wäret gelaufen
sie hätten gesagt	sie wären gelaufen
Sie hätten gesagt	Sie wären gelaufen

FUTURE SUBJUNCTIVE

ich werde sagen	ich werde laufen
du werdest sagen	du werdest laufen
er werde sagen	er werde laufen
wir werden sagen	wir werden laufen
ihr werdet sagen	ihr werdet laufen
sie werden sagen	sie werden laufen
Sie werden sagen	Sie werden laufen

CONDITIONAL

ich würde sagen	ich würde laufen
du würdest sagen	du würdest laufen
er würde sagen	er würde laufen
wir würden sagen	wir würden laufen
ihr würdet sagen	ihr würdet laufen
sie würden sagen	sie würden laufen
Sie würden sagen	Sie würden laufen

FUTURE PERFECT SUBJUNCTIVE

ich werde gesagt haben	ich werde gelaufen sein
du werdest gesagt haben	du werdest gelaufen sein
er werde gesagt haben	er werde gelaufen sein
wir werden gesagt haben	wir werden gelaufen sein
ihr werdet gesagt haben	ihr werdet gelaufen sein
sie werden gesagt haben	sie werden gelaufen sein
Sie werden gesagt haben	Sie werden gelaufen sein

CONDITIONAL PERFECT

ich würde gesagt haben	ich würde gelaufen sein
du würdest gesagt haben	du würdest gelaufen sein
er würde gesagt haben	er würde gelaufen sein
wir würden gesagt haben	wir würden gelaufen sein
ihr würdet gesagt haben	ihr würdet gelaufen sein
sie würden gesagt haben	sie würden gelaufen sein
Sie würden gesagt haben	Sie würden gelaufen sein

Passive

INFINITIVE

geliebt werden   to be loved   **gesehen werden**   to be seen

PRESENT INDICATIVE

ich werde geliebt	ich werde gesehen
du wirst geliebt	du wirst gesehen
er wird geliebt	er wird gesehen
wir werden geliebt	wir werden gesehen
ihr werdet geliebt	ihr werdet gesehen
sie werden geliebt	sie werden gesehen
Sie werden geliebt	Sie werden gesehen

PAST INDICATIVE

ich wurde geliebt	ich wurde gesehen
du wurdest geliebt	du wurdest gesehen
er wurde geliebt	er wurde gesehen
wir wurden geliebt	wir wurden gesehen
ihr wurdet geliebt	ihr wurdet gesehen
sie wurden geliebt	sie wurden gesehen
Sie wurden geliebt	Sie wurden gesehen

FUTURE INDICATIVE

ich werde geliebt werden	ich werde gesehen werden
du wirst geliebt werden	du wirst gesehen werden
er wird geliebt werden	er wird gesehen werden
wir werden geliebt werden	wir werden gesehen werden
ihr werdet geliebt werden	ihr werdet gesehen werden
sie werden geliebt werden	sie werden gesehen werden
Sie werden geliebt werden	Sie werden gesehen werden

PRESENT PERFECT

ich bin geliebt worden	ich bin gesehen worden
du bist geliebt worden	du bist gesehen worden
er ist geliebt worden	er ist gesehen worden
wir sind geliebt worden	wir sind gesehen worden
ihr seid geliebt worden	ihr seid gesehen worden
sie sind geliebt worden	sie sind gesehen worden
Sie sind geliebt worden	Sie sind gesehen worden

PAST PERFECT

ich war geliebt worden	ich war gesehen worden
du warst geliebt worden	du warst gesehen worden
er war geliebt worden	er war gesehen worden

wir waren geliebt worden   wir waren gesehen worden
ihr wart geliebt worden   ihr wart gesehen worden
sie waren geliebt worden   sie waren gesehen worden
Sie waren geliebt worden   Sie waren gesehen worden

FUTURE PERFECT

ich werde geliebt worden sein   ich werde gesehen worden sein
du wirst geliebt worden sein   du wirst gesehen worden sein
er wird geliebt worden sein   er wird gesehen worden sein
wir werden geliebt worden sein   wir werden gesehen worden sein
ihr werdet geliebt worden sein   ihr werdet gesehen worden sein
sie werden geliebt worden sein   sie werden gesehen worden sein
Sie werden geliebt worden sein   Sie werden gesehen worden sein

PRESENT SUBJUNCTIVE I

ich werde geliebt   ich werde gesehen
du werdest geliebt   du werdest gesehen

etc.

PRESENT SUBJUNCTIVE II

ich würde geliebt   ich würde gesehen

etc.

PAST SUBJUNCTIVE I

ich sei geliebt worden   ich sei gesehen worden

etc.

PAST SUBJUNCTIVE II

ich wäre geliebt worden   ich wäre gesehen worden

etc.

FUTURE SUBJUNCTIVE

ich werde geliebt werden   ich werde gesehen werden
du werdest geliebt werden   du werdest gesehen werden

etc.

CONDITIONAL

ich würde geliebt werden   ich würde gesehen werden

FUTURE PERFECT SUBJUNCTIVE

ich werde geliebt worden sein   ich werde gesehen worden sein
du werdest geliebt worden sein   du werdest gesehen worden sein
etc.

CONDITIONAL PERFECT

ich würde geliebt worden sein   ich würde gesehen worden sein
etc.

4. *Irregular Verbs.*

INFINITIVE	PAST	PAST PARTICIPLE	PRESENT 3RD SING.	PRESENT SUBJ. II
beginnen (*begin*)	begann	begonnen		
bekommen (*receive*)	bekam	bekommen		
bestehen (*consist*)	bestand	bestanden		
biegen (*turn*)	bog	ist gebogen		
bitten (*ask*)	bat	gebeten		
bleiben (*stay*)	blieb	ist geblieben		
brennen (*burn*)	brannte	gebrannt		brennte
bringen (*bring*)	brachte	gebracht		brächte
denken (*think*)	dachte	gedacht		dächte
dürfen (*be permitted*)	durfte	gedurft	darf	dürfte
empfehlen (*recommend*)	empfahl	empfohlen	empfiehlt	
entscheiden (*decide*)	entschied	entschieden		
essen (*eat*)	aß	gegessen	ißt	
fahren (*drive, ride*)	fuhr	ist gefahren	fährt	
fallen (*fall*)	fiel	ist gefallen	fällt	
finden (*find*)	fand	gefunden		
fließen (*flow*)	floß	ist geflossen		
geben (*give*)	gab	gegeben	gibt	
gefallen (*please*)	gefiel	gefallen	gefällt	
gehen (*go*)	ging	ist gegangen		
gelingen (*succeed*)	gelang	ist gelungen		
gewinnen (*win*)	gewann	gewonnen		
haben (*have*)	hatte	gehabt	hat	hätte
halten (*hold*)	hielt	gehalten	hält	
heißen (*be called*)	hieß	geheißen		
helfen (*help*)	half	geholfen	hilft	
kennen (*know*)	kannte	gekannt		kennte
kommen (*come*)	kam	ist gekommen		
können (*can*)	konnte	gekonnt	kann	könnte
lassen (*let*)	ließ	gelassen	läßt	
laufen (*run*)	lief	ist gelaufen	läuft	

INFINITIVE	PAST	PAST PARTICIPLE	PRESENT 3RD SING.	PRESENT SUBJ. II
lesen (*read*)	las	gelesen	liest	
liegen (*lie*)	lag	gelegen		
mögen (*like*)	mochte	gemocht	mag	möchte
müssen (*must*)	mußte	gemußt	muß	müßte
nehmen (*take*)	nahm	genommen	nimmt	
nennen (*name*)	nannte	genannt		nennte
rennen (*run*)	rannte	ist gerannt		rennte
scheinen (*shine; seem*)	schien	geschienen		
schlafen (*sleep*)	schlief	geschlafen	schläft	
schlagen (*strike*)	schlug	geschlagen	schlägt	
schreiben (*write*)	schrieb	geschrieben		
schwimmen (*swim*)	schwamm	ist geschwommen		
sehen (*see*)	sah	gesehen	sieht	
sein (*be*)	war	ist gewesen	ist	wäre
senden (*send*)	sandte	gesandt		sendete
singen (*sing*)	sang	gesungen		
sitzen (*sit*)	saß	gesessen		
sollen (*be supposed to*)	sollte	gesollt	soll	sollte
sprechen (*speak*)	sprach	gesprochen	spricht	
stehen (*stand*)	stand	gestanden		
tragen (*carry*)	trug	getragen	trägt	
treffen (*meet*)	traf	getroffen	trifft	
treten (*step*)	trat	ist getreten	tritt	
trinken (*drink*)	trank	getrunken		
tun (*do*)	tat	getan	tut	täte
verbringen (*spend*)	verbrachte	verbracht		verbrächte
verlassen (*leave*)	verließ	verlassen	verläßt	
verlieren (*lose*)	verlor	verloren		
verstehen (*understand*)	verstand	verstanden		
wachsen (*grow*)	wuchs	ist gewachsen	wächst	
waschen (*wash*)	wusch	gewaschen	wäscht	
werden (*become*)	wurde	ist geworden	wird	würde
wissen (*know*)	wußte	gewußt	weiß	wüßte
wollen (*want*)	wollte	gewollt	will	wollte
zerreißen (*tear to pieces*)	zerriß	zerrissen		
ziehen (*pull*)	zog	gezogen		

VOCABULARIES

The German-English vocabulary lists the plural of nouns as follows: **das Buch, ⸗er.** Genitive endings are given only for masculine and neuter nouns forming their genitive in **-n, -en, -ns,** or **-ens: der Affe, -n, -n; der Student, -en, -en; das Herz, -ens, -en.**

Principal parts are given for strong and irregular verbs. A hyphen indicates a separable prefix.

Words are stressed on the first syllable, unless the stress is indicated by a dash (**Amẹrika**) for a long vowel or diphthong or a dot (**anstạtt**) for a short vowel. Words with inseparable prefixes, however, are stressed on the root syllable.

ABBREVIATIONS

acc.	accusative	*gen.*	genitive
adj.	adjective	*impers.*	impersonal
adv.	adverb	*inf.*	infinitive
comp.	comparative	*pl.*	plural
conj.	conjunction	*prep.*	preposition
dat.	dative	*pron.*	pronoun

der **Abend, -e** evening; **am Abend** in the evening; **heute abend** this evening, tonight; **zu Abend essen** to eat supper

das **Abendessen** supper; **vor dem Abendessen** before supper; **nach dem Abendessen** after supper

abends in the evening; P.M.

aber but

ab-fahren (fährt ab), fuhr ab, ist abgefahren to leave, depart

ab-holen to fetch, get

der **Abschied, -e** departure; **beim Abschied** at parting

die **Abteilung, -en** department

acht eight

der, die, das **achte** the eighth

achtzehn eighteen

achtzig eighty

der **Affe, -n, -n** monkey

alle (*pl.*) all

allerdings to be sure

alles everything; **alles Fremde** everything strange, everything foreign

als than; when, as

also therefore, consequently

alt old

(das) **Amerika** America

der **Amerikaner, -** American

die **Amerikanerin, -nen** American girl, American woman

amerikanisch American

sich amüsieren to have a good time; **sich glänzend amüsieren** to have a splendid time

an (+ *dat.* or *acc.*) at, to, on

anderer, andere, anderes other, different

ändern to change

anders different; **anders als** different from

an-fangen (fängt an), fing an, angefangen to begin

die **Angel, -n** fishing tackle

angeln to fish; **beim Angeln** (while) fishing

die **Angelrute, -n** fishing rod

angenehm pleasant

an-kommen, kam an, ist angekommen to arrive

an-machen to put on (*light*)

an-rufen, rief an, angerufen to call up, telephone

sich an-sehen (sieht sich an), sah sich an, angesehen to look at

an-springen, sprang an, angesprungen to start

anstatt (+ *gen.*) instead of

an-stoßen (stößt an), stieß an, angestoßen to poke

die **Antwort, -en** answer

antworten to answer

an-ziehen, zog an, angezogen to dress, put on; **sich anziehen** to get dressed

der **Anzug, ⸗e** suit

der **Apfel, ⸗** apple

die **Apotheke, -n** pharmacy, drugstore

der **April** April

die **Arbeit, -en** work

arbeiten to work

ärgerlich angry

sich ärgern (über + *acc.*) to be vexed (about), annoyed (at)

der **Arm, -e** arm

arm poor

der **Arzt, ⸗e** physician, doctor

auch also, too

auf (+ *dat.* or *acc.*) on, to, in
die **Aufgabe, -n** lesson
  auf-heulen to roar
  auf-hören to stop; **er hat auf-gehört zu lesen** he stopped reading
  auf-machen to open
  aufmerksam attentive, careful
die **Aufnahme, -n** snapshot
sich **auf-setzen** to put on (*a hat*)
  auf-stehen, stand auf, ist auf-gestanden to get up, stand up
das **Auge, -n** eye
der **August** August
  aus (+ *dat.*) from, out of
  aus-sehen (sieht aus), sah aus, ausgesehen to look, appear; **gut aussehen** to look good
  außerdem besides
die **Aussicht, -en** view
  aus-steigen, stieg aus, ist ausgestiegen to get off
das **Auto, -s** car, automobile
der **Autobus, -se** bus

die **Bahnfahrt, -en** train ride
der **Bahnhof, ⸚e** railroad station
  bald soon
  bauen to build
der **Baum, ⸚e** tree
(das) **Bayern** Bavaria
der **Beamte, -n, -n** official; **ein Beamter** an official
  bedauernd regretful
sich **beeilen** to hurry
sich **bedanken** to express one's thanks
  bedecken to cover
  bedeuten to mean, signify
die **Bedeutung, -en** meaning
  begegnen (+ *dat.*) (**ist**) to meet (*by chance*)
  begeistert enthusiastic

  beginnen, begann, begonnen to begin, start
  begrüßen to greet
  bei (+ *dat.*) at the house of; **bei ihr** at her house; **bei meinem Onkel** at my uncle's (house)
  beide both
der **Bekannte, -n, -n** acquaintance; **ein Bekannter** an acquaintance
  bekommen, bekam, bekommen to get, receive
  belästigen to bother
  beleidigt offended
das **Benzin, -e** gasoline
die **Benzinuhr, -en** gas gauge
  beobachten to observe
der **Berg, -e** mountain
(das) **Berlin** Berlin
  berühmt (**wegen** + *gen.*) famous (for)
  beschreiben, beschrieb, beschrieben to describe
  besetzen to occupy
  besitzen, besaß, besessen to possess
  besonders especially
  besorgen to obtain
das **Beste** the best (thing)
  bestehen (**aus** + *dat.*) to consist (of)
  bestellen to order
  bestrafen to punish
der **Besuch, -e** visit, visitor; **zu Besuch** visiting
  besuchen to visit
  betrachten to look at, consider
  betreten (betritt), betrat, betreten to enter
das **Bett, -en** bed; **zu Bett** to bed
  bevor (*conj.*) before
  bewegen to move
  bezahlen to pay (for)

biegen, bog, ist gebogen to turn

das **Bier, -e** beer

das **Bild, -er** picture; **auf dem Bild** in the picture

billig cheap, inexpensive

binden, band, gebunden to tie

die **Birne, -n** pear

bis until

bitten (**um** + *acc.*), **bat, gebeten** to ask (for)

blättern to leaf

blau blue

bleiben, blieb, ist geblieben to remain, stay

der **Bleistift, -e** pencil

blicken (**auf** + *acc.*) to glance, look at

die **Blume, -n** flower

der **Blumenstock, ⁼e** potted plant

der **Boden, ⁼** ground, floor

der **Braten, -** roast

brauchen to need

braun brown

brennen, brannte, gebrannt to burn

der **Brief, -e** letter

die **Briefmarke, -n** postage stamp

bringen, brachte, gebracht to bring

das **Brot, -e** bread, loaf; **belegtes Brot** sandwich

die **Brücke, -n** bridge

der **Bruder, ⁼** brother

das **Buch, ⁼er** book

die **Buchdruckerkunst** art of printing

die **Bundesrepublik** Federal Republic

der **Bücherladen, ⁼** bookstore

das **Büro, -s** office

die **Burschenherrlichkeit** glory of student life

die **Burschenschaft, -en** fraternity

da (*adv.*) there; (*conj.*) because, since

dahin (to) there, thither

die **Dame, -n** lady

der **Dampfer, -** steamer, ship

der **Dank** thanks

danke thanks, thank you

danken (+ *dat.*) to thank

dann then

das that; **das sind** those are

daß (*conj.*) that

dauern to last

denken, dachte, gedacht to think; **ich denke an ihn** I'm thinking of him

das **Denkmal, ⁼er** monument

denn because, for

dennoch nevertheless

derselbe, dieselbe, dasselbe the same

deutsch German

Deutsch German (*language*)

der **Deutsche, -n, -n** German; **ein Deutscher** a German; **die Deutsche, -n** German girl, German woman

(das) **Deutschland** Germany, **nach Deutschland** to Germany

der **Dezember** December

der **Dichter, -** poet

dienen (+ *dat.*) to serve

der **Dienstag** Tuesday

dies this; **dies sind** these are

dieser, diese, dieses this, that

doch nevertheless, after all

der **Dom, -e** cathedral

die **Donau** Danube

der **Donnerstag** Thursday

das **Dorf, ⁼er** village

dort there

draußen outside

drehen to turn

drei three

dreimal three times
dreißig thirty
dreizehn thirteen
der, die, das **dritte** the third
drittens in the third place
dunkel dark
durch (+ *acc.*) through
dürfen (darf), durfte, gedurft may, to be permitted (to); **nicht dürfen** must not
Durst haben to be thirsty
das **Dutzend, -e** dozen

eben just
die **Ecke, -n** corner; **an der Ecke** on the corner, at the corner; **um die Ecke** around the corner
ehe (*conj.*) before
das **Ehepaar, -e** married couple
eigen own; **mein eigenes Haus** my own house
ein, eine, ein a, an, one
einander one another
der **Eindruck, ⁼e** impression
einfach simple, modest
einige some
einmal once
ein-schlafen (schläft ein), schlief ein, ist eingeschlafen to fall asleep
ein-schließen to enclose, lock up
ein-steigen, stieg ein, ist eingestiegen to get in, on
ein-treten (tritt ein), trat ein, ist eingetreten to enter
einundzwanzig twenty-one; **der, die, das einundzwanzigste** the twenty-first
einverstanden in agreement
der **Einwohner, -** inhabitant
einzig single; **ein einziges Mal** a single time, only once
das **Eis** ice, ice cream

elf eleven
die **Eltern** (*pl.*) parents
empfehlen (empfiehlt), empfahl, empfohlen to recommend
(das) **England** England
der **Engländer, -** Englishman
die **Engländerin, -nen** Englishwoman
Englisch English (*language*)
englisch English
der **Enkel, -** grandson, grandchild
entgegnen to reply
entlang (+ *acc.*) along; **den Fluß entlang** along the river
entscheiden, entschied, entschieden to decide
die **Entscheidung, -en** decision
entschuldigen to excuse
entschwinden, entschwand, ist entschwunden to disappear
entstehen, entstand, ist entstanden to originate
entweder ... oder either ... or
die **Erdbeere, -n** strawberry
erfahren (erfährt), erfuhr, erfahren to experience, find out, learn
der **Erfinder, -** inventor
erfreut happy
sich **erinnern (an + *acc.*)** to remember
erkennen, erkannte, erkannt to recognize
erklären to explain
die **Erklärung, -en** explanation
erleben to experience
ernst serious
erst not until, only
der, die, das **erste** the first; **heute ist der erste Februar** today is the first of February
erstens in the first place
ertönen to sound

erzählen to tell, narrate

das **Essen** meal, food

essen (ißt), aß, gegessen to eat

das **Eßzimmer, -** dining room

etwas something; **etwas Ange-nehmes** something pleasant; **so etwas** such things

(das) **Europa** Europe

fahren (fährt), fuhr, ist ge-fahren to ride, go; to drive

die **Fahrkarte, -n** (*transportation*) ticket

die **Fahrt, -en** ride, trip

der **Fall, ⁼e** case; **auf jeden Fall** in any case

fallen (fällt), fiel, ist gefallen to fall

die **Familie, -n** family

der **Farbfilm, -e** color film

farbig colored

fast almost

das **Faß, ⁼er** barrel

fassen to grasp

der **Februar** February

fehlen to be wrong, be lacking

feiern to celebrate

der **Feind, -e** enemy

das **Feld, -er** field

der **Fels, -en, -en** rock

das **Fenster, -** window

die **Ferien** (*pl.*) vacation

fertig ready

das **Fest, -e** festival, party

fest fast, tight

das **Feuerwerk, -e** fireworks

finden, fand, gefunden to find

der **Fisch, -e** fish

flach flat

die **Flasche, -n** bottle; **eine Flasche Milch** a bottle of milk

das **Fleisch** meat

fliegen, flog, ist geflogen to fly

fließen, floß, ist geflossen to flow

die **Flugkarte, -n** plane ticket

das **Flugzeug, -e** airplane

der **Fluß, ⁼sse** river

folgen (+ *dat.*) (**ist**) to follow

fort-gehen, ging fort, ist fort-gegangen to go away

der **Frack, -s** dress coat

die **Frage, -n** question; **er stellt mir eine Frage** he's asking me a question

fragen to ask

(das) **Frankreich** France

französisch French

der **Franzose, -n, -n** Frenchman

Frau Mrs.; **die Frau, -en** wom-an, wife

Fräulein Miss

die **Freiheit** freedom

der **Freitag** Friday

fremd strange, foreign; **der Fremde, -n, -n** stranger; **ein Fremder** a stranger

die **Freude, -n** joy, pleasure; **das macht mir Freude** that gives me pleasure

freuen: es freut mich I'm glad; **es freut mich, Sie kennen-zulernen** I'm glad to meet you; **sich freuen (auf** + *acc.*) to look forward to; **sich freuen (über** + *acc.*) to be pleased with

der **Freund, -e** friend

die **Freundin, -nen** girl friend

freundlich friendly

der **Friede, gen. -ns** peace

frisch fresh

der **Friseur, -e** barber

fröhlich merry

früh early; **morgen früh** to-morrow morning

der **Frühling, -e** spring; **im Früh-ling** in the spring

das **Frühstück** breakfast; **vor dem Frühstück** before breakfast;

nach dem Frühstück after breakfast

führen to lead; **dieser Weg führt zum Bahnhof** this is the way to the railroad station

der **Füllhalter, -** fountain pen

fünf five

fünfzehn fifteen

fünfzig fifty

für (+ *acc.*) for

der **Fuß, ⸗e** foot

der **Gang, ⸗e** course

ganz entire, whole, all of; **ganz Deutschland** all of Germany; **den ganzen Sommer** the whole summer (long)

der **Garten, ⸗** garden

der **Gast, ⸗e** guest

das **Gebäude, -** building

geben (gibt), gab, gegeben to give; **es gibt** (+ *acc.*) there is; there are

geboren born; **wo sind Sie geboren?** where were you born? **wo wurde Goethe geboren?** where was Goethe born?

gebraten roasted

der **Geburtstag, -e** birthday

die **Geduld** patience

gefallen (+ *dat.*), **(gefällt), gefiel, gefallen; das Haus gefällt mir** I like the house

gegen (+ *acc.*) towards, against; **gegen Mittag** around noon

die **Gegend, -en** region

gehen, ging, ist gegangen to go; **wie geht es Ihnen?** how are you? **es geht mir gut** I'm fine, well

gehören (+ *dat.*) to belong to

gelb yellow

das **Geld, -er** money

gelingen (*impers.*), **gelang, ist gelungen; es gelingt mir** I succeed

das **Gemälde, -** painting

das **Gemüse, -** vegetable

genießen, genoß, genossen to enjoy

genug enough

das **Gepäck** baggage

gerade just, right

gerne gladly; **er lernt gerne** he likes to study

das **Geschäft, -e** shop; business

der **Geschäftsmann, Geschäftsleute** businessman

das **Geschenk, -e** gift

die **Geschichte, -n** story, history

die **Geschwister** (*pl.*) brothers and sisters

das **Gesetz, -e** law

das **Gesicht, -er** face

die **Gestalt, -en** figure

gestern yesterday

gesund healthy, well

gewinnen, gewann, gewonnen to win

gewöhnlich usual

glänzend splendid

das **Glas, ⸗er** glass; **ein Glas Bier** a glass of beer

der **Glaube,** *gen.* **-ns** faith

glauben to believe

gleich same

die **Glocke, -n** bell

das **Glück** (good) luck; **Glück haben** to be lucky

glücklich happy

der **Gott, ⸗er** God

das **Grab, ⸗er** grave

das **Gras, ⸗er** grass

grau gray

die **Grenze, -n** border

grinsen to grin

groß big, large, tall

die **Großmutter,** ⸗ grandmother

der **Großvater,** ⸗ grandfather

grün green

gut good

gutmütig good-natured

das **Haar, -e** hair

das **Haarschneiden** haircut

haben (hat), hatte, gehabt to have

der **Hafen,** ⸗ harbor

halb half; **eine halbe Stunde** half an hour; **halb neun (Uhr)** half past eight (o'clock)

halten (hält), hielt, gehalten to hold; to stop

die **Hand,** ⸗**e** hand; **die Hand reichen** to shake hands

handeln (von + *dat.***)** to deal with, concern

der **Handschuh, -e** glove

der **Hase, -n, -n** rabbit

der **Hauptbahnhof,** ⸗**e** central station

die **Hauptstadt,** ⸗**e** capital city

das **Haus,** ⸗**er** house; **nach Hause** home(ward); **zu Hause** at home

heben, hob, gehoben to lift

das **Heer, -e** army

das **Heft, -e** notebook

die **Heide, -n** heath

heiß hot

heißen, hieß, geheißen to be called; **wie heißen Sie?** what's your name?; **ich heiße** my name is

helfen (+ *dat.***) (hilft), half, geholfen** to help

hell bright, light (*in color*)

heraus-reißen, riß heraus, herausgerissen to tear out

herbei-eilen (ist) to rush up

der **Herbst, -e** autumn, fall

herein-kommen, kam herein, ist hereingekommen to come in

Herr Mr.; **der Herr, -n -en** gentleman

herrlich magnificent

heute today; **heute morgen** this morning

das **Herz, -ens, -en** heart

hier here

der **Himmel, -** sky, heaven

hinaus-gehen, ging hinaus, ist hinausgegangen to go out

hin-legen to put down

hinten behind, in back

hinter (+ *dat.* **or** *acc.***)** behind

historisch historical

hoch high

hoffen to hope

holen to fetch, get

das **Holz,** ⸗**er** wood

hören to hear, listen to; **er hört Radio** he's listening to the radio

der **Hörer, -** (*telephone*) receiver

die **Hose, -n** (*pair of*) trousers

das **Hotel, -s** hotel

hübsch pretty

der **Hügel, -** hill

hundert a hundred, one hundred

Hunger haben to be hungry

husten to cough

der **Hut,** ⸗**e** hat

immer always; **immer besser** better and better; **immer mehr** more and more

in (+ *dat.* **or** *acc.***)** in, into, at, to

interessant interesting

interessieren to interest; **sich**

interessieren (für + acc.) to be interested (in)

(das) **Italien** Italy

der **Italiener, -** Italian

italienisch Italian

ja yes; **jawohl** yes indeed

die **Jacke, -n** jacket

das **Jahr, -e** year

das **Jahrhundert, -e** century

der **Januar** January; **im Januar** in January

jauchzen to cheer

je ever

je (+ *comp.*) . . . **desto** (+ *comp.*) the (+ *comp.*) . . . the (+ *comp.*) **je langsamer er spricht, desto besser verstehe ich ihn** the slower he speaks, the better I understand him

jeder (*pron.*) everyone, everybody; **jeder, jede, jedes** (*adj.*) each, every

jedesmal every time

jemand someone, somebody

jetzt now

der **Juli** July; **im Juli** in July

jung young

der **Junge, -n, -n** boy

der **Juni** June; **im Juni** in June

der **Kaffee** coffee

der **Kaiser, -** emperor

das **Kalbfleisch** veal

kalt cold

kämmen to comb; **sich die Haare kämmen** to comb one's hair

die **Karte, -n** ticket; map

die **Kartoffel, -n** potato

kaufen to buy

kein, keine, kein no, not any

der **Kellner, -** waiter

kennen, kannte, gekannt to know (*be acquainted with*)

kennen-lernen to get acquainted with, meet (*for the first time*)

das **Kilo, -s** kilogram

das **Kind, -er** child

das **Kino, -s** movies, movie theater

die **Kirche, -n** church; **in die Kirche** to church; **in der Kirche** in church, at church; **nach der Kirche** after church

klatschen to clap; **in die Hände klatschen** to applaud

das **Kleid, -er** dress, (*pl.*) clothes

klein small, little

kleinlaut dejected

klopfen to knock; **es klopft** someone is knocking at the door

das **Knie, -** knee

der **Koch, ⁼e** cook

der **Koffer, -** trunk, bag, suitcase

(das) **Köln** Cologne

Kölner (from) Cologne

kommen, kam, ist gekommen to come

der **König, -e** king

können (kann), konnte, gekonnt can, to be able to; **Deutsch können** to know German

das **Konzert, -e** concert

der **Kopf, ⁼e** head

kosten to cost

kräftig powerful

krank sick

kriechen, kroch, ist gekrochen to creep

der **Krieg, -e** war

krönen to crown

die **Küche, -n** kitchen

der **Kuchen, -** cake
der **Kugelschreiber, -** ball-point pen
die **Kunst, ̈e** art
kurz short
die **Kusine, -n** cousin (*f.*)

lächeln to smile
lachen to laugh
der **Laden, ̈** store, shop
das **Land, ̈er** country, land; **aufs Land** to the country; **auf dem Lande** in the country
die **Landkarte, -n** map
die **Landschaft, -en** landscape, countryside
lang long
lange for a long time
langsam slow
lassen (läßt), ließ, gelassen to let; **ein Haus bauen lassen** to have a house built
laufen (läuft), lief, ist gelaufen to run
laut loud
läuten to ring; **es läutet** the bell is ringing
leben to live
legen to put, lay
lehren to teach
der **Lehrer, -** teacher
die **Lehrerin, -nen** teacher (*f.*)
leicht light (*in weight*); easy
leid: es tut mir leid I'm sorry
leider unfortunately
leise softly
sich leisten to afford
lernen to learn, study
lesen (liest), las, gelesen to read
die **Leute** (*pl.*) people (*in a crowd*)
das **Licht, -er** light; **das Licht anmachen** to put on the light
lieben to love; to like

lieber rather; **lieber spielen** to prefer to play
liebsten: am liebsten most gladly; **am liebsten spielen** to like best to play
das **Lied, -er** song
liegen, lag, gelegen to lie; to be (*situated*)
links left; **nach links** to the left
locken to lure
die **Luft, ̈e** air

machen to do, make; **das macht nichts** that doesn't matter
das **Mädchen, -** girl
der **Mai** May
das **Mal, -e** time, occasion; **ein einziges Mal** only once
der **Maler, -** painter
man (*pron.*) one, people; **man sagt** one says, people say, they say
manche some
mancher, manche, manches many a
manchmal sometimes
der **Mann, ̈er** man
die **Mannschaft, -en** team
der **Mantel, ̈** coat
das **Märchen, -** fairy tale
die **Mark** mark (*German monetary unit, equivalent to approximately 25 U.S. cents*)
der **März** March
die **Medizin, -** medicine; **eine Medizin von der Apotheke holen** to get medicine from the drugstore
mehr more
mehrere several
mein my
meinen to say, think

meisten most; **die meisten Leute** most people

der **Mensch, -en, -en** man, human being, person

die **Milch** milk

die **Million, -en** million; **eine Million Einwohner** a million inhabitants; **zwei Millionen Einwohner** two million inhabitants

die **Minute, -n** minute

die **Missetat, -en** misdeed

mit (+ *dat.*) with

der **Mittag, -e** noon; **zu Mittag essen** to eat lunch (*or dinner*)

das **Mittagessen** lunch, dinner; **nach dem Mittagessen** after lunch (or dinner)

das **Mittelalter** Middle Ages

mitten (**in** + *dat.*) in the middle (of); **mitten in der Stadt** in the middle of town

der **Mittwoch** Wednesday; **am Mittwoch** on Wednesday

möchte would like to

mögen (**mag**), **mochte, gemocht** to like, care (to)

möglich possible

der **Monat, -e** month; **nächsten Monat** next month

der **Mond, -e** moon

der **Montag** Monday; **am Montag** on Monday

montags on Monday(s)

der **Morgen, -** morning; **Guten Morgen!** Good morning! **gestern morgen** yesterday morning; **heute morgen** this morning; **Freitag morgen** Friday morning

morgen tomorrow

morgens in the morning(s), A.M.

die **Motorhaube, -n** hood (*of a car*)

müde tired

(das) **München** Munich

die **Münze, -n** coin

das **Museum, Museen** museum

müssen (**muß**), **mußte, gemußt** must, to have to

die **Mutter, ⸚** mother

die **Mütze, -n** cap

nach (+ *dat.*) after, to; **nach Hause** home(ward); **fünf Minuten nach acht** five minutes after eight

der **Nachbar, -n, -n** neighbor

die **Nachbarin, -nen** neighbor (*f.*)

nachher afterwards

der **Nachmittag, -e** afternoon; **am Nachmittag** in the afternoon; **gestern nachmittag** yesterday afternoon; **heute nachmittag** this afternoon; **morgen nachmittag** tomorrow afternoon

nachmittags in the afternoon(s), P.M.

nächster, nächste, nächstes next

die **Nacht, ⸚e** night; **in der Nacht** at night

nachts at night

der **Nachtisch, -e** dessert

die **Nähe** vicinity; **in der Nähe des Turms** near the tower

der **Name, -ns, -n** name

die **Natur** nature

neben (+ *dat.* or *acc.*) next to, near

der **Neffe, -n, -n** nephew

nehmen (**nimmt**), **nahm, genommen** to take

nein no

nennen, nannte, genannt to name

nett nice, friendly

neu new

neun nine

neunzehn nineteen

neunzig ninety

nicht not; **nicht wahr?** isn't it? aren't they? don't I? etc.

die **Nichte, -n** niece

nichts nothing; **nichts Schlechtes** nothing bad; **nichts als** nothing but

nicken to nod

nie never

niemand no one, nobody

noch still, yet; **noch ein** another; **noch nicht** not yet

der **Norden** north; **von Süden nach Norden** from south to north

die **Nordsee** North Sea

normalerweise normally

der **November** November

nun now

nur only

ob whether

obgleich although

öde desolate

der **Offizier, -e** officer

oft often

ohne (+ *acc.*) without

das **Ohr, -en** ear

der **Oktober** October

der **Onkel, -** uncle

die **Ordnung, -en** order

der **Osten** east; **von Osten nach Westen** from east to west

(das) **Österreich** Austria

die **Ostsee** Baltic Sea

das **Paar, -e** pair; **ein Paar Handschuhe** a pair of gloves; **ein paar Worte** a few words

packen to pack

das **Paket, -e** package

das **Papier, -e** paper

der **Park, -s** park

der **Passagier, -e** passenger

passieren (ist) to happen

das **Pferd, -e** horse

der **Pfirsich, -e** peach

die **Pflicht, -en** duty

der **Platz, ⸚e** square, place

plaudern to chat

die **Post** mail; post office; **mit der Post** by mail

das **Postamt, ⸚er** post office

prächtig splendid

der **Präsident, -en, -en** president

der **Preis, -e** prize; price

der **Professor, Professoren** professor

prüfen to check, examine

Punkt zwölf Uhr (at) twelve o'clock sharp

das **Radio, -s** radio; **Radio hören** to listen to the radio

der **Rat** advice, counsel

raten (+ *dat.*) to advise

das **Rathaus, ⸚er** city hall

der **Ratschlag, ⸚e** (*piece of*) advice

rauchen to smoke

die **Rebe, -n** grape vine

rechnen to calculate

die **Rechnung, -en** bill

recht haben to be right; **ist dir das recht?** is that all right with you?

rechts right; **nach rechts** to the right

die **Rede, -n** speech; **eine Rede halten** to make a speech

reden to talk

regelmäßig regular

der **Regen** rain

regnen to rain; **es regnet** it's raining

reich rich
reichen to extend, hand
reif ripe
die **Reise, -n** trip; **eine Reise machen** to take a trip
das **Reisebüro, -s** travel agency
der **Reiseführer, -** guidebook
reisen (ist) to travel
der **Reisende, -n, -n** traveler; **ein Reisender** a traveler
der **Reiseplan, ⸗e** travel plan
rennen, rannte, ist gerannt to run
das **Restaurant, -s** restaurant
der **Rhein** Rhine; **am Rhein** at, on the Rhine; **an den Rhein** to the Rhine
richtig correct
die **Richtung, -en** direction; **in dieser Richtung** in this direction
das **Rindfleisch** beef
der **Ring, -e** ring
rollen to roll
die **Rolltreppe, -n** escalator
rot red
rufen, rief, gerufen to call
ruhig calm

die **Sache, -n** thing
die **Sage, -n** legend
sagen to say, tell
sammeln to collect
der **Samstag** Saturday
der **Satz, ⸗e** sentence
schade: es ist schade it's a shame
der **Schaffner, -** conductor
schauen to look
der **Schauspieler, -** actor
scheinen, schien, geschienen to shine; to seem; **die Sonne scheint** the sun is shining; **es**

scheint richtig zu sein it seems to be correct
schicken to send
das **Schiff, -e** ship
der **Schiffer, -** boatman
der **Schinken, -** ham
schlafen (schläft), schlief, geschlafen to sleep
das **Schlafzimmer, -** bedroom
schlagen (schlägt), schlug, geschlagen to strike, beat
die **Schlagsahne** whipped cream
schlecht bad, evil
schließen, schloß, geschlossen to close
schließlich finally
schlimm bad; **das Schlimmste** the worst (*thing*)
das **Schloß, ⸗sser** castle
der **Schluß, ⸗sse** end, conclusion
der **Schlüssel, -** key
schmecken (+ *dat.*) to taste (*good to*)
schmutzig dirty
schnallen to fasten
der **Schnee** snow
schneiden, schnitt, geschnitten to cut
schnell quick, fast
schon already
schön beautiful, nice
die **Schraube, -n** screw
schreiben, schrieb, geschrieben to write
die **Schreibmaschine, -n** typewriter
der **Schreibtisch, -e** desk
der **Schuh, -e** shoe
die **Schuld, -en** debt
die **Schule, -n** school
der **Schüler, -** pupil
die **Schülerin, -nen** pupil (*f.*)
schütteln to shake
schwarz black

der **Schwarzwald** Black Forest

die **Schweiz** Switzerland; **in der Schweiz** in Switzerland; **in die Schweiz** to Switzerland

schwer heavy, difficult

die **Schwester, -n** sister

schwimmen, schwamm, ist geschwommen to swim

sechs six

sechzehn sixteen

sechzig sixty

der **See, -n** lake; **am See** at the lake; **an den See** to the lake

die **See, -n** ocean, sea; **an der See** at the sea(shore); **an die See** to the seashore

sehen (sieht), sah, gesehen to see

sehr very

seit (+ *dat.*) since

die **Seite, -n** side; page; **auf dieser Seite** on this side; **auf der anderen Seite** on the other side

selbst self; even

selten seldom

senden, sandte, gesandt to send

der **September** September

servieren to serve

die **Serviette, -n** napkin

sich setzen to sit down

sich himself, herself, itself, yourself, yourselves, themselves, oneself

sicher sure, certain

die **Sicherheitsgurte, -n** safety belt

die **Sicht** sight, view

sieben seven

siebzehn seventeen

siebzig seventy

singen, sang, gesungen to sing

sitzen, saß, gesessen to sit

so ... wie as ... as

sobald as soon as

soeben right now

sofort at once

der **Sohn, ⸚e** son

solcher, solche, solches such

der **Soldat, -en, -en** soldier

sollen (soll), sollte, gesollt to be (supposed) to

der **Sommer** summer; **im Sommer** in summer

sondern but

der **Sonnabend** Saturday

die **Sonne, -n** sun

der **Sonntag** Sunday

sonst otherwise

sowohl ... als auch both ... and

(das) **Spanien** Spain

der **Spanier, -** Spaniard

spanisch Spanish

spät late

der **Spaziergang, ⸚e** walk; **einen Spaziergang machen** to take a walk

speisen to dine

die **Speisekarte, -n** menu

der **Speisewagen, -** dining car

das **Spiegelei, -er** fried egg

das **Spiel, -e** game

spielen to play

sprechen (spricht), sprach, gesprochen to speak, talk

der **Staat, -en** state; **die Vereinigten Staaten** United States

die **Stadt, ⸚e** city, town; **in der Stadt** in town; **in die Stadt** to town, downtown

die **Startbahn, -en** runway

stark strong

statt-finden, fand statt, stattgefunden to take place

stecken to put, stick

stehen, stand, gestanden to stand

stehen-bleiben, blieb stehen, ist stehengeblieben to stop
stellen to put, stand; **er stellt mir eine Frage** he's asking me a question
sterben (stirbt), starb, ist gestorben to die
der **Stern, -e** star
die **Stiefmutter, :** stepmother
die **Stimme, -n** voice
das **Stockwerk, -e** floor, story
die **Straße, -n** street
die **Straßenbahn, -en** streetcar; **mit der Straßenbahn** by streetcar
der **Strauß, :e** bouquet
das **Stück, -e** piece; **ein Stück Käse** a piece of cheese
der **Student, -en, -en** student
die **Studentin, -nen** student (*f.*), coed
studieren to study (*at a university*)
das **Studierzimmer, -** study
der **Stuhl, :e** chair
die **Stunde, -n** hour; class
der **Sturm, :e** storm
suchen to look for, seek
der **Süden** south; **von Süden nach Norden** from south to north
sympathisch likeable, pleasant

die **Tafel, -n** blackboard, tablet, plaque
der **Tag, -e** day; **acht Tage** a week
das **Tagebuch, :er** diary
tagen to meet, assemble
die **Tante, -n** aunt
die **Tasche, -n** pocket
die **Taschenlampe, -n** flashlight
die **Tasse, -n** cup; **eine Tasse Tee** a cup of tea
tausend a thousand, one thousand

der **Tee, -s** tea
der **Teil, -e** part
telefonieren to call up
teuer dear, expensive
das **Tier, -e** animal
der **Tisch, -e** table
das **Tischtuch, :er** tablecloth
der **Titel, -** title
das **Tombolalos, -e** lottery ticket
die **Tochter, :** daughter
tragen (trägt), trug, getragen to carry; to wear
treffen (trifft), traf, getroffen to meet
trinken, trank, getrunken to drink
das **Trinkgeld, -er** tip, gratuity
trotzdem nevertheless
tun (tut), tat, getan to do; **es tut mir leid** I'm sorry; **die Augen tun ihm weh** his eyes hurt
die **Tür, -en** door
der **Turm, :e** tower

über (+ *dat.* or *acc.*) above, over
überall everywhere
das **Ufer, -** bank, shore
die **Uhr, -en** clock; watch; **ein Uhr** one o'clock; **um zwei Uhr** at two o'clock; **Wieviel Uhr ist es?** What time is it?
um (+ *acc.*) around; **um zwei Uhr** at two o'clock; **um zu** (+ *inf.*) in order to
sich um-drehen to turn around
umher-führen to show around
unbedingt absolutely
und and
die **Universität, -en** university
unrecht haben to be wrong
der **Unsinn** nonsense
unten below

unter (+ *dat.* or *acc.*) under; among

unterdessen meanwhile

der **Vater,** = father

sich **verbeugen** to bow

verbringen, verbrachte, verbracht to spend

das **Verderben** destruction

verdienen to earn

die **Vereinigten Staaten** (*pl.*) United States

vergessen (**vergißt**), **vergaß, vergessen** to forget

vergleichen, verglich, verglichen to compare

verkaufen to sell

der **Verkäufer, -** salesman

die **Verkäuferin, -nen** salesgirl, saleswoman

verlassen (**verläßt**), **verließ, verlassen** to leave (behind)

sich **verlieben** (**in** + *acc.*) to fall in love (with)

verlieren, verlor, verloren to lose

verschieden different

verstehen, verstand, verstanden to understand

versuchen to try

verwahren to keep

der **Verwandte, -n, -n** relative; **ein Verwandter** a relative

verzollen to declare (*for customs*)

der **Vetter, -n** cousin

viel much; **viele** many

vielleicht perhaps

vier four

der, die, das **vierte** the fourth

das **Viertel, -** quarter; **Viertel nach sechs** quarter after six; **Viertel vor eins** quarter of one

vierzehn fourteen

vierzig forty

der **Vogel,** = bird

das **Volk,** =er people, nation

von (+ *dat.*) from, of

vor (+ *dat.* or *acc.*) in front of, before; **vor einem Monat** a month ago; **zehn Minuten vor eins** ten minutes of one

vorbei past; **am Felsen vorbei** past the rock

vor-bereiten, bereitete vor, vorbereitet to prepare

vorgestern (the) day before yesterday

vorig previous

der **Vormittag, -e** morning, forenoon; **am Vormittag** in the morning

vorne forward, up front

die **Vorspeise, -n** appetizer

vor-stellen to present, introduce

der **Vortrag,** =e lecture; **einen Vortrag halten** to lecture

wachsen (**wächst**), **wuchs, ist gewachsen** to grow

wagen to dare, venture

wählen to elect

wahr: nicht wahr? isn't it? aren't they? don't I? etc.

während (+ *gen.*) during; (*conj.*) while

der **Wald,** =er forest, woods

waldig wooded

der **Waldweg, -e** road in the woods

die **Waldwiese, -n** clearing

wann? when? at what time?

warm warm

warten (**auf** + *acc.*) to wait (for)

warum? why?

was? what?

was für (**ein**) what kind of?

waschen (**wäscht**), **wusch, ge-**

waschen to wash; **sich waschen** to get washed

das **Wasser, -** water

wecken to waken

weder . . . noch neither . . . nor

der **Weg, -e** way, road

wegen (+ *gen.*) because of, on account of

weh: der Arm tut mir weh my arm hurts

weil because, since

die **Weile, -n** while; **eine Weile** a little while

der **Wein, -e** wine

weiß white

weit far

welcher? which?

wem? (to) whom?

wen? whom?

wenig little (*in number*)

wenige few

wenn when, whenever, if

wer? who?

werden (wird), wurde, ist geworden to become, get

das **Werk, -e** work (*of art*)

das **Werkzeug, -e** tool

wessen? whose?

der **Westen** west; **nach Westen** to (the) west

das **Wetter** weather

wichtig important

wie as; **wie?** how?

wieder again

Wiedersehen: auf Wiedersehen good-by

(das) **Wien** Vienna

wieviel? how much?

willkommen welcome; **willkommen heißen** to bid welcome

der **Wind, -e** wind

der **Winkel, -** corner

der **Winter, -** winter

der **Wirt, -e** hotelkeper, innkeeper

wissen (weiß), wußte, gewußt to know

wo? where?

die **Woche, -n** week

das **Wochenende, -n** weekend

wohin? where (to)? whither?

wohnen to dwell, live

das **Wohnzimmer, -** living room

die **Wolke, -n** cloud

wollen (will), wollte, gewollt to want (to)

das **Wort** word; **die Worte** words (*in a phrase*); **die Wörter** words (*individually*)

wünschen to wish

würde(n) would

die **Wurst, ⁼e** sausage

der **Zahn, ⁼e** tooth

der **Zahnarzt, ⁼e** dentist

zehn ten

zeigen to show

die **Zeit, -en** time

die **Zeitung, -en** newspaper

das **Zelt, -e** tent

das **Zentrum, Zentren** center

zerreißen, zerriß, zerrissen to tear to pieces

zerstört destroyed

ziehen, zog, gezogen to pull; **(ist)** to go

die **Zigarette, -n** cigarette

das **Zimmer, -** room

die **Zimmervermieterin, -nen** landlady

zittern to vibrate, shake

der **Zollbeamte, -n, -n** customs official

zu (*adv.*) too, excessively; (+ *dat.*) to; **zum Vater** to the father('s house); **zur Mutter** to the mother('s house)

zuerst first
zufrieden satisfied
der **Zug, ⸗e** train; **mit dem Zug** by train
zu-machen to close
die **Zündkerze, -n** spark plug
zurück-kommen, kam zurück, ist zurückgekommen to come back
zusammen together
der **Zuschauer, -** spectator
zuviel too much

zwanzig twenty
der, die, das **zwanzigste** the twentieth
zwar to be sure
zwei two
zweimal twice
der, die, das **zweite** the second
zweitens second, in the second place
zwischen (+ *dat.* or *acc.*) between, among
zwölf twelve

a, an ein, eine, ein

able: be able to können (kann), konnte, gekonnt

above über (+ *dat. or acc.*)

account: on account of wegen (+ *gen.*)

acquaintance der Bekannte, -n, -n; **an acquaintance** ein Bekannter

acquainted: become acquainted with kennen-lernen

advice der Rat; *pl.* Ratschläge

after (*conj.*) nachdem; (*prep.*) nach (+ *dat.*); **five minutes after eight** fünf Minuten nach acht; **after all** doch

afternoon der Nachmittag, -e; **in the afternoon** am Nachmittag, nachmittags; **Sunday afternoon** Sonntag nachmittag; **this afternoon** heute nachmittag; **tomorrow afternoon** morgen nachmittag

again wieder

ago vor (+ *dat.*); **a month ago** vor einem Monat

airplane das Flugzeug, -e

alive: to be alive leben

all (*pl.*) alle; **all of Germany** ganz Deutschland; **all summer long** den ganzen Sommer

almost fast

already schon

also auch

although obgleich

always immer

A.M. morgens

America (das) Amerika

American der Amerikaner, -; **American girl, woman** die Amerikanerin, -nen; (*adj.*) amerikanisch

among zwischen (+ *dat. or acc.*)

and und

animal das Tier, -e

annoyed: be annoyed (**at**) sich ärgern (über + *acc.*)

another noch ein, noch eine, noch ein; **one another** einander

answer die Antwort, -en; **to answer** antworten

any: not any kein, keine, kein

appear aus-sehen (sieht aus), sah aus, ausgesehen

apple der Apfel, ⸗

April der April; **in April** im April

arm der Arm, -e

army das Heer, -e

around um (+ *acc.*)

arrive an-kommen, kam an, ist angekommen

art die Kunst, ⸗e

as (*when*) als; **as . . . as** so . . . wie; **as soon as** sobald

ask fragen; **ask for** bitten um (+ *acc.*), bat, gebeten

at an (+ *dat.*), bei (+ *dat.*), in (+ *dat.*), um (+ *acc.*), zu (+ *dat.*); **at the corner** an der Ecke; **at the lake** am See; **at the river** am Fluß; **at the Rhine** am Rhein; **at the sea(shore)** an der See; **at the window** am Fenster; **at her house** bei ihr; **at Mrs. Meyer's (house)** bei Frau Meyer; **at my house** bei mir; **at the uncle's (house)** bei dem Onkel; **at church** in der Kirche; **at school** in der Schule; **at one o'clock** um ein Uhr; **at one o'clock sharp** Punkt ein Uhr; **at what time?** um wieviel Uhr? **at home** zu Hause; **at parting** beim Abschied

August der August; **in August** im August

aunt die Tante, -n

Austria (das) Österreich

autumn der Herbst, -e; **in autumn** im Herbst

away: **go away** fort-gehen, ging fort ist fortgegangen

back: **in back** hinten

bad schlecht, schlimm

bag der Koffer, -

baggage das Gepäck

ball-point pen der Kugelschreiber, -

Baltic Sea die Ostsee

Bavaria (das) Bayern

be sein (ist), war, ist gewesen; **be able** können (kann), konnte, gekonnt; **be fine: I'm fine** es geht mir gut; **be glad: I'm glad** es freut mich; **be lucky** Glück haben; **be permitted to** dürfen (darf), durfte, gedurft; **be situated** liegen, lag, gelegen; **be sorry: I'm sorry** es tut mir leid; **be supposed to** sollen (soll), sollte, gesollt; **be vexed (about), annoyed (at)** sich ärgern (über + *acc.*); **be well: I'm well** es geht mir gut; **How are you?** Wie geht es Ihnen? **there is, there are** es ist, es sind; es gibt

beat schlagen (schlägt), schlug, geschlagen

beautiful schön

because da, denn, weil; **because of** wegen (+ *gen.*)

become werden (wird), wurde, ist geworden; **become acquainted with** kennen-lernen

bed das Bett, -en; **to bed** zu Bett

bedroom das Schlafzimmer, -

beef das Rindfleisch

beer das Bier, -e

before (*conj.*) bevor, ehe; (*prep.*) vor (+ *dat.*)

begin beginnen, begann, begonnen

behind (*in back*) hinten; (*prep.*) hinter (+ *dat.* or *acc.*)

believe glauben

belong (**to**) gehören (+ *dat.*)

Berlin (das) Berlin

best: **the best (thing)** das Beste

better besser; **better and better** immer besser

between zwischen (+ *dat.* or *acc.*)

big groß

bill die Rechnung, -en

bird der Vogel, ⸚

birthday der Geburtstag, -e

black schwarz

blue blau

book das Buch, ⸚er

born geboren; **Where were you born?** Wo sind Sie geboren?; **Where was Goethe born?** Wo wurde Goethe geboren?

both beide; **both . . . and** sowohl . . . als auch

bottle die Flasche, -n; **a bottle of milk** eine Flasche Milch

boy der Junge, -n, -n

bread das Brot, -e

breakfast das Frühstück; **after breakfast** nach dem Frühstück; **before breakfast** vor dem Frühstück

bridge die Brücke, -n

bright hell

bring bringen, brachte, gebracht

brother der Bruder, ⸚; **brothers and sisters** die Geschwister (*pl.*)

brown braun

build bauen

building das Gebäude, -

burn brennen, brannte, gebrannt

bus der Autobus, -se

business das Geschäft, -e; **businessman** der Geschäftsmann, Geschäftsleute

but aber, sondern
buy kaufen

cake der Kuchen, -
call: to be called heißen, hieß, geheißen; **call up** an-rufen, rief an, angerufen
can (**be able to**) können (kann), konnte, gekonnt
capital (**city**) die Hauptstadt, ⸗e
car das Auto, -s
care (**to**) mögen (mag), mochte, gemocht
carry tragen (trägt), trug, getragen
castle das Schloß, ⸗sser
cathedral der Dom, -e
central station der Hauptbahnhof, ⸗e
century das Jahrhundert, -e
chair der Stuhl, ⸗e
change ändern
chat plaudern
cheap billig
cheese der Käse
child das Kind, -er
church die Kirche, -n; **after church** nach der Kirche; **at church, in church** in der Kirche; **to church** in die Kirche
cigarette die Zigarette, -n
city die Stadt, ⸗e; **city hall** das Rathaus, ⸗er
class die Stunde, -n
clock die Uhr, -en
close schließen, schloß, geschlossen
clothes die Kleider (*pl.*)
coed die Studentin, -nen
coffee der Kaffee
coin die Münze, -n
cold kalt
collect sammeln
Cologne (das) Köln; **of Cologne** Kölner

comb kämmen; **comb one's hair** sich die Haare kämmen
come kommen, kam, ist gekommen; **come back** zurück-kommen, kam zurück, ist zurückgekommen; **come in** herein-kommen, kam herein, ist hereingekommen
concert das Konzert, -e
conductor der Schaffner, -
consequently also
consider betrachten
consist (**of**) bestehen (aus + *dat.*), bestand, bestanden
corner die Ecke, -n; **at, on the corner** an der Ecke; **around the corner** um die Ecke
correct richtig
cost kosten
counsel der Rat
country das Land, ⸗er; **in the country** auf dem Lande; **to the country** aufs Land
couple das Paar, -e
cousin der Vetter, -n; (*f.*) die Kusine, -n
cup die Tasse, -n; **a cup of tea** eine Tasse Tee

dark dunkel
daughter die Tochter, ⸗
day der Tag, -e; **day before yesterday** vorgestern; **What day of the month is today?** Der wievielte ist heute?
dear teuer
debt die Schuld, -en
December der Dezember; **in December** im Dezember
decide entscheiden, entschied, entschieden
dentist der Zahnarzt, ⸗e
depart ab-fahren (fährt ab), fuhr ab, ist abgefahren

departure der Abschied, -e

dessert der Nachtisch, -e

die sterben (stirbt), starb, ist gestorben

different anderer, andere, anderes

difficult schwer

dining car der Speisewagen, -

dining room das Eßzimmer, -

dinner (*evening meal*) das Abendessen, -; **eat dinner** zu Abend essen

direction die Richtung, -en; **in this direction** in dieser Richtung

do machen; tun (tut), tat, getan

doctor der Arzt, ⸚e

door die Tür, -en

dozen das Dutzend, -e

dress das Kleid, -er

dress an-ziehen, zog an, angezogen; **get dressed** sich anziehen

drink trinken, trank, getrunken

drive (*ride*) fahren (fährt), fuhr, ist gefahren

drugstore die Apotheke, -n

during während (+ *gen.*)

dwell wohnen

each jeder, jede, jedes

ear das Ohr, -en

early früh

east der Osten; **from east to west** von Osten nach Westen

easy leicht

eat essen (ißt), aß, gegessen; **eat lunch** (**or dinner**) zu Mittag essen; **eat supper** (**or dinner**) zu Abend essen

eight acht; **the eighth** der, die, das achte

eighteen achtzehn

eighty achtzig

either . . . or entweder . . . oder

elderly: an elderly man ein älterer Mann

elect wählen

eleven elf

enemy der Feind, -e

England (das) England

English (*adj.*) englisch; (**the**) **English** (*language*) (das) Englisch

Englishman der Engländer, -

Englishwoman die Engländerin, -nen

enter ein-treten (in + *acc.*) (tritt ein), trat ein, ist eingetreten

entire der, die, das ganze

Europe (das) Europa

even selbst

evening der Abend, -e; **in the evening** am Abend; **in the evening(s)** abends; **this evening** heute abend; **tomorrow evening** morgen abend; **Tuesday evening** Dienstag abend; **yesterday evening** gestern abend

ever je

every jeder, jede, jedes; **everytime** jedesmal; **everybody, everyone** jeder

everything alles; **everything strange, foreign** alles Fremde

everywhere überall

evil schlecht

excessively zu

expensive teuer

experience erfahren (erfährt), erfuhr, erfahren

explain erklären

extend reichen

eye das Auge, -n

face das Gesicht, -er

faith der Glaube, -ns, -n

fall (*autumn*) der Herbst, -e; **in fall** im Herbst

fall fallen (fällt), fiel, ist gefallen
family die Familie, -n
famous berühmt; **famous for** berühmt wegen (+ *gen.*)
far weit
farewell der Abschied, -e
fast schnell
father der Vater, ⸗
February der Februar; **in February** im Februar
fetch holen
few wenige; **a few** ein paar
field das Feld, -er
fifteen fünfzehn
fifty fünfzig
find finden, fand, gefunden; **find out** erfahren (erfährt), erfuhr, erfahren
fine: I'm fine es geht mir gut
first zuerst; **the first** der, die, das erste; **the first of February** der erste Februar; **in the first place** erstens
fish der Fisch, -e
five fünf
floor der Boden, ⸗
flow fließen, floß, ist geflossen
flower die Blume, -n
follow folgen (+ *dat.*)
food das Essen
foot der Fuß, ⸗e
for (*conj.*) denn; (*prep.*) für (+ *acc.*); **he has been here for a year** er ist (schon) seit einem Jahr hier
foreign fremd
forest der Wald, ⸗er
forty vierzig
forward (*up front*) vorne
fountain pen der Füllhalter, -
four vier; **the fourth** der, die, das vierte
fourteen vierzehn
France (das) Frankreich; **to France** nach Frankreich
freedom die Freiheit

French französisch; **in French** auf französisch
Frenchman der Franzose, -n, -n
Friday der Freitag; **Friday morning** Freitag morgen
friend der Freund, -e; **girl friend** die Freundin, -nen
from von (+ *dat.*); (*out of*) aus (+ *dat.*)
front: up front vorne; **in front of** vor (+ *dat.*)

game das Spiel, -e
garden der Garten, ⸗
gentleman der Herr, -n, -en
German (*adj.*) deutsch; **(the) German language** (das) Deutsch; **in German** auf deutsch; **a German** ein Deutscher; **the German** der Deutsche, -n, -n; **the German girl, woman** die Deutsche, -n
Germany (das) Deutschland; **to Germany** nach Deutschland
get (*fetch*) holen; (*receive*) bekommen, bekam, bekommen; (*become*) werden (wird), wurde, ist geworden; **get in, on** ein-steigen, stieg ein, ist eingestiegen (in + *acc.*); **get up** auf-stehen, stand auf, ist aufgestanden
gift das Geschenk, -e
girl das Mädchen, -; **girl friend** die Freundin, -nen
give geben (gibt), gab, gegeben; **it gives me pleasure** es macht mir Freude
glad: I'm glad es freut mich
gladly gerne; **most gladly** am liebsten
glance (at) blicken (auf + *acc.*)
glass das Glas, ⸗er; **a glass of beer** ein Glas Bier; **two glasses of beer** zwei Glas Bier
glove der Handschuh, -e

go gehen, ging, ist gegangen; (*travel*) fahren (fährt), fuhr, ist gefahren; **go away** fort-gehen, ging fort, ist fortgegangen; **go out** hinaus-gehen, ging hinaus, ist hinausgegangen

good gut; **good-by** auf Wiedersehen

grandchild der Enkel, -

grandfather der Großvater, =

grandmother die Großmutter, =

grandson der Enkel, -

grass das Gras, =er

gray grau

green grün

greet begrüßen

ground der Boden, =

grow wachsen (wächst), wuchs, ist gewachsen

guest der Gast, =e

hair das Haar, -e

half halb; **half an hour** eine halbe Stunde; **it's half past eight (o'clock)** es ist halb neun (Uhr)

ham der Schinken, -

hand die Hand, =e; **she is shaking hands with him** sie reicht ihm die Hand

happy glücklich

harbor der Hafen, =

hat der Hut, =e

have haben (hat), hatte, gehabt; **have to** müssen (muß), mußte, gemußt; **have a good time** sich amüsieren; **have a house built** ein Haus bauen lassen

head der Kopf, =e

health: **in good health** gesund

healthy gesund

hear hören

heart das Herz, -ens, -en

heavy schwer

Heidelberg (das) Heidelberg

help helfen (hilft), half, geholfen

here hier

high hoch, höher, am höchsten

hold halten (hält), hielt, gehalten

home: **at home** zu Hause; **homeward** nach Hause

hope hoffen

hot heiß

hotel das Hotel, -s

hour die Stunde, -n

house das Haus, =er; **at the house of** bei (+ *dat.*); **at her house** bei ihr; **to her** zu ihr; **to her mother's house** zu ihrer Mutter

how? wie?; **How are you?** Wie geht es Ihnen?; **How much?** Wieviel?

human being der Mensch, -en, -en

hundred hundert

hungry: **to be hungry** Hunger haben

hurry sich beeilen

hurt: **my arm hurts** der Arm tut mir weh; **his eyes hurt** die Augen tun ihm weh

ice (cream) das Eis

if wenn

important wichtig

in in (+ *dat.*), an (+ *dat.*), auf (+ *dat.*); **in church** in der Kirche; **in July** im Juli; **in the room** im Zimmer; **in school** in der Schule; **in (the) spring** im Frühling; **in town** in der Stadt; **in the afternoon(s)** am Nachmittag, nachmittags; **in the evening(s)** am Abend, abends; **in the morning(s)** am Vormittag, vormittags; **in the country** auf dem Lande; **in the middle of town** mitten in der Stadt

in order to um zu (+ *inf.*)

inexpensive billig

inhabitant der Einwohner, -

instead of anstatt (+ *gen.*)

interest interessieren; **be interested in**) sich interessieren (für + *acc.*)
interesting interessant
into in (+ *acc.*)
Italian der Italiener, -; (*adj.*) italienisch
Italy (das) Italien; **to Italy** nach Italien

jacket die Jacke, -n
January der Januar; **in January** im Januar
joy die Freude, -n
July der Juli; **in July** im Juli
June der Juni; **in June** im Juni
just eben

kilogram das Kilo, -s
kind: what kind of? was für (ein)?
king der König, -e
kitchen die Küche, -n
knock klopfen; **someone is knocking at the door** es klopft
know (*be acquainted with*) kennen, kannte, gekannt; **know** (*as a fact*) wissen (weiß), wußte, gewußt; **know German** Deutsch können

lady die Dame, -n
lake der See, -n; **at the lake** am See; **to the lake** an den See
large groß
last vorig
late spät
laugh lachen
lay legen
lead führen
learn lernen
leave: take leave of Abschied nehmen von (+ *dat.*)
leave (*depart*) ab-fahren (fährt ab), fuhr ab, ist abgefahren; **leave (be-**

hind) verlassen (verläßt), verließ, verlassen
left: on the left links; **to the left** nach links
lesson die Aufgabe, -n
let lassen (läßt), ließ, gelassen
letter der Brief, -e
lie (*be situated*) liegen, lag, gelegen
light (*in color*) hell; (*in weight*) leicht
light das Licht, -er; **put on the light** das Licht an-machen
like mögen (mag), mochte, gemocht; **I like the house** das Haus gefällt mir; **I like the veal** das Kalbfleisch schmeckt mir; **I like to study** ich lerne gerne; **I like best to study** ich lerne am liebsten
listen (to) hören; **listen to the radio** Radio hören
little (*small*) klein; **(a) little** wenig
live (*be alive*) leben; (*reside*) wohnen
living room das Wohnzimmer, -
long lang; **no longer** nicht mehr
look (*appear*) aus-sehen (sieht aus), sah aus, ausgesehen; **look good** gut aus-sehen; **look at** sich an-sehen (sieht sich an), sah sich an, angesehen; betrachten; blicken auf (+ *acc.*); **look for** suchen; **look forward (with pleasure) to** sich freuen auf (+ *acc.*)
lose verlieren, verlor, verloren
loud laut
love lieben
luck: good luck das Glück
lucky: be lucky Glück haben
lunch das Mittagessen; **eat lunch** zu Mittag essen
mail die Post; **by mail** mit der Post
make machen
man der Mann, ⸚er; (*human being*) der Mensch, -en, -en

many viele; **many a** mancher, manche, manches

March der März; **in March** im März

mark die Mark

may dürfen (darf), durfte, gedurft

May der Mai; **in May** im Mai

meal das Essen

mean bedeuten

meaning die Bedeutung, -en

meat das Fleisch

medicine die Medizin; **get medicine from the drugstore** eine Medizin von der Apotheke holen

meet treffen (trifft), traf, getroffen; (*by chance*) begegnen (+ *dat.*) (ist); (*for the first time*) kennen-lernen

menu die Speisekarte, -n

middle: in the middle of mitten in (+ *dat.*)

milk die Milch; **a bottle of milk** eine Flasche Milch

million die Million, -en; **a million inhabitants** eine Million Einwohner; **two million inhabitants** zwei Millionen Einwohner

minute die Minute, -n

Miss Fräulein

Monday der Montag; **on Monday(s)** am Montag, montags

money das Geld, -er

month der Monat, -e; **next month** nächsten Monat

monument das Denkmal, ̈er

moon der Mond, -e

more mehr; **more and more** immer mehr; **not any more** nicht mehr; **the more he sees the more he wants** je mehr er sieht, desto mehr will er

morning der Morgen, -; der Vormittag, -e; **Friday morning** Freitag morgen; **this morning** heute morgen; **yesterday morning** gestern morgen; **good morning** guten Morgen; **in the morning(s)** am Vormittag, morgens

most die meisten

mother die Mutter, ̈

mountain der Berg, -e

movies, movie theater das Kino, -s

Mr. Herr

Mrs. Frau

much viel

Munich (das) München

museum das Museum, Museen

must müssen (muß), mußte, gemußt

my mein

name der Name, -ns, -n; **my name is** ich heiße; **What is your name?** Wie heißen Sie? **to name** nennen, nannte, genannt; **they give their names** Sie nennen ihre Namen

narrate erzählen

nation (*people*) das Volk, ̈er

nature die Natur

near neben (+ *dat.* or *acc.*); **near the tower** in der Nähe des Turms

necktie die Krawatte, -n

need brauchen

neighbor der Nachbar, -n; (*f.*) die Nachbarin, -nen

neither . . . nor weder . . . noch

nephew der Neffe, -n, -n

never nie

nevertheless doch

new neu

next nächster, nächste, nächstes; **next month** nächsten Monat; **next to** neben (+ *dat.* or *acc.*)

nice schön

niece die Nichte, -n

night die Nacht, ̈e; **at night** in der Nacht

nine neun
nineteen neunzehn
ninety neunzig
no nein; (*adj.*) kein, keine, kein; **no one** niemand
nobody niemand
north der Norden; **from north to south** von Norden nach Süden
North Sea die Nordsee
not nicht; **not until** erst; **not any** kein, keine, kein
notebook das Heft, -e
nothing nichts
November der November; **in November** im November
now jetzt

ocean die See, -n
o'clock: one o'clock ein Uhr; **at one o'clock** um ein Uhr; **at twelve o'clock sharp** Punkt zwölf Uhr
October der Oktober; **in October** im Oktober
of von (+ *dat.*); **five minutes of eight** fünf Minuten vor acht; **in the middle of** mitten in (+ *dat.*)
officer der Offizier, -e
official der Beamte, -n, -n; **an official** ein Beamter
often oft
old alt
on auf (+ *dat.* or *acc.*), an (+ *dat.*), in (+ *dat.*); **on this side** auf dieser Seite; **on the other side** auf der anderen Seite; **on the corner** an der Ecke; **on Monday(s)** am Montag, montags; **on the Rhine** am Rhein; **on the river** am Fluß; **on Goethe Street** in der Goethestraße
on account of wegen (+ *gen.*)
once einmal; **only once** ein einziges Mal

one ein, eine, ein; **one another** einander; **one says** man sagt
only nur; (*adj.*) einzig
open auf-machen
or oder
order bestellen
order: in order to um zu (+ *inf.*)
other anderer, andere, anderes; **another** noch ein, noch eine, noch ein
out of aus (+ *dat.*)
over über (+ *dat.* or *acc.*)
own eigen; **my own house** mein eigenes Haus; **to own** besitzen, besaß, besessen

pack packen
package das Paket, -e
page die Seite, -n
painter der Maler, -
painting das Gemälde, -
pair das Paar, -e; **a pair of gloves** ein Paar Handschuhe
paper das Papier, -e
parents die Eltern (*pl.*)
park der Park, -s
part der Teil, -e
pay bezahlen
peace der Friede, -ns, -n
peach der Pfirsich, -e
pear die Birne, -n
pen Kugelschreiber, -; der Füllhalter, -
pencil der Bleistift, -e
people (*nation*) das Volk, ⸗er; (*you, one, they*) man; **people say** man sagt; (*in a crowd*) die Leute (*pl.*); (*human beings*) die Menschen (*pl.*)
permit: be permitted to dürfen (darf), durfte, gedurft
pharmacy die Apotheke, -n
physician der Arzt, ⸗e

picture das Bild, -er; **in the picture** auf dem Bild

piece das Stück, -e; **a piece of cheese** ein Stück Käse

place der Platz, ⸗e; **take place** statt-finden, fand statt, stattgefunden

play spielen

pleasant angenehm

please gefallen (+ *dat.*) (gefällt), gefiel, gefallen; **(if you) please** bitte; **be pleased (with)** sich freuen (über + *acc.*)

pleasure die Freude, -n; **that gives me pleasure** das macht mir Freude, das freut mich

P.M. nachmittags, abends

pocket die Tasche, -n

poet der Dichter, -

poor arm

possess besitzen, besaß, besessen

possible möglich

post office die Post; das Postamt, ⸗er

prefer: I prefer to eat ich esse lieber

president der Präsident, -en, -en

pretty hübsch

previous vorig

prize der Preis, -e

professor der Professor, -en

pull ziehen, zog, gezogen

pupil der Schüler, -; (*f.*) die Schülerin, -nen

put legen; (*stick*) stecken; **put a question to him** ihm eine Frage stellen; **put on** (*a hat*) auf-setzen; **put on** (*other clothes*) an-ziehen, zog an, angezogen; **put on** (*a light*) an-machen

quarter das Viertel, -; **quarter of one** Viertel vor eins; **quarter after six** Viertel nach sechs

question die Frage, -n; **he asks me a question** er stellt mir eine Frage

quick schnell

radio das Radio, -s; **listen to the radio** Radio hören

railroad station der Bahnhof, ⸗e

rain der Regen

rain regnen; **it is raining** es regnet

rather lieber

read lesen (liest), las, gelesen

receive bekommen, bekam, bekommen

recognize erkennen, erkannte, erkannt

recommend empfehlen (empfiehlt), empfahl, empfohlen

red rot

relative der Verwandte, -n, -n; **a relative** ein Verwandter

remain bleiben, blieb, ist geblieben

remember sich erinnern (an + *acc.*)

request bitten (um + *acc.*), bat, gebeten

restaurant das Restaurant, -s

Rhine der Rhein; **at the Rhine** am Rhein; **to the Rhine** an den Rhein

rich reich

ride die Fahrt, -en; **to ride** fahren (fährt), fuhr, ist gefahren

right: on the right rechts; **to the right** nach rechts; **be right** recht haben

ring der Ring, -e

ripe reif

river der Fluß, ⸗sse; **at the river** am Fluß; **to the river** an den Fluß

room das Zimmer, -

run laufen (läuft), lief, ist gelaufen; rennen, rannte, ist gerannt

salesgirl die Verkäuferin, -nen

salesman der Verkäufer, -

same derselbe, dieselbe, dasselbe

Saturday der Samstag; der Sonnabend

say sagen

school die Schule, -n; **after school** nach der Schule; **at school** in der Schule; **to school** in die Schule

sea die See, -n; **at the sea(shore)** an der See; **to the sea(shore)** an die See

second der, die, das zweite; **in the second place** zweitens

see sehen (sieht), sah, gesehen

seek suchen

seem scheinen, schien, geschienen; **it seems to be right** es scheint richtig zu sein

seldom selten

sell verkaufen

send schicken; senden, sandte, gesandt

sentence der Satz, ⸗e

September der September; **in September** im September

serve dienen (+ *dat.*)

seven sieben

seventeen siebzehn

seventh der, die, das siebte

seventy siebzig

several mehrere

shake: she is shaking hands with him sie reicht ihm die Hand

shame: it's a shame es ist schade

sharp: (at) twelve o'clock sharp Punkt zwölf Uhr

shine scheinen, schien, geschienen

ship das Schiff, -e; (*steamer*) der Dampfer, -

shoe der Schuh, -e

shop das Geschäft, -e

short kurz

show zeigen

sick krank

side die Seite, -n; **on this side** auf dieser Seite; **on the other side** auf der anderen Seite

signify bedeuten

since (*conj.*) da, weil, denn; (*prep.*) seit (+ *dat.*)

sing singen, sang, gesungen

single einzig; **one single time** ein einziges Mal

sister die Schwester, -n

sit sitzen, saß, gesessen; **sit down** sich setzen; **sit down at the table** sich an den Tisch setzen

six sechs

sixteen sechzehn

sixty sechzig

sky der Himmel, -

sleep schlafen (schläft), schlief, geschlafen

slow langsam

small klein

smile lächeln

smoke rauchen

snow der Schnee

soldier der Soldat, -en, -en

some einige, manche

somebody jemand

someone jemand; **someone is knocking at the door** es klopft

something etwas; **something brown** etwas Braunes

sometimes manchmal

son der Sohn, ⸗e

soon bald

sorry: I'm sorry das tut mir leid

south der Süden; **from south to north** von Süden nach Norden

Spain (das) Spanien; **to Spain** nach Spanien

Spaniard der Spanier, -

Spanish spanisch

speak sprechen (spricht), sprach, gesprochen

spend (*time, vacations*) verbringen, verbrachte, verbracht

splendid glänzend; **to have a splendid time** sich glänzend amüsieren

spring der Frühling, -e; **in the spring** im Frühling

square der Platz, ⸗e

stamp die Briefmarke, -n

stand stehen, stand, gestanden; **stand up** auf-stehen, stand auf, ist aufgestanden

star der Stern, -e

start beginnen, begann, begonnen

state der Staat, -es, -en; **United States** die Vereinigten Staaten

station: railroad station der Bahnhof, ⸗e

stay bleiben, blieb, ist geblieben

steamer der Dampfer, -

stick stecken

still noch; **still another** noch ein

stop (*stand still*) stehen-bleiben, blieb stehen, ist stehengeblieben; (*cease*) auf-hören

store der Laden, ⸗

storm der Sturm, ⸗e

story die Geschichte, -n

strange fremd

stranger der Fremde, -n, -n; **a stranger** ein Fremder

street die Straße, -n; **on Goethe Street** in der Goethestraße

streetcar die Straßenbahn, -en; **by streetcar** mit der Straßenbahn

strike schlagen (schlägt), schlug, geschlagen

strong stark

student (*at a university*) der Student, -en, -en; (*pupil*) der Schüler, -; (*f.*) (*at a university*) die Studentin, -nen; (*pupil*) die Schülerin, -nen

study lernen; (*at a university*) studieren

succeed gelingen (*impers.*) gelang, ist gelungen; **I succeed** es gelingt mir

such solcher, solche, solches

suit der Anzug, ⸗e

suitcase der Koffer, -

summer der Sommer, -; **in summer** im Sommer; **the whole summer (long)** den ganzen Sommer

sun die Sonne, -n

Sunday der Sonntag

supper das Abendessen; **after supper** nach dem Abendessen; **before supper** vor dem Abendessen; **eat supper** zu Abend essen

supposed: be supposed to sollen (soll), sollte, gesollt

swim schwimmen, schwamm, ist geschwommen

Switzerland die Schweiz; **in Switzerland** in der Schweiz; **to Switzerland** in die Schweiz

table der Tisch, -e

take nehmen (nimmt), nahm, genommen; **take leave** Abschied nehmen; **take place** statt-finden, fand statt, stattgefunden; **take a trip** eine Reise machen; **take a walk** einen Spaziergang machen

talk reden; sprechen (spricht), sprach, gesprochen

tall groß

taste (**good to**) schmecken (+ *dat.*)

tea der Tee, -s

teach lehren

teacher der Lehrer, -; (*f.*) die Lehrerin, -nen

team die Mannschaft, -en

tear to pieces zerreißen, zerriß, zerrissen

telephone an-rufen, rief an, angerufen
tell erzählen
ten zehn
than als
thank danken (+ *dat.*)
thanks, thank you danke
that (*adj.*) dieser, diese, dieses; der,
die, das; (*pron.*) das; (*conj.*) daß
then dann
there da, dort; (*thither*) dahin; **there
is, there are** es ist, es sind; es gibt
therefore also
these: these are dies sind
thing die Sache, -n; **such things** so
etwas
think denken, dachte, gedacht; **I
think of (about) him** ich denke
an ihn
third der, die, das dritte; **in the
third place** drittens
thirsty: be thirsty Durst haben
thirteen dreizehn
thirty dreißig
this (*adj.*) dieser, diese, dieses; (*pron.*)
dies; **this is the way to the rail-
road station** dieser Weg führt zum
Bahnhof; **this morning** heute
morgen; **this afternoon;** heute
nachmittag; **this evening** heute
abend
those: those are das sind
thousand tausend
three drei; **three times** dreimal
through durch (+ *acc.*)
Thursday Donnerstag
tie die Krawatte, -n
time die Zeit, -en; (*occasion*) das
Mal, -e; **every time** jedesmal;
once einmal; **twice** zweimal; **three
times** dreimal; **to have a good
time** sich amüsieren; **to have a
splendid time** sich glänzend amü-

sieren; **What time is it?** Wieviel
Uhr ist es? **At what time?** Um
wieviel Uhr?
tired müde
to an (+ *acc.*), in (+ *acc.*), auf
(+ *acc.*), nach (+ *dat.*), zu (+
dat.); **to bed** zu Bett; **to church**
in die Kirche; **to the country** aufs
Land; **to Germany** nach Deutschland; **to her house** zu ihr; **to the
lake** an den See; **to the left** nach
links; **to the mother('s house)** zur
Mutter; **to the post office** zum
Postamt; **to the Rhine** an den
Rhein; **to the right** nach rechts;
to the river an den Fluß; **to
school** in die Schule; **to the sea-
(shore)** an die See; **to Switzerland** in die Schweiz; **to town** in
die Stadt; **to the west** nach
Westen; **to the window** ans
Fenster
today heute
tomorrow morgen; **tomorrow morning** morgen früh
too (*also*) auch; (*excessively*) zu
tooth der Zahn, ⸚e
tower der Turm, ⸚e
town die Stadt, ⸚e; **in town** in der
Stadt; **to town, downtown** in die
Stadt
train der Zug, ⸚e; **by train** mit dem
Zug
travel reisen (ist)
traveler der Reisende, -n, -n; **a
traveler** ein Reisender
tree der Baum, ⸚e
trip die Fahrt, -en; die Reise, -n; **to
take a trip** eine Reise machen
trousers die Hose, -n
trunk der Koffer, -
try versuchen
Tuesday der Dienstag

turn biegen, bog, ist gebogen
twelve zwölf
twentieth der, die, das zwanzigste
twenty zwanzig
twenty-one einundzwanzig
twice zweimal
two zwei
typewriter die Schreibmaschine, -n

uncle der Onkel, -
under unter (+ *dat.* or *acc.*)
understand verstehen, verstand, verstanden
United States die Vereinigten Staaten; **to the United States** nach den Vereinigten Staaten
university die Universität, -en
until bis; **not until** erst
up front vorne
usual gewöhnlich

veal das Kalbfleisch
vegetable das Gemüse, -
very sehr
vex: to be vexed (about) sich ärgern (über + *acc.*)
vicinity die Nähe
Vienna (das) Wien
view die Aussicht, -en
village das Dorf, ⸗er
visit besuchen

wait (for) warten (auf + *acc.*)
waiter der Kellner, -
walk der Spaziergang, ⸗e; **to take a walk** einen Spaziergang machen
want (to) wollen (will), wollte, gewollt
warm warm
wash waschen (wäscht), wusch, gewaschen; **to get washed** sich waschen
watch die Uhr, -en

water das Wasser, -
way der Weg, -e; **this is the way to the railroad station** dieser Weg führt zum Bahnhof
wealthy reich
wear tragen (trägt), trug, getragen
Wednesday der Mittwoch; **on Wednesday** am Mittwoch
week die Woche, -n; **a week** acht Tage
well gut; **I'm well** es geht mir gut; (*healthy*) gesund
west der Westen; **to the west** nach Westen
what? was? **what kind of?** was für (ein)? **at what time?** wann? **What time is it?** Wieviel Uhr ist es?
when (*conj.*) als, wenn; (*whenever*) wenn; (**at what time?**) wann?
where wo; (*whither*) wohin
whether ob
which? welcher?, welche?, welches?
while die Weile, -n; **a little while** eine Weile; (*conj.*) während
white weiß
who? wer?
whole ganz; **the whole summer (long)** den ganzen Sommer
whom? wen?; (**to**) **whom?** wem?
whose? wessen?
why? warum?
will (*to want to*) wollen (will), wollte, gewollt
willingly von Herzen gern
win gewinnen, gewann, gewonnen
wind der Wind, -e
window das Fenster, -; **at the window** am Fenster; **to the window** ans Fenster
wine der Wein, -e
winter der Winter, -; **in winter** im Winter
wish wünschen

with mit (+ *dat.*)

without ohne (+ *acc.*)

woman die Frau, -en

woods der Wald, ⸗er

word das Wort, Wörter (*individually*), Worte (*in a phrase*)

work arbeiten

work die Arbeit, -en; (*of art*) das Werk, -e

worst: the worst thing das Schlimmste

write schreiben, schrieb, geschrieben

wrong: to be wrong unrecht haben

year das Jahr, -e

yellow gelb

yes ja

yesterday gestern; **(the) day before yesterday** vorgestern

yet (*nevertheless*) doch; (*still*) noch

young jung

your dein; euer; Ihr

Index

GLOSSARY

Accusative: The case of a noun, adjective, or pronoun which indicates the direct object.

Adjective: A word that describes or modifies a noun or pronoun.

Adverb: A word that modifies a verb, an adjective, or another adverb.

Antecedent: The word to which a later word refers.

Auxiliary Verb: A verb which helps in the conjugation of another verb (he *has* left, you *must* leave).

Cardinal Number: A numeral which answers the question "How many?"

Case: The form of a noun, pronoun, or adjective which indicates its relationship to other words (nominative, genitive, dative, accusative).

Clause: A group of words containing a subject and predicate. A main (independent) clause can form a sentence in itself; a subordinate (dependent) clause can function only with an independent clause.

Comparison: The change in the form of an adjective or adverb showing degrees of quality: positive (*old*), comparative (*older*), superlative (*oldest*).

Conjugation: The inflections or changes of form in verbs showing tense, mood, voice, person, and number.

Conjunction: A word used to connect words, phrases, or clauses. Coordinating conjunctions connect expressions of equal value. Subordinating conjunctions connect a dependent clause with a main clause.

Dative: That case of a noun, adjective, or pronoun which makes it an indirect object.

Declension: The inflections or changes in a noun, pronoun, or adjective showing case, gender, and number.

Definite Article: der, die, das.

Der-Words: Words declined like the definite article.

Ein-Words: Words declined like the indefinite article.

Finite Verb: The conjugated verb form showing person, number, tense.

Gender: The grammatical distinction of nouns and pronouns (masculine, feminine, neuter).

Genitive: The case denoting a possessive relationship.

Imperative: The mood of a verb expressing a command.

Indefinite Article: ein, eine, ein.

Indicative: The mood of a verb expressing a fact.

Indirect Discourse: A statement that is merely reported, rather than quoted directly.

Indirect Question: A question in indirect discourse.

Infinitive: The form of the verb which expresses its general meaning without distinction as to grammatical person or number.

Inflect: To change the form of a word to indicate gender, number, case, person, tense, etc.

Interrogative: An adjective or a pronoun used to ask a direct or indirect question.

Intransitive Verb: A verb expressing an action or state that does not require a direct object.

Inversion: A reversal of the normal sequence: subject–verb.